Digital Humanities in Latin America

Reframing Media, Technology, and Culture in Latin/o America

Digital Humanities
in Latin America

EDITED BY
HÉCTOR FERNÁNDEZ L'HOESTE
AND JUAN CARLOS RODRÍGUEZ

University of Florida Press
Gainesville

Publication of this paperback edition made possible by a Sustaining the Humanities through the American Rescue Plan grant from the National Endowment for the Humanities.

First cloth printing, 2020
First paperback printing, 2023

28 27 26 25 24 23   6 5 4 3 2 1

Library of Congress Cataloging-in-Publication Data
Names: Fernández l'Hoeste, Héctor D., 1962– editor. | Rodríguez, Juan
   Carlos, (Associate Professor), editor.
Title: Digital humanities in Latin America / edited by Héctor Fernández
   L'Hoeste, Juan Carlos Rodríguez.
Other titles: Reframing Media, Technology, and Culture in Latin/o America.
Description: Gainesville : University of Florida Press, 2020. | Series:
   Reframing media, technology, and culture in Latin/o America | Includes
   bibliographical references and index.
Identifiers: LCCN 2019040202 (print) | LCCN 2019040203 (ebook) |
   ISBN 9781683401476 (hardback) | ISBN 9781683401759 (pdf) |
   ISBN 9781683403753 (pbk.)
Subjects: LCSH: Digital humanities. | Humanities—Research—Latin America.
   | Humanities—Latin America—Electronic information resources.
Classification: LCC AZ195 .D555 2020 (print) | LCC AZ195 (ebook) | DDC
   001.30285—dc23
LC record available at https://lccn.loc.gov/2019040202
LC ebook record available at https://lccn.loc.gov/2019040203

University of Florida Press
2046 NE Waldo Road
Suite 2100
Gainesville, FL 32609
http://upress.ufl.edu

UF PRESS
UNIVERSITY
OF FLORIDA

Contents

Illustrations

Figures

Table

Acknowledgments

Our deepest thanks go to everyone involved in this project. We sincerely couldn't have asked for a more enjoyable and intellectually thriving group of academic colleagues and participants. The team at the University of Florida Press—Stephanye Hunter, Marthe Walters, Rachel Doll, Victoria Reynolds, and many others—was a godsend. In both cases, we're truly appreciative of your generosity and patience. Many thanks also go to our reviewers for their thorough reading and precious feedback.

Juan would like to thank the School of Modern Languages and the Office of the Dean of the Ivan Allen College, specially Dean Jacqueline Royster, for providing support to the event and participating in the sessions. Juan also would like to recognize the stimulating dialogue with colleagues Alex Gil, Lauren Klein, Yanni Loukissas, Janet Murray, Nassim Parvin, Brad Rittenhouse, the Caribbean Digital community and the DILAC Lab at Georgia Tech; these conversations have enriched his perspective on digital humanities in the context of Latin American Studies. Special thanks go to Marc Zimmerman for his friendship and mentorship in all these years. This project would have not been possible without the support of my family and friends. I would like to thank my wife Cynthia, my son Gustavo, my mom, my sisters, and my family and friends from Puerto Rico, Cuba, and the US for their love and support.

Héctor would like to thank the Office of the Dean of the College of Arts & Sciences at Georgia State University for its support of an event that brought together so many effervescent minds. Thanks also go to Brennan Collins and the Student Innovation Fellowship team: Nagi Gatla, Venkatesh Chintapandu, and Thomas Breideband. Endless gratitude goes to my sisters in Denver, who many times put up with their brother's solitary inclination at the Schlessmann Family Branch Library of the Denver

Public Library during spring, summer, and holiday visits. As always, special thanks go to my son Sebastián for bearing with dad and sharing my enthusiasm for technology (and its many cultural implications). Finally, long-delayed thanks go to Los Andes for sparking my lifelong relationship with things Apple.

Introduction

In and Out of Digital Humanities

Nations, Networks, and Practices in Latinx America

HÉCTOR FERNÁNDEZ L'HOESTE AND JUAN CARLOS RODRÍGUEZ

Since his intervention with *Café Internet del Tercer Mundo* (2000), an installation that was part of the 7th Havana Art Biennial, Cuban artist Abel Barroso has created many wooden versions of technological artifacts, including personal computers, cellphones, and even pinball machines. Barroso's *tecnología de palo* (literally, stick technology) provides an ironic comment on the meanings of the technological imagination in a place like Cuba, where the digital divide is more pronounced than in many other Latin American societies—with cellphone penetration below 30 percent (GSMA 2016). In Cuba, there is a dramatic contrast between those few with access to the technological means provided by the government and the vast majority lacking access to the internet or even the basic means for a functioning communication device—an altogether rarer event in the rest of the region, where the rate of penetration of the cellphone network tends to be relatively high, even by worldwide standards (Cuen 2010). Barroso's art speaks volumes about the way the digital divide materializes in societies where the gap between modernity and periphery is openly patent, as is the case in many locations around the western hemisphere. Yet, just as those from other peripheral regions, Latin American users have been characterized frequently as passive consumers of new technologies

(Medina and da Costa 2014). Barroso's wooden computers question the role of technological innovation within the geopolitics of knowledge. At the same time, his work highlights the fact that the digital divide is not simply a matter of epistemic limitations but also of economic inequality. A setting may bear the basic technological know-how and even the level of education necessary for its operation, but, without the appropriate economic means or infrastructure, little remains feasible. It is precisely this type of comment on the Latin American and Latinx condition that motivated us to engage research related to the impact of media, technology, and culture on Latin American and Latinx societies.

Technology in Latin America is informed on the basis of exchanges with a multipolar world (the European market; Asian *qǐyè jítuán, keiretsus,* and *chaebols*; and even protectionist policies addressing the development of a national and/or regional industry, as in Brazil). Moreover, the variety of circumstances and contexts available throughout the hemisphere dictates the asymmetric nature of its embrace and implementation. It is very hard to speak here of homogeneity and/or even standardization in the description of a relationship with technology, compared to the US, where conditions remain relatively even in comparison to other corners of the world.

Inequality in Latin America accounts for a less homogeneous relation with modernity than is commonly the case in richer countries, where certain online services (such as Twitter, as promoted by a resident of the White House) and products (Apple is substantially more visible in the US than in Latin America, given its premium cost) embodying principal constructs of technology and power attain marked protagonism, as opposed to different ones in Latin America, where research by Swedish giant Ericsson lists WhatsApp, Chrome, YouTube, Facebook, and Gmail among the top five smartphone apps based on monthly active users (Ericsson 2015). In the world of emerging economies, the internet is less regulated than in the US, Europe, Japan, and Korea—SIM cards, for instance, were switchable in Latin America years before they were in the US. Also, witness the popularity of alternative products and services like Kodi and Ubuntu in places all over the southern end of the western hemisphere, attaining levels of attention unheard of in the US. Despite the internet's bent toward breaching borders, there is a qualitative difference between the use of technology on the part of US monolingual nationals, whose communication focuses less on international exchange, and US bi-national/

international individuals—including many Latinxs, obviously—whose usage is almost explicitly in favor of pragmatic transgression when it comes to geopolitical boundaries. In due time, considerations of this nature attained materiality for us, as the opportunity came up to organize and celebrate events that would promote research and scholarship more in line with these concerns, questioning the nature of factors granting greater efficacy to the relationship between technology and culture up and down the continent.

In the fall of 2015, sponsored by three units of our academic institutions, the Center for Latin American and Latino/a Studies at Georgia State University, and the School of Modern Languages and the Ivan Allen College of Liberal Arts at the Georgia Institute of Technology, we met with a group of scholars in the city of Atlanta. Our object was to celebrate a meeting that would serve to establish a bond among a few of us interested in the study of the implications of culture, media, and technology in the Americas. A good mix of voices, including veterans of the field like Chilean communications expert Angharad Valdivia, from the University of Illinois at Urbana-Champaign, and Colombian media scholar Cristina Venegas (UC Santa Barbara); emergent academics, such as Peruvian GA Tech professor Paul Alonso and Spelman College faculty member Anastasia Valecce; and even Cuban digital activist and blogger Orlando Pardo Lazo generated a vibrant conversation about Latin American and Latinx digital culture in the wake of digital humanities. We invited colleagues to think about the links between their critical works in Latin American cyberculture and its potential connections to digital humanities. Instead of focusing our discussion exclusively on DH in the Latin American and Latinx context, participants offered overviews of their investigations and then proposed ways in which their work could relate to digital humanities or challenge its assumptions. Though our research headed in many directions, it was evident that the ultimate results had more in common than in disparity. Morgan Ames, for instance, had superb fieldwork on the impact of affordable laptops (in particular, the OLPC initiative headed by the MIT Media Lab's Nicholas Negroponte) in Paraguay; Anita Chan shared some of her enthralling research on digital culture in Peru, where technology has played a major role in adding efficiency to the economy and lifting many out of poverty; and Ricardo Domínguez wowed us with a performance at Georgia Tech, in which the intricacies of his militant approach through the Electronic Disturbance Theater were rendered obvious. This book is a collection of essays that were the product of our symposium.

Digital Practices and New Media Studies in Latinx America

Our symposium was in part inspired by the robust corpus of critical works devoted to digital practices in Latin America. During the 1990s, the emergent field of digital practices in Latin America was informed by many tendencies; however, in our view, two prevailed. On the one hand, a technocratic discourse served as a frame for the adoption of ICT (Information and Communication Technologies) infrastructure, which in turn led to the development of digital practices linked to e-government, e-commerce, and technology-infused educational efforts (Bonilla and Cliche 2004; Gascó Hernández 2007). On the other hand, a political and aesthetic discourse aligned with critical practices and informed by notions such as cyberculture, e-literature, and hacktivism stimulated a hemispheric dialogue expressed through performance and militancy. On the side of politics, the Ejército Zapatista de Liberación Nacional (EZLN) stands as one of the pioneering organizations embracing digital technologies to communicate its messages across the world. On the performance side, we have cultural practitioners like Guillermo Gómez-Peña, who questioned the commodification of Latinx and Latin American identities on both sides of the border (Gómez Peña 2001), while the Electronic Disturbance Theater enacted virtual sit-ins as a critique of institutional co-optation and violence by the Mexican state (Lane 2003).

By the turn of the century, cellphone technology served clearly as a platform to popularize the use of new technologies, accelerating the transition onto a Web. 2.0 standard (2004). In consequence, the rise of the blogosphere, online video databases, video game platforms, and social media, which increasingly relied on the browser as user interface, attained critical mass. The blogosphere empowered the dissemination of opinions, transforming a variety of individuals into authors, and it facilitated new forms of civic journalism that offered alternative reports of events from perspectives that contrasted with mainstream media. Among its many roles, online video databases served as a new archive of images that allowed for the remixing of popular traditions and memories. In turn, video game platforms evolved in a way such that they allowed increased communication and connected participation from distant corners of the world. Lastly, social media managed to revolutionize the boundaries between the public and private spheres by establishing social networking as a mediation that reshapes both spaces. In addition, they simultaneously crank-started online income generation for millions.

The field of Latin American digital studies has emerged in dialogue with the evolution and shifts of digital practices in the region. Instead of reproducing an uncritical techno-deterministic agenda that merely celebrates the development of new technologies, Latin American digital studies have emerged at the intersection of critical debates in fields such as cultural and media studies, which take as point of departure the hybrid and uneven nature of Latin American modernity. In response to the limited technocratic views of e-government scholarship, titles like Eden Medina's *Cybernetic Revolutionaries* (2011) and Cristina Venegas's *Digital Dilemmas* (2010) propose critical readings of the intertwined histories of Latin American states and computer infrastructures. Both authors take the discussion of power and knowledge in Latin America beyond Ángel Rama's model of the *ciudad letrada*, a model still dependent on a notion of technology based on writing and analog culture (Rama 1984). Both books highlight how the state in Latin America envisioned a *sui generis* application of digital technologies and information systems.

While Medina's book emphasizes the role of the computer as a technology of control and centralized processing of information, Venegas offers a narrative of Cuban technologies that gradually move from state control and centralization to civic adoption and participation in digital networks that lead to decentralized practices. The public debate on decentralized digital practices in Latin America goes beyond academic circuits, as demonstrated by books focusing on the Cuban blogosphere, such as Yoani Sánchez's *Havana Real: One Woman Fights to Tell the Truth About Cuba Today* (2011) and *WordPress: Un blog para hablar del mundo* (2011), which contain translated blogs from platforms like Sánchez's own Generation Y. Conversely, the public debate on decentralized digital technologies that focuses on blogs has also left a mark in academic debates. Books such as Osvaldo Cleger's *Narrar en la era de las blogoficciones* (2010) represent a critical tendency to connect blogs to new literary practices, while Hilda Chacón's *Online Activism in Latin America* (2018) underscores the contribution of blogging as an element of political change. As the protest has migrated to social media, a number of academic reflections explore the role of YouTube and Facebook in redefining Latin American politics.

Prior to the blogging boom, the decentralized cultural practices associated with new technologies captured the critical attention of veteran thinkers coming from the fields of Latin American cultural studies. Since the success of *Hybrid Cultures* (1995), Argentinean-Mexican anthropologist Nestor García Canclini has updated his reflections on modern technologies in his books *La globalización imaginada* (1999), *Diferentes, desiguales y desconectados* (2004), and *Lectores, espectadores e internautas* (2007), in which he discusses the new tendencies of cultural consumption emerging among *desconectados* and *internautas* (internet navigators) from Latin America. Another veteran voice of Latin American cultural studies, Spanish-Colombian media expert Jesús Martín-Barbero has suggested that new information technologies transform not only the way we communicate with others, but our understanding of our location in the world (*Oficio de cartógrafo* 2002). Along the way, coming from a disciplinary outlook of televisual studies, Martín-Barbero has embraced theorization related to more data-driven flows of communication. By the turn of the century, it was clear that the field of Latin American cultural studies had gradually migrated from the lettered city to the cybercity.

This reorientation becomes even more evident upon considering volumes like Jairo Lugo's *The Media in Latin America* (2008), which serves as a first-decade-of-the-century inventory of the media industry throughout the hemisphere, clarifying how, gradually but consistently, the shift in technologies is affecting and transforming the way we understand and consume media. Lugo's book also settles accounts with the transformation of media following the implementation of neoliberal policies in the 1990s, which brought forth a loosening of the grasp of the state and the growing influence of the private sector. Lugo's book provides hard evidence confirming the theoretical perspectives offered by García Canclini and Martín-Barbero's expanded attention to wider informational flows.

In his text "Latin American Cyberliterature: From the Lettered City to the Creativity of its Citizens," the foreword to the collection of essays *Latin American Cyberculture and Cyberliterature* (2007), edited by Claire Taylor and Thea Pitman, Martín-Barbero considers Latin American cyberculture as a strategic opportunity emerging at the intersection of aesthetic and political practices. For Martín-Barbero, Latin American cyberculture is a political scenario that "could lead to the transformation of an education system" and to "the creation of new forms of performative citizenship and mediation" that, in turn, "could mean that the democratization of our societies reaches the culture of the majority" (xv). Although Martín-Barbero's text ends on a techno-optimistic note, his position is more complex, as it also contains a warning about the ambivalent effects of technologies. When he refers to the role of the internet in *mestizaje* (miscegenation), he points out that "the internet reveals, at the same time, all its capacity for subversion of the status quo, and its deceptive and effective ways of legitimizing the current exclusionary practices of our societies. And what is worse: the new opacity of certain *mestizajes* and cybercultural visibilities means we cannot know for certain where one ends and the other begins" (xvi).

In Martín-Barbero's view of new media, technophilia and technophobia are condensed in a construction that not only reveals the ambivalence of new technologies but also the ambivalent responses they incite in the academic community. Martín-Barbero suggests that *mestizaje*, a cultural category that already speaks of unstable racial and cultural formations, is subject to new modalities once it goes through digital networks that alter its meanings.

While García Canclini and Martín-Barbero explored the impact of digital technologies in the rearticulation of social identities, critics Debra Castillo and Edmundo Paz Soldán, in their edited collection of essays *Latin American Literature and the Mass Media* (2000), began interrogating the role of new technologies in Latin American literary worlds and argued that the current situation required a rethinking of Latin cultural production beyond Rama's model of the lettered city. Other books on Latin American online literature, like Matthew Bush and Tania Gentic's *Technology, Literature, and Digital Culture in Latin America* (2015), invite us to consider the impact of technology on the role of affect in the production and reception of digital literature. While the field of Latin American digital studies has produced a number of books on literary and textual practices, including Luis Correa Díaz and Scott Weintraub's *Poesía y poéticas digitales* (2016), it has also helped give shape to the study of new digital genres. For example, Philip Penix-Tadsen's *Cultural Code: Video Games and Latin America* (2016) investigates the production of video games in Latin America "by providing a preliminary mapping of the cultural history of video games in Latin America, as well as a critical guide to the history of Latin American cultural representation in video games" (2).

The role of Latin American cyberculture as a zone of exploration and experimentation that serves to destabilize or reshape cultural categories such as nation, region, identity, and community is the focus of various books published by Claire Taylor and Thea Pitman, two pioneers of the field of new media studies in Latinx America. The works of these authors represent a great contribution to the study of political and aesthetic discourses that align digital technologies with critical practices. In their first volume together, *Latin American Cyberculture and Cyberliterature* (2007), Taylor and Pitman defend a view of cyberspace as a zone of negotiation: "It is a zone of negotiation that provides the potential for Latin American Cyberculture; through a strategic use of cyberspace and of globalised internet technologies, Latin American practitioners are negotiating (temporary) spaces for the expression of localised identities" (19). As manifested in the essays included in this collection, this zone of negotiation opens a space for the remixing of politics and aesthetics in projects dealing with new identities linked to cyborgs and web performances, with new collectivities defined by cyberart and online communities, and with protean practices such as grassroots computing and the "other internet." However, cyberspace also allows for the digital reconfiguration of the Latin American literary canon as well as for the emergence of experimental textual practices.

In *Latin American Identity in Online Cultural Production* (2013), Taylor and Pitman continue the discussion on Latin American digital practices by exploring "how the defining discourses of Latin America are reconfigured online" (2), a critical effort that involves engaging with pre-digital and digital practices that invite us to define "the complex ways in which Latin American identity is renegotiated online, and analyse how these founding discourses are at times challenged and at times revitalised in their contemporary configurations" (27). The authors offer a reconceptualization of Latin America online cultural production as a possible post-regional phenomenon, not only to account for the tensions of the local and the global created by digital technologies, but also to incorporate within their framework the questioning of regional master narratives coming from theorists in the field of Latin American cultural studies:

Latin American cultural production online, as "Latin American post-regional practice," is thus a practice which works through the dismantling of the conventional conceptualizations of Latin America, all the while taking up, engaging with, and reworking, tropes and discourses of Latin Americanness . . . In this way, Latin American online cultural practices play with presence and absence enabled by new media technologies, and we can find within it [*sic*] a simultaneous tactical use of online fluidity and border-crossings, coupled with a tactics of reterritorialisation, reaffirmations of place, and reworkings of locality. (21–22)

In her book *Place and Politics in Latin American Digital Culture* (2014), Claire Taylor expands her investigation of locality in Latin American cultural production online by focusing on place-based net art projects that offer alternative representations of locations while engaging in the recuperation of cultural memory. Taylor's book offers a hemispheric constellation of case studies involving the use of digital technologies in different contexts and for different purposes: memory and human rights activism in Chile and Argentina; gaming and democracy in Colombia; migration and border-crossing in Mexican and US Latino contexts. Our own project of promoting a dialogue about Latin American and Latinx digital culture in the wake of digital humanities is in part inspired by Taylor and Pitman's push to rethink cyberculture in the Americas.

More recently, in "Where is the ML in DH? And Where is the DH in ML? The Relationship between Modern Languages and Digital Humanities, and an Argument for a Critical DHML" (2017), Pitman and Taylor explore the transdisciplinary intersections of modern languages and digital humanities in the anglophone context, inspired in part by discussions about the need to give impetus to a global DH community that is at once heterogenous, inclusive, and interested in cultural criticism. Concurring with Mexican DH expert Isabel Galina Russell, one of the contributors to our book, Pitman and Taylor argue that "it is time for all the various and different versions of DH to compare and contrast their situatedness globally, hopefully eschewing the construction of any sense of centre/periphery or 'one true DH' as the exercise unfolds" (2). In their discussion of DH definitions, Pitman and Taylor align their project with conceptions of DH that emphasize the critical and transgressive potential of the field

(Pitman and Taylor 2017, 3; Thompson Klein 2015). They conclude the article with a call to develop a common language between DH and ML. The very fact that their well-intended suggestions emerge, just like ours, from a disciplinary, geopolitical context hints at the implicit difficulty of avoiding constructions of a partial nature. We share a common interest in dismantling binaries like the center/periphery dualism; however, we cannot forget that our desire, just like the desire that inspires Taylor and Pitman, is, perhaps unconsciously, influenced by our locus of enunciation in metropolitan centers like the UK and the US.

Latinx American Media Studies "in the Age of Digital Humanities"

We consider that Pitman and Taylor's article offers a valid and stimulating assessment of the existing and potential links between ML and DH. Even if there are many points of convergence between their project and some arguments in this book, however, there are also some significant differences worth discussing, as they underscore the location of our project within the field of new media studies in Latinx America. In contrast to Taylor and Pitman's focus on the disciplinary convergence of DH and ML in the anglophone context, the symposium that served as the origin of this book focused on the existing and potential links between DH and Latinx American Studies, as both fields are practiced not only in the US, but also in Latin America. Our symposium, entitled "Latin/o American Media Studies in the Age of Digital Humanities," invited participants to examine the consequences and implications of this digital turn in the humanities for the study of Latinx and Latin American culture. Conscious of the many constraints implicit in our efforts, this symposium intended to address—but was not limited to—questions of the following nature:

- What opportunities can digital humanities offer to scholars investigating Latinx and Latin American media and culture?
- How can digital humanities, as an interdisciplinary field initially associated with English departments, be compatible with area studies?
- What could be the challenges of embracing this platform in Latinx American media and cultural studies?
- How should digital humanities address the possibility that it may be perceived in other latitudes as an academic agent of hegemony?

Could Latin American and Latinx brands of digital humanities suggest a decentering of the trend away from an anglophone tradition or a reversal of dynamics contributing to the consolidation of further academic hegemony in the anglophone world?

- How can digital humanities become a platform for inter-hemispheric collaboration without reproducing or augmenting the current digital divide?
- Can digital humanities become an alternative platform for the circulation of knowledge? Or are digital humanities simply another means for the appropriation of the cultural production of the South by the academic machines of the north?
- In comparison to other academic areas, there has been much criticism of the apolitical nature of digital humanities. Technology tends to be viewed uncritically, as though communication devices and internet paraphernalia lacked corresponding connotations in terms of identity. In addition, as an academic field of inquiry, digital humanities exhibit a latent lack of attention to issues of class, race, gender, and sexuality. Is it possible to practice digital humanities as a form of cultural resistance?
- Digital humanities may be perceived as an academic project with a strong messianic nature. Are digital humanities a new branding strategy to save the humanities in the context of neoliberal economic restructuring?
- With these questions in mind, how do you envision your work in the context of digital humanities and/or Latinx American media/cultural studies? Given the interdisciplinary nature of your work, where would you locate it?

Our questions were motivated by some debates that have given shape to the field of digital humanities. Implicit in them is an interest in exploring the role of digital humanities in the production of knowledge in the Latinx American context. For Schreibman, Siemens, and Unsworth, digital humanities could play an important role in the "representation of knowledge" ("The Digital Humanities" 2004). In contrast to this modest aspiration, Chris Berry ("The Computational Turn" 2011), basing his arguments on Bill Readings's book *The University in Ruins* (1996), expresses a higher ambition when he considers DH to be part of an epistemic transformation that could redefine the university in the context of a global computational turn (Berry 2011, 5–13). Rather than simply emphasizing the epistemic role of DH in academic settings, our questions explore the political and economic dimensions of DH not only as they affect digital academic practices but as they are linked to broader social processes. While some debates in DH assume the production of knowledge as a neutral process, we are interested in highlighting that DH, like any other emerging field, is subject to being shaped by political, economic, and social forces. Neither representing knowledge nor transforming the epistemic foundation of the university is a disinterested operation isolated from other areas of the social world. We invited participants to engage with our questions and explore the political, economic, and geopolitical ramifications of DH in the Latinx American context, because we wanted to stress that operations of knowledge production and representation, as well as those of epistemic transformation, occur within the context of competing ideologies, worldviews, and structural adjustments. As political and economic processes affect operations of knowledge, these very political and economic processes are reciprocally affected by the production, representation, and circulation of knowledge.

Although area studies have been criticized as an inadequate paradigm for the production of knowledge (Mignolo 2000; Avelar 2000; Moreiras 2001; Mato 2003), Latin American studies, as a network of scholarship, has been strong in cultural criticism. Digital humanities, on the other hand, has been criticized for a lack of interest in cultural criticism (Liu 2012). Asking about the links between digital humanities and Latin American studies is another way of asking about the possibility of elaborating a brand of digital humanities that will benefit from contextual approaches to cultural criticism. Our hemispheric orientation toward a Latinx American Studies paradigm could contribute to complicating questions about the construction of social identities based on race, ethnicity, and gender.

Some questions we sent to participants in preparation for the symposium focused on the relationship between digital humanities and the geopolitics of knowledge. They were informed by debates about inclusion and exclusion in the digital humanities: Is DH an Anglo-European way of saving the humanities or a global project that allows us to rethink digital scholarship as a heterogeneous and diverse field? Tara McPherson's well-known article "Why Are the Digital Humanities So White?" (2012) highlights some of the very tangible tensions between a normative Anglocentric view of the field and one that allows for the inclusion and participation of groups that embody alternate forms of identity and disciplinary practice (that is, those with a different conception of DH in mind). This tension took a geopolitical twist in 2011 with the creation of a global map of DH centers that reproduced an Anglocentric view of the field, dominated by US, British, and Canadian universities—the fact that the map starts with a projection that privileges the Global North, denoting lack of critical geographic assessment, does not help—offering a very visual incarnation of a hegemonic drive, compounded by the uncritical combination of technological proclivities and the cultural isolationism that is customary of work in certain sectors of the hard sciences (Terras 2011). This motivated a series of discussions about the monolingual disposition of the field that also underscored the concerns about how DH's Anglocentrism could end up invisibilizing DH initiatives created in other parts of the world (Galina Russell 2013; Priego 2012). In an effort to render more visible the global nature of DH practices, a special interest group, "Global Outlook :: Digital Humanities," was created as part of the Alliance of Digital Humanities Organizations. Dominican DH scholar Alex Gil, along with a group of practitioners collaborating in this collective, launched the project "Around DH in 80 Days," a global map of DH initiatives that covers all continents—including a number of Latin American sites, like Brazil's Hímaco, Colombia's Biblioteca Virtual, and Peru's Memora—and reframes DH as a culturally diverse set of practices.

As we have seen, the geopolitical imagination plays an important role in DH debates. Scholars such as Gil, Galina, and Fiormonte have promoted the idea of a "Global DH" network or "DH from a Global Perspective" to defy the Anglocentric domination of the DH field (Fiormonte 2014). As "Around DH in 80 Days" suggests, we cannot limit ourselves to an understanding of the digital humanities as they are conceived of in the Anglosphere because this will only lead us to reproduce previous tendencies, which in themselves have not produced a very constructive rapport for Latinx American scholars and practitioners. If we continue emulating metropolitan models, we will be embracing a theoretical straitjacket and adopting categories of research that are already evincing limitations within their inceptive contexts. Our contention is that, by framing the study of digital objects and practices in an ampler manner, less susceptible to dualisms and direct oppositions that validate the Anglocentric practice as the dominant one in the hemisphere, technology can play a significant role in the qualification of difference. It is crucial to discuss digital humanities in the context of the geopolitics of knowledge that regulates, among other things, the digital divide between center and periphery, north and south, the US and Latin America. Slogans such as "Your DH is not my DH" (Murray, quoted in Risam 2015) are very powerful arguments in favor of a global DH network that affirms diversity and contextual specificity. But what happens when questions such as "Are Digital Humanities about 'building' (Ramsay 2013) or sharing?" (Sample 2011) move south of the border and are complicated by concerns involving the international division of labor, the translation of cultural artifacts, unequal access to cultural patrimony, and the extractive practices of cultural appropriation? Just as it is crucial to ask "Why Are the Digital Humanities So White?" (McPherson 2012), it is also crucial to ask whether digital humanities constitute an opportunistic, strategic, and instrumental version of academic imperialism in the Americas, or whether they have the potential to become a critical, reflexive, transgressive, or counterhegemonic practice in the regions (see Thompson Klein 2015). All of this has more to do with the question "What do we want DH to be?" than with the question of defining DH, a question that has obsessed the field for some time and, ultimately, been left unresolved in many publications (see Nyhan, Terras, and Vanhoutte 2013, 1–7).

In Latin America, the interest in conceiving of DH as a global practice that depends on local, national, regional, and transnational networks has inspired the creation of the Asociación Argentina de Humanidades Digitales, the Red Colombiana de Humanidades Digitales, and Mexico's Red de Humanidades Digitales, among others. The Asociación Argentina de Humanidades Digitales defines itself as "a community of open practices" constituted by scholars from different Argentine universities. It promotes research and the sharing of knowledge between DH and other disciplines. In the case of Colombia, the Red connects a group of individuals interested in digital humanities with no particular academic affiliation and highlights a number of national DH projects, including Senderos Digitales, the Mapoteca Digital of the National Library of Colombia, and Gaboteca, the latter a virtual reference room devoted to the works of Gabriel García Márquez. The network of Mexican scholars from different universities promotes events, workshops, and publications, and includes projects such as the Digital Library of New Hispanic Thought (BdPn), a textual lab composed of editions marked in TEI/XML as well as digital tools to examine these books and other documents of the seventeenth century on the practices of astrology and astronomy (Galina Russell 2014).

Some DH projects in Latin America respond to the more traditional need to preserve cultural patrimony, while others, like Cantos Cautivos and Centros Clandestinos, emerge from efforts to promote human rights in the region through the combination of academic work and civic interventions. Even if the Latin American projects manifest the specific alliances, tensions, and disputes that inform the symbolic articulations of the social contexts in which they are produced—and even if they look very different from American, British, or Canadian DH projects—they still operate within a digital preservation and tool-making paradigm (see Unsworth 2002; Ramsay 2013) that, at times, does not allow for the problematization of digital disparities whose impact includes institutional practices of cultural preservation, but is also linked to broader questions of power, inequality, participation, and access as they relate to other digital practices. Just as we are interested in the application of digital technologies to the preservation of cultural patrimony with humanist value, we are also interested in examining how digital practices engage humanist topics that would lead us to think of DH beyond the digital preservation and/or systematization of humanities-oriented collections. Consequently, we are interested in the contributions that various humanist and critical perspectives may offer not only to the context of Latinx and Latin American studies, but also to the field of DH as it is already evolving and as it exists across the hemisphere.

Inspired by Galina Russell's conception of the need to rethink DH as a global and heterogenous landscape of critical practices, Pitman and Taylor's views on the links of modern languages and DH open the door to situating discussions of DH within the debates concerning the geopolitics of knowledge. We welcome Pitman and Taylor's critique of the area studies paradigm (2013; 2017), just as we welcome Galina Russell's call for a heterogenous global DH. And we are also inspired by the way Pitman and Taylor complicate the geopolitics of knowledge by looking at Latin America as a post-regional and hemispheric configuration that includes US Latino and Latin American practices. It is evident that their gaze, like ours, comes from a location that also differs from Galina Russell's, and this difference in location endows each project with particular focuses.

For instance, rather than focusing on poetic and aesthetic digital practices that challenge geopolitical paradigms and offer alternative or utopian scenarios, we would like to shift the focus to consider how digital practices rearticulate geopolitical paradigms such as the nation, the region, and even the idea of area studies, in ways that reveal persistent patterns of inequality, injustice, exploitation, and social conflict. We are more interested in investigating how digital networks relate to, and at times become part of, the real problems of our existence than in finding a digital fix to the real problems of our region. Although rethinking Latin America as a post-regional configuration is provocative, stimulating, and can generate momentum for utopian social justice projects, the truth is that the operations made possible by geopolitical constellations such as the nation and the region do not simply vanish or go away with the help of lucid epistemic calibrations, but persist and inform the way we experience digital practices. The fact that area studies or Latin Americanism is no longer trendy does not necessarily mean that we have to disregard the material, economic, and sociopolitical differences that help to create patterns of inequality in our region and across the world, and in the digital realm.

Although our questions took DH as a turning point to open a discussion on Latin American cybercultures, they did not assume that participants self-identify as DH practitioners (on DH self-identification see Pitman and Taylor 2017, 2; and Nyhan, Terras and Vanhoutte 2013, 2). Instead of reproducing the dogmatic self-definition strategies of some Anglo DH brands—the question of who's in and who's out of DH (Unsworth 2002) based on what participants do (build, code, design, etc.)—our questions invited participants to explore different types of engagements with DH without having to rely on a commitment to the field. Rather than encouraging a passive acceptance of DH's foundational concepts, we encouraged participants to examine, redefine, contextualize, and challenge their assumptions. Some participants engaged these questions actively and offered possible avenues toward the establishment of a variety of projects under the umbrella of digital humanities, while others expressed their skepticism about the implications of the adoption of a notion that did not necessarily fit within the conventional understanding of digital practices, cultural policies, and institutional fields contributing to the digital turn in Latin America. In this latter part of the conversation, the difference in approaches to technology from a variety of cultural dispositions became evident. Also, we encountered a lack of consensus about the roles the digital humanities could play in the Latinx American context, a hybrid imagined space combining Latin American and Latinx cultural practices. What became evident after our meeting was that the notion of speaking exclusively within and from a disciplinary viewpoint of DH could be productive, but it was not enough. Some authors collaborating on this volume (Ames, Chan, Fernández L'Hoeste, Valdivia, Valecce, Venegas) warn not only about the dangers of reproducing hegemonic ideologies in digital media, but also about the risk of transforming digital media into a new form of hegemonic articulation. In contrast, other authors included in this book (Alonso, Arriaga, Domínguez, Lozano, Pardo Lazo, and Rodríguez) invite us to consider simultaneously the potential and limitations of alternative and counter-hegemonic practices that open a space for critical reflection on digital media.

Instead of simply calling for the creation of a common language between two transdisciplinary configurations, as Pitman and Taylor suggest when discussing links between DH and ML, which is in fact a legitimate strategy, we prefer to take a step back to think about the factors that enable but also complicate the convergence between DH and Latinx American Studies. The essays in this book reveal different degrees of engagement with the question of the role of DH in Latinx American studies, expressing various approaches and attitudes that highlight why transdisciplinary heteroglossia and constant shifts in the locus of enunciation are as important as the development of a common language. Before committing to a digital humanities agenda, we note the need for the definition of multiple critical frameworks that allow for the understanding of digital practices in their full complexity and with their specific context in mind. This obviously involves consideration of digital pedagogies and digital criticism, advancing critical views that touch upon aspects relevant to the DH discussion, but also reaching beyond these matters, proposing a more tangential view of the field. That explains why the phrase "in the Age of Digital Humanities" expresses neither a goal nor a point of departure, but instead suggests an unstable constellation of perspectives and practices from which to rethink the dilemmas that give shape to new media studies in Latinx America. One may find works, networks, and communities relevant to DH in unexpected places. Not all digital practices relevant to humanities frameworks go through the ritual of self-identification with DH. Along with a DH-ML common language, what Taylor and Pitman call a critical DHML approach, it is imperative to map DH from the standpoint of its ample ramifications and discover wider contexts in which DH do not perform a protagonist role but insinuate themselves as possibilities in coexistence with other academic fields, public debates, and digital practices that operate in disparate domains such as activism, arts, civic engagement, journalism, etc. In contrast to an exclusive commitment to DH as the single approach, we call for the incubation of multiple strategies that go in and out of DH and allow for an intersectional engagement with its potential and shortcomings.

A Brief Overview

This book is divided into four sections and a coda: digital nations, transnational networks, digital aesthetics and practices, and interviews with Latin American DH scholars. The first segment focuses on the influence of technology on the way the nation is imagined and enacted by a group of people, usually in open contrast to the efforts of the state and/or the corporate sector. The second portion, titled "Transnational Networks," alludes to the manner in which technology contributes to overcoming the barriers of the state in its capacity as alleged representative of the interests of the nation, occasionally dealing with ethnicity and/or race. While the first segment concentrates on analysis within a set of boundaries, the second part emphasizes transgression and/or surpassing of these thresholds. The third section is more founded on the empirical aspect of cultural and technological practices, describing cases in which the digital is employed as critical device. The fourth section comprises three interviews with renowned Latin American DH scholars who discuss the development of DH in their corresponding national contexts: Argentina, Brazil, and Mexico. We conclude the volume with a short coda discussing potential opportunities and challenges in the context of digital humanities in Latinx America.

This volume takes on a number of tasks: a redefinition of the nations' symbolic territories, which implies their exploration as digital contexts, experiments, media products, or even as uneven battlefields; a reexamination of the role of transnational networks in the configuration of new identities and/or communities, as exemplified by the cases of the Andean, Latin, and Afro-Latin networks discussed in this book; and a highlighting of the importance of cases that complexify the interaction between national territories and transnational flows through the remixing of aesthetic and political codes. This explains why contributors to this volume engage issues such as digital infrastructures (Venegas); distribution and adoption of digital technologies, as well as the gaps between corporations and users that affect the implementation of digital pedagogies (Ames); the ways in which corporate structures are contributing to the privatization of national identities, which intensifies prevailing inequities between the state and the people (Fernández L'Hoeste); the use of digital networks as mechanisms of control and surveillance, but also of opposition and contestation (Valecce); the embracing of the digital as a utopian narrative that erases alternate identities and materialities (Valdivia); the inscription of ethnicity in the redefinition of participatory culture (Lozano); the role of new media in the creation of community links that add visibility to marginal accounts of race (Arriaga); the use of corporate pressure to impose an informatic ideal that excludes forms of solidarity and epistemic equity (Chan); the tense convergence of documentary and digital conventions as manifested by computer interfaces that also reveal the digital dilemmas of the nation (Rodríguez); the local, regional, and transnational dimensions of digital humor (Alonso); the challenges of electronic civil disobedience in the context of cyberwar rhetoric (Domínguez); and a testimony of cyber-resistance amid authoritarian repression (Pardo Lazo). As a matter of context, the three interviews at the end of the volume, by Gimena del Río (Argentina), Ana Lígia Medeiros (Brazil), and Isabel Galina Russell (Mexico), provide Latin American perspectives on digital humanities as they are practiced today. While Del Río and Medeiros emphasize the economic gap in the state's investment in digital humanities and the impact of the political crisis on everything Brazilian, respectively—though they're both adamant about the dynamism of local efforts in DH—Galina Russell explains the ways in which projects in digital humanities existed in Mexico long before the label was popularized in the US or Europe.

In the end, one of this volume's key contributions is that it tries to set a series of lines of flight that allow for a rethinking of the role of media, technology, and culture within those areas of the humanities and the social sciences, in which, up to now, digital humanities have attained prevalence. In this sense, we cannot advocate for a particular direction for the field. Though we do not claim to know which directions are the most promising for the field, we wish to kindle awareness of a more expansive array of possibilities. For the most part, the digital humanities have oscillated between two drives: a commemorative impulse toward the digitized preservation of canonical and/or canonically emergent cultural goods and legacies, and a computational impulse toward the creation of digital tools and systems that apply principles of big data research and visualization design for the study, curation, and archiving of cultural collections. Our book proposes a different orientation that has less to do with the question of how new technologies can be integrated and/or applied to the humanities and more to do with how the humanities can help us rethink a critical framework that may reveal the potential complexity of diverse digital genealogies in a wider context. Each of the chapters in this book offers a contextualized analysis of social transformations within concrete digital trajectories that may inspire new links between digital technologies and the humanities in the future. This could give way to a new set of practices leading to a critique of digital humanities' potential conversion into a mechanism of cultural brokerage and distinction; the exploration of a convergence between digital humanities and different forms of civic engagement, including online activism and artivism; the politicization of digital humanities to the extent that it may attenuate and/or alleviate epistemic and infrastructural disparities across a wider spectrum of digital divides and protocols of control; and the promotion of digital humanities into a feasible option for an alternative pedagogy of the technologically disenfranchised. Perhaps it is less a matter of coding and data viz than of raising awareness of the challenges and opportunities inherent in our relationship to new technologies, lest we turn out more digital than human. This is a mission too important for us to allow hacks to jeopardize it. Not to evoke Bioy Casares, but it may even help produce a promising future.

I

Digital Nations

1

Tech Disruption as Knowledge Production

Cuba and the Digital Humanities

CRISTINA VENEGAS

The questions guiding the theme of this collection consider how digital humanities (DH) research has attended to Latin/o American issues and to potential challenges.[1] This focus on digital scholarship and scholarship about the digital raises implications for the production of knowledge, politics, the writing of history, self-expression, and activism. The digital has expanded not only the amount of information arriving at our computers, but the potential for preservation, circulation, documentation, and the expansion of previous notions of archives. This potential resonates in non-Western environments when the collection and dissemination of content have been impeded by unequal flows of information, economic restrictions, or political repression. Documenting alternative forms of knowledge through dedicated digital spaces challenges previous dominant understandings of cultures. Diana Taylor notes one such area where digital repositories and archival practices decenter dominant claims: the archive has "become the site of such contestations of power as we move into the digital age" (2012). She notes that "Digital technologies constitute yet another system of transmission that is rapidly complicating Western systems of knowledge, raising new issues around presence, temporality, space, embodiment, sociability, and memory (usually associated with the repertoire) and those of copyright, authority, history, and preservation (linked to the archive)" (ibid.).

Taylor argues that one way to harness the enormous power of the digital archive is to use the expanded capacity for digital preservation, recording, copying, and storing to transmit embodied work from the Americas. She wonders: Do digital technologies move us into different systems of knowledge and subjectivity? Or do they "merely extend what we do in embodied and print/material cultures (the repertoire and the archive) into cyberspace?" (ibid.). Taylor responds to this challenge in the collaborative digital archive housed in the Hemispheric Institute's Digital Video Library at New York University, which contains over 600 hours of free and non-downloadable material of recorded performances that would otherwise have remained ephemeral, and thus gain new "life" through digital preservation—both of the performance and of the digital copy itself. The nature of copying and commissioned "live" performances, born-digital materials, and archived videos questions the user's relationship to traditional notions of archives as well as to the act of copying itself. Yet digital technologies also contain contradictory dimensions: they empower individual expression and state surveillance; they multiply points of access to public life and enhance censorship; they put production in the hands of individuals and expand the realm of digital capitalism; they also multiply and transform archival and curatorial practices. To help articulate the multiple meanings of the digital, we look to the points of overlap and continuity with the past, for instance in policy or legislation, as well as to the new systems of knowledge being produced. We seek methods to understand the relation between technology and culture, politics and media, race and representation, labor and economic models. An understanding of digital media content should consider the material structures through which said content circulates and that thereby transform its use and meaning.

This chapter highlights some of the important work in digital humanities that addresses race, gender, and class in the context of the digital as a way to set a foundation for a discussion about the ongoing dilemmas of the digital in Cuba. As a new era of transnational relations emerges in Cuba, digital technologies are playing a key role in the transformation of Cuban society. Attention to evolving material and social infrastructures enabled through telecom policies, economic partnerships, and the proliferation of digital devices reveals new forms of social and political mediations of the digital. Indeed, across the Americas, new research is taking up questions that include an understanding of how digital social networks mediate Latinx immigrant sociality and activism, and articulate the problems of digital segregation.

Lisa Nakamura and Peter Chow-White's *Race after the Internet* gathers scholarship that locates race inside and outside digital structures to propose that "race itself has become a digital medium, a distinctive set of informatic codes, network mediated narratives, maps, images and visualizations that index identity" (5). The violent and racially motivated deaths of Michael Brown in Ferguson, Missouri, Freddie Gray in Baltimore, Maryland, and Eric Garner in Staten Island, New York, in 2014 and 2015—and, indeed, other deaths in other locations—tragically remind us that social inequality and racist brutality continue to be part of everyday life, no matter the power of the digital in our society.[2] Indeed, digital media played an important role in the organization and proliferation of citizen campaigns calling for investigations into the wrongful deaths of black citizens at the hands of police, witnessed through a mobile phone camera. Nakamura and Chow-White's observation that "the digital is altering our understandings of what race is as well as nurturing new types of inequalities along racial lines" (2) is a haunting reminder of these events and of many others yet to come. Discussing issues hidden in digital structures, Tara McPherson expresses concern with why the digital humanities are so white by considering the relationship between technology system-design, in this case the UNIX programming language, and the modularity of segregated spaces. She looks inside the systems that make up the digital, and suggests that modes of thinking overlap with those of racist discourse (2012b, 140). Joseph Straubhaar, Jeremiah Spence, Zeynep Tufecki, and Roberta Lentz locate the question of race and technological inequity in the history of development of Austin, Texas. They examine "Austin as a segregated city, its turn toward becoming a technopolis," what was done to address the digital divide, and how different groups were affected by those programs (2012, 1). Their situated research and strong theoretical insights connect the city's segregation to the digital divide that became evident thereafter by tracing it to urban policies and the application of managerial concepts used to develop the future of the city.

Turning to social media as a key space for Latino DREAM activism, Cristina Beltran's ethnographic research "shows the many ways social media operate as spaces of confrontation, contemplation, and self-assertion"

(2014, 246). Demonstrating that race has become digital, Carlos Jimenez focuses on the web interface regulating access to the television show *It's Always Sunny in Philadelphia* to determine how ethnic humor and viewing experiences of this controversial comedy show are altered from one media platform to another (2011). A shift in the geopolitical lens uncovers a history of computing applied under a socialist political system. Eden Medina's book *Cyber Revolutionaries* tells the story of how the science of cybernetics—in particular the work of Stafford Beer—helped to create practical solutions for the socialist transition in Chile under Salvador Allende's government in the early 1970s. Project Cybersyn, as it was dubbed by Allende's team of experts, was "the 1970s Chilean computer network for economic management." Medina's research weaves together biography, computing history, economic and political history, and international scientific collaboration to investigate "how countries outside the geographic, economic, and political centers of the world used computers" (2011, location 64). Artists and writers, including contributors to this volume, are using creative social practices, like those archived in the Hemispheric Institute's Digital Video Library, to deal with the potential of groups and individuals across communities to address social and political issues directly, and creatively intervene in everyday experiences. Our investment in understanding the role of the digital must then look to the places and spaces where global culture and politics meet, fueled by migration and transnational mobility across the Americas. And we must examine human and material infrastructures as they relate to technology and media nodes and networks to understand the impact and overlapping forms that emerge across different scales and locations. Turning our attention to regional and racially inflected political concerns in the Americas means understanding the place of technology in the history of geopolitical interactions.

Thinking specifically and geopolitically about constructions of the digital leads us to examine how different societies participate in and negotiate the speed and location of technological change, alongside political crises and unequal economic development. Smartphones have become essential tools for thousands of immigrants and displaced peoples who embark on risky voyages over land and sea. In 2015, European nations once again responded to the arrival of refugees from war-torn areas with a mix of policies that excluded and welcomed them (Brunwasser 2015). Survivors of harrowing journeys relied on tech tools to soften and orient their arrival, facilitate transactions, and trace a path to safe locations. What role do smartphones perform in these confounding scenarios of social inequality, insecurity, and ingenuity? How can we understand the ethical implications of cheap mobile technology, embroiled as they are in stories of death and survival? How does this type of mobility determine new practices of technological use? How could an archive of emergency phone calls, say from the US border region, inform research into processes of law enforcement, geographies of migration, humanitarian resources, and telecommunication networks? And what does the record of the digital transmission mean in the context of the infrastructure that it makes visible? For instance, the investigative documentary *Muriendo por cruzar* (Telemundo Network, Weather Channel 2014), about migrant deaths 70 miles north of the US-Mexico border, revealed that cellphones functioned as lifelines for people crossing the desert in extreme heat, but weak GPS signals delayed the locating of distressed callers. The record of the calls makes the contours of migration more audible and visible, but it also captures the limits of tech tools in inhumane circumstances while leaving a recording of the caller's death.

Digital practices also invite greater interconnectedness and coordination of power among activists and the public, as we saw in 2011, when social media networks facilitated the organization of protests and transmission of events from places inaccessible to global corporate news media during the Arab Spring. These same digital bits from all over the Middle East are indexed and archived in Laila Shareen Sakr's R-Shief Initiative, in which thousands of semantic units can be analyzed and visualized to study patterns of information diffusion (Lindsey 2015).[3] The complexity of experience in contemporary life includes both the promise and perils of digital technology, so we must constantly interrogate the way we ask questions about the digital as well as the assumptions underlying our studies and methodologies. The geopolitics of migration, seen from the perspective of mobile signals, tell different stories depending on the location of the charging station, be it in an airport terminal, a refugee camp, or a space under siege.

The explosion of digital technologies has already demonstrated the enormous challenges and opportunities for transforming learning environments and teaching methods, for pedagogical objectives, and for knowledge production and dissemination. All over the world, governments and individuals grapple with obstacles and opportunities brought about by the spread of digital technologies on different scales and in uneven circumstances. The DH debates over the future of the humanities certainly reflect the political and cultural concerns affecting the humanities as shifts in state and federal funding for public education in the US force universities to search for new revenue sources and lean more toward market-oriented bottom lines. At the same time, DH as a field promotes the use of new methods and modes of research based on the increasing analytic power of search engines and visualization technologies, to name just two examples. On the way to embracing digital tools for research, teaching, and learning, a new type of scholar and scholarship has been created that pushes back against traditional institutional criteria for evaluation and for the proliferation of open-access knowledge dissemination. In all of this, we tackle the digital alongside our own anxiety about obsolescence.

Tech in Cuba

In my research, I have been interested in media forms and how they are embedded in networks of uneven power and varying configurations. My book *Digital Dilemmas: The State, the Individual and Digital Media in Cuba* investigates digital culture in Cuba, its emerging internet infrastructure in the 1990s and the relationship between politics and technology. I examined a wide range of interlocking topics from infrastructures of power and media technologies to discourses of progress and freedom (2010a). I considered the impact of political ideologies on attitudes toward media and its new "liberating" potential, and linked the debates about democracy to digital technology from national and transnational perspectives. I also examined what people did with technology, whether it was to support, refute, or ignore hegemonic ideas.

The research began when internet use was being adopted in Cuba and continued through the first years of the new century, thus providing an important historical perspective on the competing forces at work and the heated debates now largely focused on access. As in other nations that censor internet use and crack down on citizen journalists, the expansion of internet access in Cuba is a highly politicized issue in which independent bloggers call for the liberation of the internet from strict government restrictions, document abuses of individuals, follow evolving media networks, or comment on sui generis solutions to economic problems

(Venegas 2010b). Through long visits to Cuba over many years, face-to-face interviews with academics, filmmakers, writers, journalists, doctors, psychologists, tourism consultants, students, politicians, and engineers, and exchanges with fellow researchers, I wove together the story of the complicated alliances and decisions made in the context of economic crisis, political ideology, and solutions to local problems.

Early websites functioned as virtual communities and as textual registers of Cuban identity, establishing the significance of the virtual in navigating the paradoxes inherent in the production and use of digital media. Websites provided, then and now, a form of digital access that facilitates investigation from outside Cuba of what can sometimes be barely viewed from within the island. As virtual entry points, website analysis revealed an aspect of the production of content, but analysis at a distance did not solve the problem of identifying the characteristics of source, tone, and network configurations, and the resulting ideological experience. On-site investigation provided the opportunity to exchange viewpoints with Cuban scholars and understand the human dimension alongside concrete political and economic concerns like censorship or harassment. I found myself not only researching, but constantly bringing tech tools to the island for donation, teaching, and reference. These human and technological exchanges made clear the problems of system interoperability, of infrastructure limits, and of the value of new relationships forged in solving them. The work was not inspired by the concerns of the emerging field of digital humanities in the US—after all, the research began in the mid-1990s. To be sure, DH-oriented research seeks to connect the potential of technology to the development of new questions for the study of the humanities; to devise new research tools that help us understand the impact of our digitally mediated social environment or create new understanding of analogue culture. However, lest we get lost in defining the borderlines of a new academic field determined in the annals of North American academic institutions, our questions should instead be generated by real situations occurring not only in technologically rich areas of the world, but also in the places where the power imbalances of these modes of research are made manifest.

Using website analysis also proved valuable in understanding media transitions in relation to geopolitical contexts as they were defined by cold-war policies. As we know, websites are ephemeral, unstable, and not always archived, so many of the sites I analyzed no longer exist, or are catalogued only in the Internet Archive. Ironically, I printed and saved some of them on paper. Dealing with the evanescence of the digital object is part of the complexity of developing a methodology that apprehends the traces of evolving online practices and catalogues their histories. It is as much a philosophical issue about the writing of history—accounting for the irrecoverable object and the missing link to the past—as it is an issue of methodology. For example, in a critical investigation of the original online exile narratives and their relationship to Cuba's early internet use, I compared the textual content and style of the websites and read them against the prevailing zeitgeist. Early Cuban and Cuban-American websites oftentimes crudely, but creatively, expressed painful histories of Cuban migration. Like films, literature, and talk radio shows on the topic, their content focused on traumatic dramas, nostalgia, and regime condemnation. The enthusiasm of users was evident in the early adoption of websites as new forms of sharing individual histories emerged. These practices have since been boldly extended by a Cuban blogosphere that through great difficulty has established a consistent presence on the internet, on social networks, and in international human rights forums as the new venues for convening political communities.

Without adhering to a spurious aim of technological utopianism, the research focused on the ineffable quality of individual emotional dramas of survival facing dispersed populations. This early approach, informed by debates about Cuba's survival, the official reinvention of socialism, and the crippling effects of the US embargo, stands as a snapshot of early web analysis and the challenges of digital scholarship.

My use of digital research tools was incidental to the magnitude of the subject matter, for the digital encompasses all aspects of society, from the economic and political to the social and personal. The intention was to consider the overall context for the introduction of digital technologies without falling into the trap of conflating technology with progress while concurrently understanding the use of narratives of progress. Technologies have their own histories shaped by individuals, institutions, and events. For my research, this meant being attentive to how the adoption of computing technologies at different historical moments of the nation was characterized as a force of economic development, and to the obstacles that economic limitations and political necessity created. Moreover, the patterns of hypertextual associations provided a roadmap to the story of the competing interests among political leaders, journalists, medical doctors, businesspeople, computer scientists, and dissidents. Like Medina's analysis of the Cybersyn Project in Chile, I am interested in how these types of histories reveal technological investment in developing countries regardless of economic capacity. Technologies are imagined as necessary tools for control and power, and in the case of Cuba, there is a veiled acceptance of the inevitable double-edged sword of technology. These types of questions complicate our understanding of the place of technology in national projects, for diasporic groups, for Indigenous communities, and for peaceful or repressive political projects. This work is taking place in the humanities, communication studies, sociology, science studies and more, expanding the focus to different cultural, political, and transnational contexts.

The internet infrastructure that emerged in Cuba, with its centralized structure, demonstrated in 1996 that the relationship between politics and technology would continue to be defined by political, economic, and social needs. Some analysts then and now see centralization of the internet in Cuba as a key obstacle for greater diffusion and openness (Roberts Biddle 2013). Centralization of the infrastructure, telecommunication scholars argue, inhibits the development of greater use by non-experts while it expands the bureaucratic organizational infrastructure of a ministerial body that stipulates policies of access (Press et al. 1998). Though the Cuban government embarked on a course of ICT development in the late 1990s, it also lacked access to the key sources of economic investment that could fuel expansive large-scale infrastructure projects, as it continued to operate under a siege mentality fueled in part by the continued policies of the US embargo. The cataclysmic collapse of the economy after the disintegration of the Soviet Bloc set the Cuban government on a path to maintain its socialist course while adopting capitalist economic tools. The development of the internet continues to follow this organizational logic, expanding the market for ICT services across sectors including domestic customers, the Cuban government, business, science, medicine, and tourism, to name the most prominent.

The government also supported education in computer science and engineering, graduating thousands of skilled software developers, network managers, data center specialists, help desk representatives, and security service workers while concurrently limiting the internet access pipeline to a narrow user base. These policies reveal that the government prioritizes developing a labor force whose members, wittingly or not, and because of limited employment opportunities, have left the country, are private consultants, or work for the state. The contradiction inherent in maintaining strict controls on internet access while also training hundreds of high-tech workers has been noted by citizen journalists, bloggers, intellectuals, and artists alike. It is an important investment that has not gone unnoticed by tech analysts, and this human resource that has been generated will no doubt have repercussions as digital networks continue to evolve. While there has been expansion of the system in terms of bandwidth capacity, local networks, and the number of Wi-Fi service locations, the infrastructural, economic, and political challenges are significant. In the meantime, as was made clear before and after President Obama's historic visit to Havana in March 2016, one of the "normalization" strategies toward Cuba since 2009 has been pressuring the Cuban government to increase internet access. The focus on telecommunications has been a centerpiece of the rapprochement underway since December 17, 2014, between the two governments. The Trump administration created a Cuba Internet Task Force that supports expanding Internet development. A report on "Cuba's Readiness for IT Transformation" by Nearshore Americas, a "multi-channel business" focused on providing information on and analyses of the Americas' tech potential, is one example of how Cuba's tech workforce is valued by external forces interested in capitalizing on the Cuban government's investment (Nearshore Americas 2015).[4]

The announced rapprochement was followed by concrete actions by both governments. The US announced new rules to ease sanctions in January 2015, and by early March ETECSA (the country's state-owned Cuban telecommunications company) had reestablished telephone service between the island and the US after a 15-year absence. Netflix launched its service in Cuba in February of that year, and in July the Cuban government opened public Wi-Fi hotspots in Havana. Also in 2015, the official five-year National Strategy for the Development of Broadband Infrastructure was released, which proposed to expand telephone, fiber optic, and wireless networks throughout the country, prioritizing system security and economic development. As the text of the policy makes clear, this rollout of infrastructure is not meant to translate to universal access. What is at stake for the Cuban government in maintaining the current model of internet access, with its contradictory policies, is political control over process, investments, profits, and securing future strategies for economic development—all of this under the historical specter of ideological war with US-style capitalism.

It has been amply established that Cuba has one of the lowest rates of internet penetration in the Americas (International Communications Union 2013). Yet Cuban researchers and journalists are studying the effects of the digital, even in its truncated form. Moreover, they are participating in broader professional networks as research fellows at European and US universities and research centers like Harvard, the Nieman Foundation for Journalism, and the Berkman Center. New projects have turned their attention to improving citizen journalism, the analysis of legal infrastructures, processes of sociality, and emerging networks of media distribution. There is also a consideration of the bureaucratic armature that sets the policies of limited access, the socialization of youth through the activities of the Joven Club de Computación (Domínguez García et al. 2014), and an ongoing study of media distribution—such as *el paquete semanal*, a weekly terabyte of pirated digital content packaged and distributed throughout the island, as well as issues related to material infrastructure and the diplomatic change currently under way. Added to the voluminous writings of bloggers and activists, this research imparts a local perspective and methods that reveal the deep meaning of living outside digital architectures, the limits of centralized planning, the experience of living across the island in rural and urban areas, the work of farming, and racial discrimination in Cuba.

Cuban researcher and journalist Milena Recio Silva examines the public policies governing the internet in the country. In a report to the Latin American Council of Social Sciences (CLACSO) in 2013, she looks at the numerous government decrees that establish parameters for security, regulation, and access to the internet, and argues that "the sociocultural situation that we live in imprints on our social relations and our mental horizons the trace of the digital, the virtual and the global, which is embodied in the internet even though access to this network is deferred" (2013, 5).[5] The physical disconnection from the internet is thus not a direct result of cultural disconnection. However, Recio observes that the low rate of access to the internet in Cuba, even if its social design is meant to favor government, education, health, sciences, and the economy, actually impairs development. Broader access would drive its development and that of Cuban society much farther. Turning to the text of the policies, she notes that "citizen rights relative to ICT access are not regulated in the Constitution of the Republic nor any other document the authors were able to study. Moreover, the abundance of policy norms—more than 100 documents—needs to be elevated to a juridical plan of greater status" (23). This is especially so since the government had announced Cuba would have a telecommunications law by 2011.

Recio Silva's observations can also be applied to the National Broadband Plan of 2015, the objective of which focuses on infrastructural development that privileges the security of the system and expansion of capacity, yet has scant mention of the "last mile" service, which alludes to private home use. Debates over the internet have taken place since the late 1990s, sometimes encompassing opposing views between intellectuals and hard-liners as well as activists and journalists. They have been covered in the pages of journals like *Temas* as well as in blogs (Venegas 2010a, 20–25). More recently, Recio Silva's work, and that of Cuban bloggers like journalist Elaine Díaz (*Polémica digital* blog), Yoani Sánchez (*Generation Y* blog and *14yMedio*), Cuban Voices, and the *Havana Times* blog have discussed telecom policy developments or policy-related issues that aim to formalize and contribute to a comprehensive telecommunication policy. These virtual discussions and scholarly commentaries expand a realm of participation that, like the INFORMATICA conferences begun in the late 1990s and the February 2015 First National Workshop on Information and Cybersecurity, has been open only to specialists in the field. Broader public discussion of the concepts used in formulating internet policy might help broadband appear as a utility (see numerous debates about net neutrality), which would open the system up to different avenues for activism and establish the purpose of control. For now, Cuban policy makers have to deal with entrenched perspectives alongside those of well-intended supporters of expanded use.

We must also continue to pose questions about the relations among economic, political, and social change and digital technology; censorship and the internet; or the relationship between diplomacy and technology. How does digital technology mediate and shape social structures? Is racial inequity embedded in technological design of digital infrastructure? How can the study of Cuba's ICT infrastructure development help us to understand the materiality of technology and its relationship to the social? Where do we locate the evidentiary traces for studying the histories of social computing on the island? What is the relation of global internet governance policies to the actual use of media technologies? How do the limits of digital technology affect higher education in Cuba? What is at stake for the constitution of digital archives in and outside of Cuba? How are educational initiatives transformed through the creation of new digital markets for Cuban intellectual products? There is more to address in this research context that also extends to topics pertinent to DH disciplinary wrangling, such as new forms of knowledge production, technological literacy, access, and education brought about by the digital, which all go to the heart of pedagogical and political concerns regarding transformations of society writ large. Our approaches must be driven by how digital technologies matter both within the halls of academia and outside in the segregated streets, unwired schools, digital labor shops, and censored territories of the digital age.

One of the areas worthy of further study, as I have already mentioned, is in the arena of infrastructure. Existing research already documents the operational infrastructure of the internet, its shifts and articulations. Recent studies of media infrastructure call for "a critical analysis of infrastructure [that] involves interrogating the standards and formats necessary to route content across these systems, whether compression technologies or internet protocols" (Parks and Starosielski 2015, 5). The history of Cuba's networks presents an account of international cooperation, needed circumvention of US embargo hurdles, patterns of signal traffic routing, and national political control. An examination of the physical routing of connections reveals the combined use of satellite and terrestrial systems, their operational struggles, and that Cuban territory is isolated from the underwater sea cables that connect the Caribbean to global nodes. The type of cooperation necessary to connect to this network of signal transmission was hard to enact politically prior to the rapprochement. But the exercise also demonstrates the "inevitability" that signals will pass through US territory no matter what political agreements stipulate. As Doug Madory, Director of Internet analysis for Oracle Dyn, an internet performance company, points out:

Almost all of Cuba's international Internet traffic has been passing through the United States for as long the Internet has existed in Cuba. For example, the satellite ground stations for the satellite service they currently use are on the East Coast of the United States. [Note: Tata service to Cuba was formerly via satellite and used a ground station in Canada. Of course, Canada also primarily connects to the outside world through the US.] The Telefónica and Tata service across the ALBA-1 cable eventually makes its way to Miami to reach the global Internet. For technical reasons and not necessarily political, it is very hard to avoid the gravitational pull of the United States when routing international Internet traffic in the western hemisphere. (2014b)

Such analysis helps tell the story of the "mystery" cable, a project between Venezuela and Cuba that would finally connect Cuba to South America and to global internet networks (Madory 2013). The ALBA-1 cable, as it is called, runs from the coast of Venezuela to Siboney Beach in Santiago de Cuba. The mystery of the cable was the inexplicable delay in its operability, as the cable lay dormant after its installation had been completed in 2011. On January 14, 2013, Madory noticed changes in internet routing and speeds in Cuba and determined that the ALBA-1 fiber optic cable was finally operational (2014a). Providing greater connection speeds and security to the Cuban system, the construction of the ALBA-1 submarine connection is also a story of political alliance between the Hugo Chávez and Fidel Castro governments, of corruption scandals, and of international telecommunication agreements with the companies that carry and extend the signals (Telefónica and Tata). A focus on infrastructure, as Lisa Parks and Nicole Starosielski suggest, "brings into relief the unique *materialities* of media distribution—the resources, technologies, labor, and relations that are required to shape, energize, and sustain the distribution of audiovisual traffic on global, national, and local scales" (2015, 5, emphasis in text). Adopting a focus on these overlapping forces and bringing it into humanist analysis expands our understanding of media and its circulation.

I have tried to reflect here on how our research objectives and perspectives benefit from expanded modes of investigation that allow scholars to address race, power relations, and geopolitics in the context of internet development, social media networks, mobile devices, and emerging communities of producers and users. For our specific context of Latinx American media studies, the challenges brought about by the framework of DH do not have to preclude advancing transmedia projects with colleagues across the Americas, or examining the myriad ways in which digital media and devices have altered the way we produce art and politics. They can still challenge the actions of authoritarian governments, and uncover the missing pieces of our past through histories of technologies. The research can also effectively guide policies about technological development and provide an additional bridge from academia to public policy. It is this kind of analysis within the technologically rich US that effectively exposes flaws in the foundations of our socioeconomic and political structures, and provides a comparative perspective on the ongoing dilemmas of the digital in Cuba.

Notes

1. This essay was originally presented at the Latin/o American Media Studies in The Age of Digital Humanities symposium at the Georgia Institute of Technology and Georgia State University, March 26–27, 2015, Atlanta, GA.

2. Michael Brown was shot on August 9, 2014, by Ferguson police in Missouri; Freddie Gray died while in police custody in Baltimore, Maryland, on April 19, 2015.

3. See also Sakr 2009.

4. Nearshore Americas specializes in outsourcing processes in Latin America and the Caribbean.

5. The original in Spanish: "la situación sociocultural en la que nos desenvolvemos imprime a nuestras relaciones sociales y a nuestros horizontes mentales la huella de lo digital/virtual global encarnado en toda su amplitud en Internet, aunque el acceso a esta red esté diferido." My translation.

2

The Media Machine

One Laptop per Child in Paraguay

MORGAN AMES

When I arrived on foot thirty minutes before the morning session of school started, on a chilly day in August 2010 during my fieldwork in a small Paraguayan town 50 kilometers east of the capital, Asunción, students in white shirts and blue pants and pinafores were trickling into the schoolyard alongside me, chatting and roughhousing with their friends. Some boys played a pickup *fútbol* game in the central courtyard. One girl swept out a classroom and the open-air hallway in front of it. Other children simply ran around the yard pell-mell or stood in small clusters in classroom doorways or hallways facing the courtyard, watching each other and talking with friends. A few lingered around the school cantina in the corner of the courtyard, buying candy or cups of hot, milky tea to combat the still-chilly winter air. A couple of girls recognized me and ran up for a quick hug, a common expression of affection that many Paraguayan adults, especially teachers (which I was considered by many students, who did not really understand "researcher" or "ethnographer"), gave freely to children.

Around a dozen small clusters of boys or girls (rarely a mix—in Paraguay, as in the United States, children were socialized into exclusionary gender roles early and often self-segregated) crouched around their sticker-covered "XO" laptops, giggling and hiding their screens when any adult approached, even though the teachers who occasionally passed by never tried to see what they were doing. These laptops, designed by the One Laptop per Child (OLPC) project, had been given to the children about a year and a half before by Paraguay Educa, an Asunción-based non-governmental organization. When I asked them what the children were up to on their laptops, a few of these groups replied "nada"—nothing—and hid their screens, but most let me see. Four small groups of boys were playing/watching "juegitos" (little games): two, a side-scrolling game called Vascolet; one, a game called "Wear the Shirt" (a *fútbol* game); and one, Super Mario Brothers in WINE, a Windows program loader ported to the XO. This game-playing was quite social: for each boy using a laptop, several more clustered around, their steamy breaths mingling, to watch his screen. Another boy sitting by himself searched for "juegos con motos" (games with motorcycles) on the XO Planet website. A girl nearby searched for hip-hop music and two boys searched for reggaetón music to play on the tinny XO speakers in the classroom or on the walk home from school. The characteristic "cha, ch-ch-cha" reggaetón backbeat emanated from a few XOs around the courtyard, adding to the din of the voices of children at play.

This vignette shows that One Laptop per Child's laptops were indeed popular among some students. It also highlights what most unsupervised laptop use actually looked like. One question often asked about OLPC is: Do these uses constitute learning? In my research on the project, I often saw promotional pictures of children hunched over OLPC-designed XO laptops, just like those I saw that chilly morning in August 2010, used as evidence in themselves of the kinds of learning that OLPC promised. A closer examination of just *what* children are doing on their laptops, however, brings up more complicated questions of just what we mean by "learning" and whether what these children were doing counts.

This chapter describes the most captivating uses of OLPC's XO laptops, which were not "productive" or programming-centric, as OLPC's developers hoped, but "consumptive" and media-centric, focused on music, videos, and video games. This chapter explores this use in the broader context of OLPC's utopian dreams, Paraguay's sociopolitical realities, and concerns about media imperialism by transnational corporations interested in marketing to these children to probe the question of whether these uses constitute learning. By closely attending to the messy realities of day-to-day use (Suchman 2007; Dourish and Bell 2011) and the meanings developed on the ground, this chapter contextualizes both utopian and dystopian discourses about OLPC by accounting for children's agency in deciding how to use their laptops on the one hand, and how that agency is circumscribed and shaped on the other.

Background on OLPC and Paraguay Educa: Utopian Ideals, Messier Realities

In 2008, two young Paraguayans—one a recent graduate of Tufts University in Boston and the other of a computer science program in Paraguay's capital, Asunción—started Paraguay Educa, a non-governmental organization (NGO) with a mission to bring One Laptop per Child's specially designed computers to children in their country. The organization was not able to secure financial support from the Paraguayan government as they had hoped, but with donations from the Swift Group, Itaipú Dam, the Inter-American Development Bank, and others, the NGO purchased and distributed 4000 first-generation laptops in April 2009 and 6000 second-generation laptops in May 2011. They then gave these laptops to every elementary-school student, from first grade to sixth, and their teachers in the district around the small town of Caacupé, about 50 kilometers east of the capital, Asunción. Per OLPC's recommendations, these laptops became the personal property of these children and teachers.

In September 2008, as the project in Paraguay was just getting off the ground, the NGO Paraguay Educa explained the project in an article in *ABC Color*, one of Paraguay's two major newspapers (*ABC Color* staff 2008), drawing directly from OLPC's promotional materials. They listed the laptop's advertised features, including low power consumption, customized learning software, rugged construction, and a state-of-the-art screen (OLPC staff 2011), and touted OLPC's Five Core Principles of child ownership, low ages, saturation, connection, and free/open-source software (OLPC staff 2012c).

More importantly, the two organizations, Paraguay Educa and the Cambridge, Massachusetts–based OLPC Foundation, shared a vision for the project: OLPC's specially designed XO laptops could by themselves make up for the lack of local educational opportunities and produce children who were adept at the kind of mathematical thinking valued in computer engineering cultures (Papert 1993; Negroponte and Bender 2007; Ames and Rosner 2014; Ames 2015; Ames, Rosner, and Erickson 2015). From the project's announcement in January 2005, OLPC founder Nicholas Negroponte and other OLPC leaders and affiliates often stressed that OLPC's XO laptops would overhaul education in the Global South (Bender 2007; Papert 2006; Negroponte 2006; Negroponte and Bender 2007) and create a generation of technology-literate freethinkers by using MIT professor and OLPC co-founder Seymour Papert's do-it-yourself educational philosophy, constructionism (OLPC staff 2012b).

Developed over some forty years, and borrowing tenets from Piaget's theory of constructivism, Papert's (similarly spelled and often-confused) constructionism focuses on child-driven learning-by-doing with the help of "objects-to-think-with," particularly computers (Papert 1980; Papert and Harel 1991; Papert 1993). Papert brought constructionism to a wider audience in his two best-selling books *Mindstorms* (Papert 1980), in which he describes constructionism in detail and proposes having a computer for every child, and *The Children's Machine*, in which he pushes the idea of one computer per child more strongly and denounces traditional classroom-based education as "slow, boring, and frankly out of touch" (Papert 1993, 5). In both of these books, Papert describes children who took to computers naturally and learned their inner workings with playful gusto when given unrestricted access to a machine with his learning program Logo installed on it. By learning computers' inner workings, Papert argued, these children would also learn how to *think* like a computer (Papert 1980)—how to think mathematically—overcoming a culturally ingrained fear of mathematics. They would fly past the clueless adults in their lives (Papert 1993), instead connecting with other like-minded children in person and online to follow their passions and continue to learn.

Constructionism was built into OLPC's XO laptop from the ground up, inspiring its design and core principles (OLPC staff 2012a; Kane et al. 2012; OLPC staff 2012c). Its ruggedized case was designed to withstand the rigors of children's use (Warschauer and Ames 2010; Rosner and Ames 2014). Its hardware and software were geared toward encouraging children to explore and create, like the computers and game systems the project's developers used in their own childhoods (Ames and Rosner 2014; Ames 2015). The machine was underpowered and had a very small hard drive: one gigabyte in the first-generation machine, four gigabytes in the second. These limitations helped keep costs down—and if children were using the content provided, they would not need much more storage or speed.

After an initial school year of little laptop use, Paraguay Educa added extra support to try to realize OLPC's goals. The NGO hired full-time teacher trainers who spent their days in the schools, helping teachers design curriculum with the laptops and manage laptop use in the classroom. With backgrounds in education and technology, they were instructed particularly to encourage the use of the laptop's more constructionist programs, such as Scratch (http://scratch.mit.edu), though they did so with limited success. This program ran from 2010 to 2012, when it began to be discontinued gradually due to lack of funding (Ames 2014). Paraguay Educa also hosted a number of festivals, summer camps, and other out-of-school events, including one of the largest "Scratch Days" (a once-yearly event in late May) in the world. Though these initiatives were expensive and thus difficult for the small NGO to maintain, and they moreover broke with OLPC's claim that the laptop itself would be enough to enact change, Paraguay Educa felt that promoting constructionist learning was important enough to be worth the investment, as long as they could afford to make it.

Paraguay Educa is not the only one to have found OLPC's and constructionism's promises seductive. Like Dewey, Montessori, Piaget, and others before him, Papert's faith in children to direct their own learning seems admirable, putting children on Romantic-era pedestals as noble, pure, and true to themselves—above culture (Ames and Rosner 2014; Ames 2015). But in light of OLPC's mission to bring these ideas to children across the Global South, constructionism and OLPC could also be seen as imperialist, and Paraguay Educa's faithful adherence to OLPC's vision as problematic (Luyt 2008; Ananny and Winters 2007; Toyama 2010). After all, the NGO uncritically adopted a set of ideals largely developed at an elite institution, MIT, in a country with a history of both military and cultural imperialism in the region, the United States (Marques, Holmes, and Medina 2014; Takhteyev 2012; Chan 2014). They moreover chose to invest in an untested technological intervention instead of food, vaccinations, working bathrooms, or any number of other kinds of much-needed aid (Toyama 2010). In light of these concerns, we may ask: Were OLPC's promises—or their neocolonial ambitions, depending on one's perspective—coming to fruition? Just what were children doing with OLPC's laptops?

Learning with the XO Laptop

To begin to answer these questions, we can return to the vignette that opened this chapter, which shows that the day-to-day use of OLPC's XO laptops in Paraguay often did not coincide with the hopes of either OLPC or Paraguay Educa. Instead, those children who used their laptops at all were almost uniformly interested in finding ways to use it not as a constructionist tool for teaching themselves mathematical thinking, as OLPC and Paraguay Educa had hoped, but as another machine through which to consume media. Nearly all voluntary (non-teacher-directed, non-homework-related) XO use that I witnessed—whether before and after school, during recess, at home, or even during class—did not involve engaging with the constructionist programs that OLPC had installed on their laptops. It instead focused on game-playing, video-watching, music-listening, and other media consumption.

The aggregated records of entries in the "Journal" program (a record of programs opened on the laptop) across all students with OLPC laptops in Paraguay provide quantitative data to corroborate these qualitative results. Fully 32.6 percent of the program-opening events recorded in the XO's Journal were "unrecognized." This would include both WINE (a program that can load and run Windows programs) and Gnome (an alternate Linux desktop environment), from which students could launch games or video players. The next most popular program opened was the XO's browser, which accounted for 13.4 percent of events recorded. Jukebox and Tam Tam Mini, the options for playing music in Sugar, the XO's default environment, accounted for 5.78 percent of the events recorded, though because I witnessed students also playing songs through Gnome and WINE, this underestimates the frequency of music-playing. On the "productive" side, the word processor and office suites, both frequently used in the classroom, together accounted for another 9.38 percent of events, and the Record program, which allowed students to take and view pictures and videos, rounded out the top five. Overall, these five types of programs, out of the 152 total programs logged, accounted for over two thirds of recorded program-opening events, as summarized in Table 2.1.

Table 2.1. The five most popular types of programs opened

Program Name	# Recorded Openings	Percentage
Unrecognized (Gnome, WINE, etc.)	58828	32.60%
Web Browser	24228	13.42%
Word Processor, Office	16931	9.38%
Record (camera, webcam)	13515	7.49%
Jukebox, Tam Tam Mini	10429	5.78%

Source: As recorded in journal in February–August 2010.
Note: Programs include the browser, Office suite, camera/webcam, music players, and unrecognized programs, which together account for 68.67 percent of the events recorded.

Three quarters of the rest were opened so infrequently that they accounted for less than 0.2 percent of the events recorded, and half accounted for less than 0.02 percent each (often being opened just once), making up a very long, slim tail.

Many of the teachers supervising these children were aware of their leisure activities on the computer. Still, not many wanted to control what children did in their free time, and some felt that any laptop use was teaching the children about technology and was therefore good. This view, which we will revisit as the chapter concludes, is echoed by "new media literacy" and "connected learning" literature (such as Jenkins 2006; Ito et al. 2010), though critiqued elsewhere (see Warschauer and Matuchniak 2010; Sims 2017). "Outside of the classroom," one teacher at a small rural school explained, "kids will listen to music and play" (Ames 2010)—and that, in her view, was okay. However, their leisure use had sullied her view of the project at first: she continued, "Last year I thought it was just a toy, not a tool for classes—more for games and music." A teacher at another small rural school matter-of-factly described what students at different ages did, and how it had changed over time, though not without a note of disapproval in her voice. "The older children visit prohibited [pornographic] sites," she told me, grimacing. "The younger children are interested in games. At first they were interested in downloading rude/gross [*grosero* was the word used here and in other interviews] things, and they would show me. After that, it was music and video clips" (Ames 2010).

On the one hand, this brings the agency of those using the technology day-to-day back into narratives about OLPC, which early on were dominated by either utopian (Papert 2006; Bender 2007; Kane et al. 2012; Negroponte 2006) or dystopian (Vota 2007a; Ananny and Winters 2007; Luyt 2008) predictions of subsuming local cultures and individual practices for a brave new technological world created in OLPC's image. Clearly, children were finding their own uses for the machine in spite of what OLPC had planned for them. On the other hand, we will see that their use was instead channeled into capitalist and consumptive ends by large media corporations—much like their existing use of television and radio, both ubiquitous in Paraguay—and similar use has been condemned among professionals and many middle-class parents in the United States as simply "screen time" (Ames et al. 2011). In the next sections, I first detail the types of use I saw, and local understandings of each. I then discuss the elements of self-directed learning in this use, and then explore its broader implications.

Games

Videogames in particular were wildly popular among the students who did use their laptops, boys and girls alike. Almost all children I interviewed and observed had their favorite games, whether they were an online Barbie dress-up game or a car-racing game played in Windows. For instance, one seventh-grade student explained to me, "I play Flash internet games. My favorite is Barcelona [a soccer game]—it has matches and two penalties and so on. We use WINE a lot for games" (Ames 2010). Other favorites that I saw and heard about during my fieldwork included Vascolet, Super Vampire Ninja Zero, Mario Brothers (which came with the WINE Windows program loader), Tux Kart (an open-source version of the popular Nintendo game Mario Kart featuring Tux, Linux's penguin mascot), and various soccer-playing games. Before my fieldwork started, the classic first-person shooter game Doom circulated into, and then out of, popularity as well; most adults who mentioned it roundly condemned its violence.

Parents and teachers seemed to be divided on whether all of the game-playing their students were doing was educational or not. Many agreed that up to a certain point, games helped students become more proficient using their laptops, but some felt that most students reached that level of proficiency fairly quickly and that further game-playing was just leisure, not learning—a critique that will resurface as this chapter concludes. One teacher and mother of five children, three of whom were in the laptop program, noted that games that were too much like studying were not popular, but ones that were easier—like watching television—were: "The educational games are like studying, and they do not like them—they consider them boring. The others they like because they do not require much mental processing—for this they prefer them because they are very easy, like watching television" (Ames 2010).

Music and Videos

Not far behind videogames in popularity were music and videos, which children downloaded to their hard drives and played offline on their XOs. During fieldwork observations, I found that music in particular was nearly ubiquitous. Some students played music in the background off of their XO while they surfed the internet during recess, while they walked home from school, while they played at home, and even while they worked on schoolwork in class (if their teacher was lax enough), adding a soundtrack of their choice to all of these activities—much like many young people in the United States add a soundtrack to their daily activities with phones and MP3 players. One student said that she liked to download music to dance to at home. One mother commented, "They play, watch TV, or use the computer if we are at home to listen to music off of their pen drive [USB memory stick]. . . . They just like music and soccer" (Ames 2010).

Rap-like reggaetón music was most popular, and students often mentioned Daddy Yankee as a favorite musician. During my 2010 fieldwork I also heard a lot of Shakira's World Cup "Waka Waka" theme song, as Paraguay was gripped by World Cup fever in celebration of their first-ever ascent to the quarterfinals. I also heard many other pop songs in both Spanish and English, including familiar US-based pop stars such as Lady Gaga, Miley Cyrus, and Michael Jackson. Many of the videos that students played and shared were music videos for favorite songs.

Though music was fairly ubiquitous all around town, not all parents or teachers liked that their children used their laptops to play it. One teacher objected to the distraction a new song could make in the classroom. "The main negatives are the music and video websites—they will get distracted and not pay attention to class or their work. It is especially so when a new song is available—then they will focus on it," she explained (Ames 2010).

Teachers also complained that students filled as much of their one-gigabyte hard drive as they could with songs and videos, often deleting activities that teachers wanted to use in class. In fact, one aspect of students' computer use that I found particularly striking, coming as I did from a culture of obsessive data backups, was their cavalier attitude toward data loss. Not only were many students unperturbed when Sugar software updates deleted all of the school projects and other work on their laptops, some actively deleted them themselves, along with programs, to make space for memory-hogging media. A few students told me that they had lost the small amount of interest they had in creating when their projects were accidentally deleted in a software upgrade, suggesting that data impermanence accentuated practices of consumption over creation. If students could not trust that their projects would not be accidentally deleted, why should they bother putting lots of time into them?

Pornography

Finally, I heard stories about one of the most worried-about topics for children on computers: access to pornography. Though every school had an internet filter in place to block as much sexual content as it could, no filter is perfect, and one technician admitted that the logs on the school server confirmed that not all pornographic sites were effectively blocked. I did not ask students about this directly, and none ever talked to me about it or showed me anything, but I did ask parents in interviews whether they had any worries about the internet. Many talked about their concerns about "prohibited" or "inappropriate" content, though none knew whether their own children were viewing anything in this category. However, one teacher trainer employed by Paraguay Educa told me about catching a student showing cartoon pornography to friends not once, but three times.

Pornographic content was ubiquitous enough on the internet that at times it was hard to avoid, even with a filter. A fifth-grade teacher described an incident that had happened during a lesson in class, when she had instructed students to research parts of a flower on the internet. One student found a picture of a penis when he searched for "pistil" (possibly misspelled) and gleefully showed it to the students around him, resulting in uproar. In another incident, a teacher tried her search ahead of time, but for something far less suggestive. She explained, "I was searching for information on the sense of smell, and suddenly these rude things appear! If a child saw that and asked 'What is that?,' their innocence would be lost very fast. So that is why I want to monitor—that is my fear. I know you have to learn these things in life, but all in due time—I do not want them to hurry" (Ames 2010).

This teacher's thoughtful point about maintaining innocence for as long as possible is in stark contrast to the glib remarks several OLPC employees and contributors made after news broke of pornography-watching in a Nigerian OLPC pilot program in July 2007 (Vota 2007b). Even before that, Seymour Papert claimed in a 2006 interview that children would simply moderate themselves in looking at salacious content (which the interviewer called "weirdness") on the XO: "We envision 100 million laptops being in the hands of children in a few years' time. It is impossible for us to even think about moderating what all these children are doing. . . . The proper kind of moderator is the children themselves. The children themselves should be the control over the best use of the computers, and preventing what you call weirdness" (Papert 2006).

Thus, while the general public was predictably shocked over news of the 2007 pornography scandal, and while Paraguayan teachers and parents were concerned about ongoing access to pornography, the (largely male) OLPC community shrugged, stating that pornography is a large part of the internet—and since children will encounter it eventually anyway, why try to regulate it?

These opposing viewpoints characterize two sides of the debate on pornography and children and the regulation of children's media more broadly. On the one hand, parenting organizations such as the American Academy of Pediatrics match the view of the parents and teachers quoted here in their focus on protecting children from what is considered harmful media content, however that is culturally defined (see, for example, AAP staff 2015). Methods for implementing this protection are sometimes focused on the individual, but often include government regulation or technical solutions such as content filtering. On the other hand, Papert and OLPC's view matches the stance often taken in the US technology industry and championed by the digital rights group Electronic Frontier Foundation that any attempt at censorship—even for content that is widely considered reprehensible or audiences that are widely considered vulnerable—is technically bound to fail due to the abundance of technological workarounds (as the failures of Paraguay Educa's filters shows), and legally could lead to a slippery slope that begets more censorship (see, for example, https://www.eff.org/issues/content-blocking).

Some who hold this latter view advocate for self-regulation, as Papert does above; elsewhere in his writings, he indicates a mistrust of most parents and other adults when it comes to understanding children's interactions with technology (Papert 1993). Others are more equivocal on parents' roles, suggesting that parents could monitor and restrict their children's media exposure manually, in accordance with their personal values. Both of these approaches either trust the market to follow popular sentiment or place the onus on the individual to self-regulate. The ongoing debate on these matters shows that no solution is perfect. We will revisit the media's role in these debates, as well as their possible imperialist implications, in the conclusion.

Practices of Retrofitting and Pathways of Information Sharing

What elements of learning appeared in these media-centric uses? Recall that XO laptops were not designed to be media machines. In addition to their small hard drives, low-quality speakers, and lack of dedicated video- or audio-playing software (the Jukebox or the Tam Tam music suite programs were designed to engage children more in creating their own music than consuming it), both Flash (a fairly common format in 2010 for online videos, music, games, and interactive websites) and YouTube (one of the largest sources of video on the internet) were blocked. Blocking YouTube in particular was a difficult decision, one teacher explained, but necessary because of children watching what she described as "aggressive" videos. "It is too bad for other kids who are not interested in those things," she lamented. This suggests an interesting cultural difference, one that will be explored further in this chapter's conclusion: while YouTube aggressively filters sexual content to make it "kid-safe" according to cultural values in the US, cultural values in Paraguay also condemn violence, where US cultural values are more equivocal on the topic.

Even so, a number of XO-dedicated websites quickly popped up that explained how to install workarounds and provided installation files for download. Many of these sites were hosted in Uruguay, where a large, active software developer community provided the country-wide project of well over half a million XOs with volunteer technical support (see sites such as http://rapceibal.info), training classes, and lots of how-to websites in Spanish. These sites were supplemented by (and sometimes drew on) US-based websites created by enthusiasts who bought first-generation XO laptops during OLPC's "Give One, Get One" programs during Christmas 2007 and 2008, and posted their own workarounds for the XO's hardware and software limitations. Several of the games popular in Paraguay, including Doom (Blizzard 2006) and Super Mario Brothers (Murph 2006), were originally ported to the XO by US-based programmers. Others were developed closer to home, including several versions of Vascolet (http://ww1.nestle.com.uy/vascolet), sponsored by Nestlé Corporation, which starred a character the company developed in 1974 to promote chocolate milk powder across Latin America, and Super Vampire Ninja Zero, both created by Montevideo-based Batovi Game Studios (http://www.batovi.com).

These sites were easily discoverable through web searches, and their tutorials would spread first to a few of the most technically savvy children in the school, who were generally also the oldest with laptops (sixth and seventh graders during my 2010 fieldwork), and from them to others. Some students also asked Paraguay Educa's teacher trainers or technicians for tips on what to do with an overly full journal or to download and install new programs. From these sources, videogames, movies, music, song lyrics, jokes, and more circulated from student to student on pen drives, which also allowed the students who could afford them (a handful at wealthier private schools, sometimes none at rural public schools) to supplement the small one-gigabyte memory capacity of their XO. "There are two or three students in every room who are really good at searching the internet and finding games and other pages you would never imagine existed," one teacher trainer explained. "They share with the other students. They also know how to get around the school's firewalls and download music," some of them doing so with home internet connections (Ames 2010). In a group conversation, several other teacher trainers commented that new songs or games could spread throughout the schools where they worked within a day, starting before school, continuing at recess, and jumping to the afternoon session via students from the morning session who stayed late to surf the internet overlapping with students in the afternoon session coming in early to do the same (Ames 2010).

Students, too, discussed the social sources of their media with me. "My classmates showed me Vascolet—they gave it to me on a pen drive," said one fourth-grade student in a larger rural school (Ames 2010). A second-grade student in a large private school told me, "My favorite thing to do is download music in WINE. I do not know how to [do this] myself, but friends help me at school" (Ames 2010). Information also flowed between siblings and cousins, again generally from older to younger, which allowed it to jump between school sessions and schools as well.

In sum, these quotes, as well as the groups I saw huddled around laptops before school, both attest that students often used their laptops in ways that were not individual, but profoundly social—and that much of this social interaction happened face-to-face among friends at school and family members at home, rather than online. Students learned about sources of media and software, as well as instructions for installation and strategies for memory management, from one another. While the observation that learning is a deeply social process is nothing new to education or sociology (Brown et al. 1989; Lave and Wenger 1991; Ito 2009; Ito et al. 2010), many technologically driven education projects—from OLPC to the Khan Academy (Khan 2011)—often talk about technology-assisted education as a primarily individualistic endeavor, something that takes place between the student and the machine. This account shows otherwise, but it also highlights the centrality of the products of media corporations in these children's lives. We will next explore some of the implications of media in the One Laptop per Child project.

Media and the Legacy of OLPC

Media-centric use may well be the most important legacy of the OLPC project. XO laptops were not being used as programming machines, as the computers discussed in Papert's books *Mindstorms* or *The Children's Machine*. Instead, the children in Paraguay whom I encountered in my fieldwork were using their XOs like many around the world use computers today: as media-rich, internet-connected sources of entertainment. Despite the custom-designed laptops coming pre-loaded with lots of educational programs, children were using their XOs like they would use any other computer.

One teacher trainer spoke to me about some students' proficiency in downloading games and other content, even when the same students struggled with using educational programs such as Scratch, one of the featured constructionist programs on the XO. "They are super-smart only when it is convenient for them, when they want to—only when they are motivated," the trainer observed, with equal parts admiration and exasperation (Ames 2010). "It is amazing—kids who cannot read or write know how to download games, sometimes even in English. They memorize what to write—click here, copy and paste there, follow the links. They follow directions well. But if you give them directions on the computer for something you want them to do, they cannot do it. It is amazing" (Ames 2010).

This teacher trainer's comment highlights the fact that in using their machines for media, these children are still engaging the machine. Though it may not involve using some of the more constructionist programs, they were nonetheless learning about the laptop. Still, the terms for this learning were not set by OLPC or teachers, but by multinational companies who created or sponsored the games, music, and videos that appealed to these children. Large media players such as Nestlé and Nickelodeon have vested interests in steering children's leisure time toward particular forms of branded consumption that benefit their corporate bottom lines. While most children in Paraguay already had access to a television and were surrounded by the music and products of these media corporations before the laptop program started, XO laptops allowed unsupervised media consumption by more children, at younger ages, via avenues that their teachers and parents were told were educational. In this way, transnational corporations could move into OLPC projects in Latin America and take advantage of this new market of young proto-consumers.

Learning, the Internet, and the Legacy of OLPC

Media-centric computer use can be problematic, and has in fact been vilified in the United States under the rhetoric of "screen time" (Guernsey 2007). Still, there is a silver lining in Paraguay. With almost all students only having access to the internet at school, teachers and school directors lauded the program for increasing attendance. At times I even found children sitting just outside school buildings after school hours or on weekends for internet access. One teacher corroborated this excitement about the internet, saying, "Students who did not come to school regularly now do, so they can get on the internet and download games and music" (Ames 2010). Even so, this teacher was not sure about the long-term effects of this media exposure. "Games have their place," she explained, "but it should be a small part of their lives, so they can practice mathematics, which just is not as fun" (Ames 2010). The portrait of laptop use described at the beginning of this chapter corroborates this concern: the laptop *was* often a distraction in the classroom. In my observations I almost always saw at least one child eschew listening to a teacher or doing schoolwork to surf the internet, listen to music, check on the status of downloads, or discuss with classmates the latest song, game, or video that was circulating around the school instead.

On the other hand, these students had more technical proficiency than they would have had otherwise. Their skill at finding content, installing software, playing media, and teaching one another—even if such proficiency was selective and possibly limited—may well translate into increased comfort with technology more generally, as smartphones and other computing devices become more affordable and popular across Paraguay. The children who are part of this program may have a similar familiarity with technology as middle-class children in the Global North; though they may not all be the programmers OLPC envisioned, they have a head start on basic technological literacy. Moreover, though Paraguay's economy is still largely agrarian (Federal Research Division 2005; Hetherington 2009), Paraguayan technologists and futurists hope to develop more demand for computer skills with a shift to high tech, though it is uncertain whether this will come to fruition.

These results echo other studies on computer use in classrooms, which often find that computer access modestly increases student literacy and decreases truancy and attrition (Silvernail 2005; Warschauer 2008). However, those studies, like this one, also suggest that there may be some limits to the benefits that computers can confer. After all, facile media consumption of any kind—whether via television, radio, game console, or computer—can be a lot more fun and easy than more intellectually challenging pursuits.

Concluding Remarks

One Laptop per Child championed their XO laptops as machines to enable children to teach themselves about mathematics and programming, and local NGO Paraguay Educa tried to promote programming-centric uses among the Paraguayan students and teachers who were using the laptop day-to-day. Even so, across seven months of ethnographic observations I found that approximately two-thirds of students in the program hardly used the laptops at all outside of the classroom, and most of the rest wanted to use the laptop as a media machine, not as a programming machine. Videogames, music, movies, Spanish song lyrics, jokes, and even pornography circulated from websites and on USB drives, past the school's internet content filters and from student to student.

This centrality of media differs markedly from the constructionist learning model that inspired OLPC. Seymour Papert's writings (perhaps purposefully) seem to exist in a cultural vacuum, where media influences have little role in children's lives, and learning through creative play is the natural focus—at least for the few precocious children in each class on which his narrative is focused (Ames and Rosner 2014). This is laudable as a goal, but in the face of vested interests in steering children's leisure time toward particular forms of branded consumption that benefit corporate bottom lines, it seems naïve to say the least to expect children to manage or critically assess, much less resist, these media influences on their own.

Though many educators and parents in the United States may critique and limit consumption-oriented, media-centric computer use, and though Paraguayan teachers and parents often had mixed feelings about this consumptive focus as well, there were several aspects of this use that were considered positive locally, and would generally be considered "learning" in the educational community. In addition to increasing attendance (even as they increased distraction) and helping students develop some technical proficiency, students learned from one another, from project staff, and from OLPC-focused websites. This social use appears to fit several other frameworks for technology-enabled informal learning that have been developed independent of (though were possibly influenced by) constructionism, such as connected learning (Ito et al. 2010) and new media literacy (Jenkins 2006). In these models, children learn how to interact with technology—though generally on a more basic and media-focused level than Papert proposes—by pursuing their own interests rather than through prescribed "assignments." Like constructionism, these models do not completely eschew adult guidance, though both insist on letting children's interests guide inquiry.

However, it is unclear how the media-centric uses described in this chapter fit with the goal of connected learning, which is to expand a student's "educational, economic, or political opportunity"—especially when the same media properties as children saw on television recurred on their laptops. As the parent quoted earlier in this chapter indicates, without guidance, children's leisure laptop use generally focuses on easy games and content consumption, heavy on stimulus but light on reflection. My own observations corroborate her view that the games and activities that are more "like studying" are eschewed for those that are more like "watching television."

More broadly, early critiques of OLPC's ideological imperialism (Luyt 2008; Ananny and Winters 2007; Toyama 2010) generally focused on analyzing OLPC's promotional materials or news stories about the project, but lacked on-the-ground use data, and thus did not account for how seldom the project's vision is taken up in practice. As we have seen, children exhibited more agency in their laptop use than these more technologically determinist narratives suggested. But this does not mean that imperialist influences were absent from the project, because the tone of engagement was instead set by the corporate interests of media producers and platforms. Companies that create or host media, such as YouTube, often do so with US cultural values in mind. These values become the default against which variations might be introduced to appeal more to the cultural values of larger and more lucrative markets worldwide. Markets that are smaller or less lucrative, however, may get no tailoring, and the tailoring that does happen may still be consumption-focused and beholden to imperialistic assumptions. Paraguay Educa's block of all of YouTube in response to media violence represents one (albeit extreme) act of agency that local actors can take in the face of mismatches in cultural values.

Thus, while the influence of media corporations in Paraguay predates the XO laptops—saturated as the country is with televisions and radios—it was certainly accentuated by them. Critical communication and media scholars have long decried the "cultural imperialism" that often US-centric media seem to exhibit overseas, as American movies, stars, and media models (such as reality television or coordinated media "properties") seem to subsume local practices (Fejes 1981). These models are problematic in that they often presume a one-way flow of media products from a culturally aggressive United States to passive and often Othered recipients elsewhere, rather than acknowledging that such uptake is an active cultural bricolage of meaning-making, aspiration, and agency—and, moreover, that this bricolage has been ongoing for hundreds if not thousands of years (Wolf 1982). Still, an element of media critique creeps back in when we consider children's media in particular, and its contentious role in families and communities around the world, the US included. As our discussion of the cultural battles over pornography indicated, many feel that the stakes are high and that there are no clear answers for how to moderate children's media access.

Overall, it can be easy to be seduced by OLPC's starry-eyed vision, just as it can be difficult to assess the learning that actually takes place with a program like OLPC, focused as it is on learning outside of the classroom. This chapter has explored what happens to an idealistic education reform project in the messy, negotiated realities of everyday life.

3

Nation Branding

Neoliberalism, Identity, and Social Media

HÉCTOR FERNÁNDEZ L'HOESTE

In "Neoliberalism as Political Technology: Expertise, Energy, and Democracy in Chile," Manuel Tironi and Javiera Barandiarán critique the ways in which neoliberalism was implemented in the energy sector of the Chilean government (2014). The fact that Chile served as beachhead and laboratory for many policies eventually replicated in other corners of the world contributes to a critique of the manipulation of public policies in favor of the interests of a few. As they reiterate, the process has been documented extensively (Foxley 1983; French-Davis 1980; Liverman and Vilas 2006; Portes and Roberts 2005; Ossandón 2009; Sabatini 2000). Yet the novelty of their approach lies in how they describe the process—on a case-by-case basis and with thorough detail. Too frequently, neoliberalism has been described and spoken of in broad terms, as though it entailed an evident but immaterial presence; this is clearly not the case with their text.

A product of our times, instigated in Latin America by the policy adjustments of the Chicago Boys—the group of right-wing, University of Chicago–trained economists commissioned by Pinochet to overhaul the Chilean economy—and, on a more global level, by deregulation fostered by the Reagan (1981–1989) and Thatcher (1979–1990) administrations (though one could argue US financial deregulation started as early as

1978, with *Marquette v. First of Omaha*), neoliberalism has been viewed largely as an epochal and abstract force, rather than as a set of concrete, tangible practices (Sherman 2009). Its main contention is the introduction of the market as a measure of performance. In Tironi and Barandiarán's text, the objective is to discuss two specific examples of neoliberalism as enacted policies, portrayed as examples of "political technology": the end of the Chilean nuclear energy program and the implementation of a hydroelectric project in the southern portion of the country. As "political technology," neoliberalism surfaces as a distinct, pragmatic application of knowledge that seeks to change the order of things in the state and society. By identifying neoliberalism in this manner, they define it as a practice well in sync with the redefinition of duties and responsibilities of many members of society, which comprises occupations as varied as engineers—the Chilean case—or academics—our own—all thanks to the providential intervention of actuaries, economists, statisticians, technocrats, and business managers (and even people from other disciplines who have internalized this mindset). Within this scheme, it becomes possible to quantify anyone's occupational performance, regardless of social, disciplinary, or non-economic considerations, and transform it along a quest for ulterior, hypothetical administrative and economic efficiency.

Quoting Foucault, not exactly a paladin of left-wing politics, Tironi and Barandiarán highlight how a technology, especially a political one, focuses on "techniques and practices that give a concrete form to this new political rationality" (Foucault 2001, 410). In this specific case, the new political rationality entails the neoliberal state, or rather, a new way of imagining the materialization of the idea of nation in accordance with statistical efficiency. Even so, the challenging and rather disheartening theoretical leap is the embracing of technology as a way to transcend ideologies, which, in the case of neoliberalism, with society at large at the service of the market, is clearly a fallacy. That certain ideologies may be transcended does not hide the fact that, ultimately, another ideology, at the service of a particularly callous type of capitalism, is at the helm. Because what is this quasi-Randian delusion regarding the optimization of resources and superior statistical efficiency but a latter phase in the instrumentalization of political conservatism?[1] Replacement of one ideology by another does not speak of the abolition of ideology. Instead, that is precisely why it wishes to insinuate itself as the implementation of a series of concrete measures at the service of alleged managerial efficiency, à la Hayek.

Then again, in the cases discussed by these scholars, the implementation of neoliberal policies follows three distinct steps: 1) the redefinition of social goods; 2) the redefinition of the role of the state; and 3) the redefinition of the role of experts. In our actual case, these threefold dynamics will be reproduced with precision. In my exposition, I explain how these three acts of redefinition entail the replacement of a more socially driven understanding of identity with an act of commercial prestidigitation by way of nation branding; the pertinent state entities will be replaced by advertising and image consultancy firms; and, lastly, scholars of various disciplines will be replaced by advertising and PR executives. As is painfully evident, neoliberalism is a practice founded on the notion of the redefinition of the roles of members and elements of the state. Through this redefinition, a new relationship is suggested between the idea of nation as imagined community and the reality of the state as a material expression of the concept of nation. Change one and the other will follow, even if it involves a matter of reverse engineering.

Following the Chilean pair's example, my object is to propose the practice of nation branding as a political technology, as a recent example of an implementation of neoliberalism in which the definition of national identity, previously the realm of the social sciences and humanities, becomes the newly gained turf of business managers and advertising executives, thanks to the auspices of technologies associated with social media. This definition conceals the first step in the implementation of neoliberal policies: the redefinition of social goods. In short, following neoliberalism, identity is reinterpreted as brand. Identity no longer results from the never-ending and instantaneous negotiation among a multiplicity of parties, representative of myriad aspects relevant to the configuration of individuals and communities, but is rendered instead as the quantifiable, concrete result of a variety of transactions. While social scientists and humanists define identity in a broad sense, resulting from a series of social exchanges and cultural processes, in branding, identity is abridged—subsumed, rather—into a logo, as a marketing campaign, with direct financial implications. It boils down to the capability to transform everything into a distinct form of capital. Anyone who has walked through a US university can be quite aware of this process, as the constant presence of branding, a process not very visible until recently on campuses in other latitudes—such as Europe and Latin America—becomes plain.[2] In the US, thoroughly branded higher education institutions are usually entities that have endured the onslaught of neoliberalism. My own academic institution suffers from an acute case of branding, à la John Sexton's NYU, in which many buildings within a certain quadrant of downtown Atlanta display a logo. The US academic sector is, to put it mildly, keenly aware of identity branding as a manipulation of cultural and, most importantly, economic capital. Thus I argue that nation branding features an inroad into the realm of culture and identity.

Nation branding, a practice that has risen in consonance with the implementation of neoliberalism, is rooted in the creation, measurement, development, and management of a reputation for a country, in the same spirit as any commercial product, including the design and elaboration of a logo and its accompanying marketing campaign. In nation branding, nationality ceases to be a matter of anthropological, artistic, cultural, geographic, historical, linguistic, political, psychological, religious, and sociological experiences, mutating into a product almost entirely defined in terms of a reductive understanding of economic capital. It is of British origin, fostered by the winds of change promoted by Thatcher, the strong-willed daughter of a greengrocer. In nation branding, whereas national identity used to be discussed as an object of study with many imperatives, usually defined and/or prioritized per the interest of a research team, it is now reborn as a marque, as a construct immediately quantifiable by the amount of capital it generates, be it via tourism, exports, or direct investment. While it is possible to argue that individuals associated with fields like communication, political science, and the arts and humanities can participate in an effort of this nature, it is important to note that their role remains markedly tangential, if present at all, and that, ultimately, decision-making in nation-branding campaigns habitually resides in the hands of corporate executives and the advertising sector, holding the reins of the process firmly. As in the second case discussed by Tironi and Barandiarán, nation branding involves a co-optation of the state, since, while the state is at the center of the strategy—after all, most nation-branding campaigns, while concocted by the private sector, are enacted by government entities—this only happens after the corresponding logic has been internalized. Thus, nation branding advocates for a state utterly "convinced" of its limitations, which are propitiously handled by the private sector. To circumvent the limitations of the state, the private sector suggests greater appreciation for technologies immediately at hand: social media, which, properly administered, should lead to a wealth of information related to the understanding and perception of any national condition. Hence, nation branding is a nationalism à la internet, with technology playing the crucial role of partner in crime to the privatization of the politics of identity.

In "Humanistic Theory and Digital Scholarship," her contribution to the renowned volume *Debates in the Digital Humanities*, Johanna Drucker argues for the cultural authority of the humanities in a digital world (2012). In a few words, she discusses the inclusion and greater impact of theory on the making of digital objects, emphasizing how the humanities are observer-dependent rather than entity-defined, ambiguous rather than empirical. To fulfill this task, she suggests, it is imperative that we demonstrate the critical purchase of the method and theory of the humanities, focusing on the structure of technology rather than on its effects. With this thought in mind, she reiterates, "Data mining in the digital humanities has largely depended on counting, sorting, ordering techniques—in essence, some automated calculations" (n.p.).

My object in this text is not to reproduce these automated calculations—though the research I describe here could involve data mining at a later stage—but rather to shed some light on how the construction of national identity in Latin America and the fostering of nationalism in many locations rely not only on poor observation but also on the appropriation of technology that stands as flawed for these purposes from its very inception. For this reason, I concentrate instead on the makeup of technology. In other words, paying heed to Drucker, my object here is to show how digital media fixed upon modes of social relations are not necessarily ideal vehicles for the promotion of subtler theoretical concepts associated with national identities. Along the way, I contend that technology is being used as a justification for socially questionable ventures, bent on the promotion of contrived undertakings, rather than as a sensible tool for the ways in which Latin American states embrace the practice of nation branding as an instrument to advance their identities in the context of institutional interests. Within this framework, that which Drucker argues—that the bearing of the theoretical upon positivistic, deterministic practices be augmented, particularly in terms of the making of technology—becomes clear and radically consequential.

As conceived by British author Simon Anholt, who contributed to the establishment of the term through the 1990s—though the practice dates from a decade earlier—a nation brand is the sum of people's perceptions of a country across areas like exports, governance, tourism, investment and immigration, culture and heritage, and people. In December 2013, the British brand consultancy firm Brand Finance published its annual report on nation brands. Of Latin American countries, only Brazil and Mexico figured among the top twenty most valuable nation brands of the world, in eighth and 15th place respectively (2013). Such a finding seems predictable given the size and bearing of both economies on the world stage. However, the Country Brand Index (or CBI) for 2014–2015, published by Future Brand, the brand consultancy branch of the McCann-Erickson WorldGroup, does not list a single Latin American nation within its rankings (2014). In fact, within Future Brand's index, not a single Latin American nation figures as a country brand, a category defined in its report as "countries that have above average perceptions across both the Status and Experience dimensions and have measurable competitive advantages over their peers as a result," where "Status" and "Experience" are dimensions understood according to attributes relating to value system, quality of life, and business potential, and heritage and culture, tourism, and "Made in" expertise, respectively. Under these methodological assumptions, only 22 of the 75 countries included in this report qualified as "country brands." Yet in Future Brand's own 2013 Country Brand Index for Latin America, ten out of 21 Latin American nations emerge as top performers in terms of nation branding: in descending order, Brazil, Argentina, Costa Rica, Chile, Peru, Mexico, Uruguay, Panama, Colombia, and Puerto Rico (2013).[3] That is to say, according to the consultancy, while at the global level Latin American nation brands lacked leverage, when it came to a regional arena, there was a clear order to be contemplated. (It might be only a coincidence that Future Brand has handled three of the most profitable brands: those of Argentina, Costa Rica, and Peru.) The order of the ranking stands in sharp contradiction to later findings by Future Brand for 2014–2015, in which Puerto Rico and Costa Rica stand as the highest-ranked Latin American nations, in 33rd and 37th place respectively. How can nation brands perform better at the global level than on a regional scale, one would feel compelled to ask? Not to be outdone, the Chilean monthly *América Economía*, one of the most reputable economics publications in the region, published its nation brand rankings in December

2013, with distinctive results. Similar journals, like the Colombian *Dinero* or the Peruvian *Gestión*, also follow nation branding idiosyncratically. Despite such an eclectic mix of research, there are commonalities. While all these rankings are quite explicit about their independent methodologies, they all employ a combination of government statistics, consensus forecasts, and analyst projections to quantify the variables contemplated for each study, resulting in an overall brand rating.

Now, I will not question the nonsensical idea that the very industry offering consultancy in branding services is the one in charge of quantifying overall brand effectiveness; I will focus instead on how Latin American nations have embraced and put into practice various mechanisms to advance the notion of nation branding.[4] For reasons of brevity, rather than focus on 21 countries, I will center on the ten suggested in Future Brand's ranking as the better performers. Each of these countries has a nation-branding campaign in which it invests considerable funds. In 2005, Mexico spent 18 million dollars on the launch of its nation brand (Barriendos 2006). In the case of Colombia, following the debacle of its flawed and amply criticized "Colombia es pasión" (Colombia is Passion) campaign (which had already involved substantial investment), the country launched a new nation-branding campaign titled "La respuesta es Colombia" on September 7, 2012, before an audience of 46,500, during the playoffs of the 2014 World Cup in Brazil, to the tune of $3.8 million (assigned to accounts with Omnicom solutions and WPP Colombia).[5] Peru, a key player in this area, invested more than $10 million just during the second half of 2014, largely relying on the sheer import of its nation brand.[6] In the case of Costa Rica, the government paid $650,000, a large sum for a small country, just for research for its 2013 brand—that is, this did not involve the actual launch of any campaign (González Sandoval 2013). Clearly, nation branding involves large sums of money. In terms of investment, it is key to recognize nation branding as an established commercial concept.

Countries like Peru have had nation-branding initiatives since 2009, though the concept was suggested as far back as the mid-1980s. In each case, the respective nation-branding campaign relies heavily on social media presence, frequently involving a dedicated website as well as feeds through venues like Facebook, Twitter, LinkedIn, Instagram, etc. Within the commercial and cultural practice that is nation branding, social media are construed as idealized channels of interaction between the public and campaign content. Hence, social media are thus taken as a logical outcome of the utilitarian nature of technology, facilitating an idealized perception of the world according to branding prerogatives. Social media play a key role in the dissemination of the brand and is integral to it being embraced by national and international audiences, never mind the fact that many of these platforms were initially conceived as outlets having little statistical weight. Following this mindset, it becomes painfully clear that the second phase of Tironi and Barandiarán's model—a redefinition of the role of the state—has taken place. At this point, the state has accepted its "limitations" and ceded ground to the private sector, agreeing the latter is better-suited to the management and assessment of national identity, effectively partaking in a policy-oriented game that limits its responsibilities and degree of accountability with respect to the overall population. To put it plainly, the state has succumbed to peer pressure—it has drunk the Kool-Aid, one could say—embracing nation branding as a surrogate for an expanded and better-documented understanding of national identity. In spite of everything, one could easily argue that countries with strong brand identity, such as Italy, Japan, Germany, or the US, managed to establish their particular character as the result of extensive investment in infrastructure, historically driven political and social processes, and judicious concern for general welfare, rather than advertising campaigns.

Among the top-ranked Latin American countries, the entities in charge of the promotion of these campaigns are, respectively: the Instituto Nacional de Promoción Turística (Inprotur) in Argentina; the Instituto Brasileiro de Turismo (Embratur) in Brazil; the Fundación Imagen de Chile in Chile; ProColombia in Colombia; the Instituto Costarricense de Turismo (ICT) and Procomer in Costa Rica; the Secretaría de Turismo (Sectur) in Mexico; the Autoridad de Turismo in Panama; the Comisión de Promoción del Perú para la Exportación y el Turismo (PromPerú) in Peru; the Puerto Rico Tourism Company in Puerto Rico; and the Ministerio de Turismo y Deporte in Uruguay. It is notable that, while these government agencies are "in charge" of campaigns, the actual design and implementation of each campaign is contracted to a firm from the private sector, most likely one of the local representatives of or a local agency linked to any of the five major advertising agencies in the world: the WPP Group (UK), Omnicom (US), Publicis (France), Interpublic (US), and Dentsu (Japan).

Each nation-brand campaign is embodied by the use of a corresponding slogan, usually identifying the complementary Facebook, Twitter, Instagram, or Pinterest feeds. Slogans are meant to convey a nexus between the values recognized and promoted by each campaign and its followers. They are as follows: Late con vos (Argentina); Brasil sensacional! (Brazil); Sorprende, siempre (Chile); La respuesta es Colombia (Colombia); Esencial Costa Rica (Costa Rica); Vive hoy, vive lo tuyo (Mexico); Visit Panama (Panama); Perú (Peru); The All-Star Island/La Isla Estrella (Puerto Rico); and Uruguay Natural (Uruguay). These slogans supposedly convey the gist of the identity of a country—its affective core, if you will—or the features that allegedly manage to represent it best, a claim that I find, at the very least, hard to fathom.

With minute variations, each country relies on a wide array of social media in the promotion of its nation brand (Argentina: Facebook, Twitter, Google, Instagram, Pinterest, Foursquare, and YouTube; Brazil: Facebook, Twitter, and Instagram; Chile: Facebook, Twitter, and YouTube; Colombia: Facebook, Twitter, Google, and YouTube; Costa Rica: Facebook, Twitter, YouTube, Pinterest, and Instagram; Mexico: Facebook, Twitter, YouTube, Instagram, Pinterest, and Google; Panama: Facebook, Twitter, Instagram, and Blogger; Peru: Facebook, Twitter, YouTube, and Google; Puerto Rico: Facebook, Twitter, and Pinterest; and Uruguay: Facebook and Twitter, with RSS and TV feeds). According to the inclinations of the advertising agencies, presence on these various platforms supposedly proves crucial to the advancement and promotion of a new profile-raising identity for each country. Beyond doubt, at the time of writing this piece, Facebook and Twitter appear as the prevailing social media, as nation-brand campaigns for all top-ranked Latin American countries have proprietary accounts. In fact, Facebook and Twitter figure as the only two distinctive social media outlets shared by all campaigns, adding to their degree of relevance in terms of campaign effectiveness. Beyond them, there is a marked preference for Instagram (in the cases of Argentina, Brazil, Costa Rica, Mexico, and Panama), Google (Argentina, Colombia, Mexico, and Peru), Pinterest (Argentina, Costa Rica, Mexico, and Puerto Rico), and YouTube (Argentina, Chile, Colombia, Costa Rica, Mexico, and Peru). Several entities also embrace RSS feeds or TV streaming feeds, but the use of these resources is more sporadic. Moreover, the fact that there is no consensus on the use of these other platforms highlights the widespread degree of reliance on Facebook and Twitter. Nowadays, given the scale of visibility intended by advertising agencies bent on transnational outreach, Facebook and Twitter, imagined as cyber non-places, are viewed as central to any symbolic effort. Given their omnipresence, these media figure as more fetishized indicators of the amount of interaction between the public and the nation-brand campaign than printed media or even the actual content being developed by any of the consulting firms.

That personally oriented websites tailored to institutional interests are being deployed with nationalist fervor appears deceitful, for what is nationalism but the expression of the love of nation in the language of the state? The theorization of such categories in the humanities far surpasses the way they are conceived of and interpreted within the world of advertising, where they are assessed in a concrete, functional manner. This aspect is worth mentioning, given its duplicitous nature. Furthermore, while a detailed examination of the behavior of the corresponding pages on Facebook or Twitter may evince limitations, in view of the way they are being embraced and deployed by nation-branding campaigns, the alleged claim is that they attest to the degree of penetration and effectiveness of each operation, regardless of particular considerations with respect to the nature of friends and followers. At the very least, this is what such an extensive usage of social media seems to suggest. The fact that at first glance it is not feasible to identify germane properties such as the origin and nature of "likes," "friends," or "followers" for specific feeds, elements that could provide precious information regarding the actual performance of any campaign, provides food for thought. Even in a relatively straightforward case like Chile or Costa Rica, given these countries' relatively low migration rates to the US, it is not feasible to tell much from the names associated with "likes" or "shares," nor the "retweets" or "follows" of any post (that is, when one looks further into the lists of participants). Further data mining could perhaps yield some insight into these aspects, but initial examinations do not provide much information.[7] Nonetheless, even at a superficial level, there are ways to question the manner in which parties involved in pursuits associated with nation branding have appropriated these media.

The following pie charts provide a better interpretation of the information ostensibly available through Facebook and Twitter. In the first case, the graphic illustrates the number of "likes" for the corresponding page of each nation-brand campaign. Though Twitter is more generous than

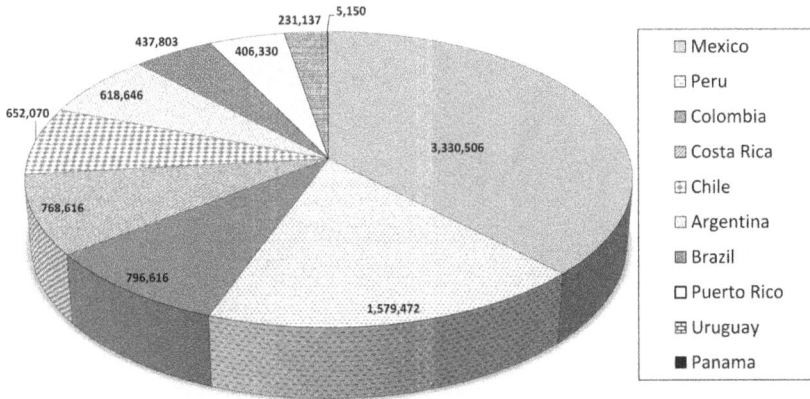

Figure 3.1. Number of Facebook "Likes" per country.

Facebook in terms of data, disclosing the number of tweets, the number of people currently following tweets, the overall number of followers, the number of people who have listed a feed as a favorite, and the number of lists on which a Twitter feed appears, for purposes of clarity, the second pie chart favors the overall number of followers as a key piece of information. Considering the highly malleable nature of Twitter—as opposed to Facebook's less-fluctuating temperament regarding information—it is important to contemplate data consistent to a comparable degree. It is also important to consider that, whereas activity in a Facebook feed can rely more on various sources (that is to say, the actual influence of friends or other individuals affecting the timeline of a feed), Twitter is more reliant on self-promotion or dedicated communication by an individual or party. Thus, data from Twitter, though more dynamic than data from Facebook, reflects to a greater extent the amount of work or effort coming from a single agent. Data from Facebook and Twitter can also benefit from a comparative vetting process. For purposes of control and comparison, I am using a third chart, which includes the number of arrivals (whether tourist or otherwise) in each country during 2012, the latest year for which, at the time of writing this text, all countries have provided reliable data on travel.[8]

What emerges as readily apparent from the first two images is that, when it comes to Facebook, Mexico, Peru, and Colombia stand out, comprising well over half of the activity related to nation-branding campaigns on Facebook. The results for the remaining countries, though lesser in

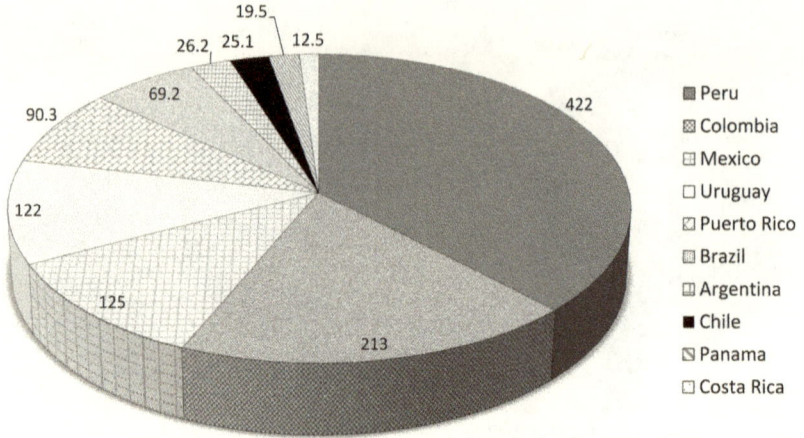

Figure 3.2. Number of Twitter followers (in thousands) per country.

magnitude, also provide relevant information. While the number of likes for a country like Chile is significant, the likes for Costa Rica represent a greater achievement, given its population and the size of its economy. Proportionally speaking, Costa Rica generates a number of "likes" that compares well to a sixth of its population, while Chile stands far behind. Then again, were Future Brand or any of the other agencies to disclose some information pertinent to the national origin of these "likes," perhaps

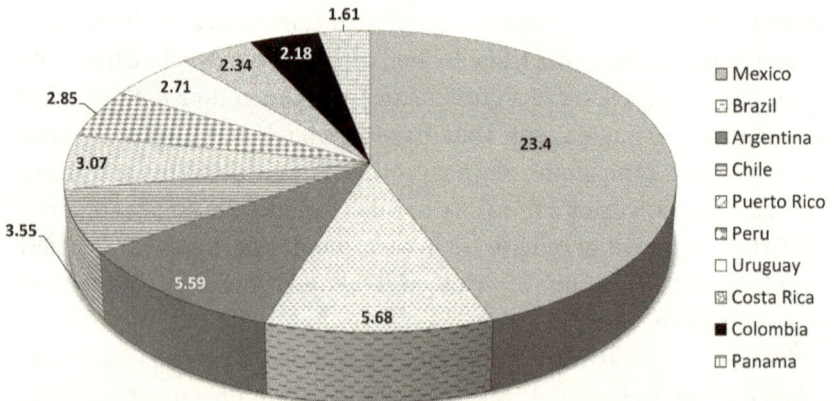

Figure 3.3. Number of arrivals (in millions) per country in 2012 (source: The World Bank).

Chile would come out faring better. This latter consideration points to a further, much-needed area of research into nation-branding campaigns.

When it comes to Twitter, Peru, Colombia, and Mexico (in this order) stand once again as heavy hitters, in this case covering almost three-quarters of the pie. Uruguay, a country that ranked low regarding Facebook, trades places with Costa Rica. The rest of the group remains in the mid-pack. The numbers for the remaining Southern Cone nations as well as for Brazil are rather dismal, a surprising fact considering the degree of digital literacy and access to technology in this part of the continent, higher than the regional average.[9] Data for Panama and Costa Rica show a definite lag in terms of Twitter activity, despite the fact both countries are quite active in this area. The official account Essential Costa Rica tweets content daily, whereas Visit Panama tweets several times a day. Still, the magnitude of the overall response to their tweets (19.5K and 12.5K, respectively) fails to attain critical volume, most likely a reflection of scant international reach and a nationally limited outcome.

The numbers for tourist arrivals stand in sharp contrast to the data resulting from social media. In terms of 2012 arrivals, Mexico remains at the head of the pack, while Peru and Colombia are relegated to the mid-pack and tail of the group respectively. Argentina and Brazil rise in numbers and move ahead, while arrivals surpass half of the population in countries like Costa Rica. Tourist arrivals do not necessarily embody information in terms of trade or governance, alternative fields targeted by nation branding, but, given their consistency, they provide a reasonably reliable measure of information in terms of international perception. It is very telling when a small country like Costa Rica manages to bring in well over half of its population's numbers in visitors. To imagine a comparable figure for Brazil or Mexico would result in very sizeable numbers. In terms of travel, given its proximity to large markets in the Americas, Mexico has traditionally outperformed other Latin American nations, even in times of instability and societal violence. Along the same lines, the need for nation branding does not appear as imperative in the case of a country like Peru, with an economy intent on catching up, economically and politically, with other South American countries; there are, one could argue, more pressing issues in terms of investment. Argentina and Brazil have usually come next, the former for historical reasons (the prioritization of European heritage, relative safety and affordability, etc.) and the latter for its rising profile (emerging as one of the top markets in the world).

A rise in numbers, such as Colombia was able to attain between 2012 and 2014, almost doubling its number of visitors without the assistance of important international events, represents a far better indicator of a shift in international perception than social media data, despite the claims of the advertising sector (Alsema 2015). Careful consideration of figures for tourist arrivals account better for statistical anomalies like the 2014 World Cup, which increased Brazil's figures by a million arrivals (Marcopoto 2014). In other words, when it comes to a shift in the degree of perception of a national image, numbers from social media are better consumed in context, just like arrivals. If we fail to consider events like the World Cup, which introduces a statistically anomalous spike in the data, results may appear to be dumbfounding. What, we are left to ask, justifies the consideration of a judicious context for the data?

On the whole, the consequences of nation-brand investment are supposed to surface in many ways, not just as arrivals, tourism, or trade. Yet the fact that Facebook and Twitter are favored as means of support for these campaigns and report data with scant correlation to the actual circumstances of consumption of national imagery points to the limited impact of digital media on more complex and ample aspects of identity. With this thought in mind, it is feasible to conclude that social media might prove particularly unsuitable to enterprises of this nature. Additional data mining, by means of environments like R (GNU S) or Dapper, or a pay service like Gnip or Datasift (for historical—that is, not real-time—data), could further complexify this picture. Yet what stands as unquestionable is that, when it comes to the sensible investment of government funds in a region deprived of elemental necessities, the shallow combination of identity politics and digital means makes for an utterly unreliable mix. It is equally perplexing that Latin American political establishments have fallen so rapidly and willingly for efforts of this nature, and that the parties involved have not demanded more accurate ways to substantiate the validity of their work. Mark Twain once famously asserted, "You can't depend on your eyes when your imagination is out of focus" (*A Connecticut Yankee in King Arthur's Court*, n.p.). This could easily be the case with nation brands in Latin America.

On July 6, 2017, the Costa Rican economic periodical *El Financiero* proudly published a story titled "Estudio: Marca país Esencial Costa Rica es la de mayor crecimiento en América" (Case Study: Esencial Costa Rica

Nation Brand is the Largest Growing One in the Americas) (Fernández Mora 2017). The article explains how, according to the firms Bloom Consulting and Place Matters, "experts in the evaluation of a country's standing in foreign markets," the value of the Costa Rican nation brand had risen twelve slots in terms of tourism and five for commerce and investment over the last three years (2015 through 2017 inclusive). Bloom Consulting is a Spanish-based firm specializing in nation branding that has the city of Miami among its clients; Place Matters is a British consultancy specializing in place branding with economic interests in Canada, the UK, and the US. According to their data, online searches from 2015 to 2017 increased 23 percent for tourism, 19 percent for investment opportunities, and 16 percent for exports. Both firms base their results on 63 million online searches over the same period, using three languages and 86,500 keywords. The results include 900 interviews with journalists, press agencies, tourism professionals, international recruiters, international organizations, multinational representatives, etc. Fifty-three percent of those interviewed allegedly recognized the Esencial logo and considered the concept of "essential" added value to tourism and business opportunities. Despite the debatable nature of these contentions, from a cultural perspective, the main flaw in Costa Rica's nation branding campaign resides in its promotion of essentialism, equating nationality with a set of intrinsic characteristics. This feature alone reveals the very superficial understanding of identity implicit in its implementation. For one, to think there is an essence is contrary to everything the humanities and social sciences claim when it comes to a more detailed assessment of identities, as the thought of all people related to a territory containing a fixed set of characteristics not only borders on perilous bio-determinism, but also suggests a very shallow understanding of the circumstances of a people as nation. In addition, one could argue that to think of essentialism as something positive and affirmative is akin to licensed prejudice. Also, the claim to an outstanding performance of the nation brand campaign by entities belonging to the same sector of the economy as its creators brings us to the third premise of Tironi and Barandiarán's study: the redefinition of the role of the expert. While members of the private sector are now identified as experts in national identity management, the work of previous experts—government personnel linked to the social sciences and/or humanities, perhaps even to cultural or policy-promoting entities associated with the state—is now relegated to a sanctioning of efforts by advertising or business professionals, assuming and legitimating their command of the subject matter.

Then again, on July 9, 2017, only three days after the article in question appeared in *El Financiero*, the newspaper *La Nación*, flagship of the homonymous media group, published a story titled "Ingreso de turistas de EE.UU. bajó este año en Costa Rica" (US Tourist Arrivals Decreased this Year in Costa Rica) (Barquero S. 2017). The drop was most likely the outcome of the increasing cost of travel to Costa Rica, given its conservative exchange rate policy, which has rendered life in the country—in many aspects—more expensive than in Europe. In light of the claim of the successful performance of the nation branding campaign, the complexity of identity becomes fully evident. Are we to conclude that, to the advertising executives, the alleged success of the campaign ratifies their assessment of Costa Rican identity? Are the many tourists visiting the tiny country all thinking about it in such a narrow manner? I beg to differ. It takes more than advertising campaigns to manage well the image of a nation. The key consideration is what most scholars involved in cultural studies understand well: identity is the result of a variety of complex issues. To attempt to encapsulate it within sets of very concrete quantifiers is entirely misleading. In this way, anything that stands beyond these parameters appears as an outlier, and I am not sure that is the nature of the mentality that any twenty-first century nation is willing to embrace to engage its population in a more effective fashion. Rather than defend the interests of a population, what this approach manages to accomplish is the validation of a reductive understanding of identity, enshrining know-nothingism and prescriptive thinking proper to the times by way of approaches that may work well in selling individual products, but that fall exceedingly short when it comes to engaging the more intangible nature of social and cultural constructs, even if adequately accompanied by technological dexterity. To view a national identity as a brand, to replace the bodies of the state previously dedicated to the promotion of folklore and culture—even if on a commercial basis—and to embrace advertising personnel (of all people, from a discipline dedicated to trickery and fabrication) as experts on identity, when their prescription for the idiosyncrasy of a people is encapsulated in a few lines and visual iconography founded on the playful conjugation of shapes and colors, comes across as a risky proposal. To suggest technology is a competent and reliable tool to back this bet to an inordinate degree sounds even more contemptible, particularly in the age of neoliberalism.

Notes

1. As in Ayn Rand, the author.

2. European and Latin American universities may also have endured neoliberalism, but branding seems less evident there as a symptom of this process. Globalization, though, is swiftly taking care of this aspect, as more universities around the world are beginning to market their identities.

3. For a brief review of some Latin American nation brands, see http://www.brandemia.org/latinoamercia-en-marcas/.

4. Among others, Future Brand is in charge of Argentina's nation brand, relaunched on September 3, 2013 (it was officially created in 2008), according to the website Brandemia. See Igor Iriarte, "Argentina renueva su marca país," *Brandemia*, October 3, 2013, http://www.brandemia.org/argentina-renueva-su-marca-pais. Accessed Feb. 27, 2019. It also created brands for Peru and Costa Rica, as well as those of other private-sector companies, like American Airlines. See Modesto García, "Futurebrand rediseña la marca turística de Costa Rica," *Brandemia*, September 17, 2013, http://www.brandemia.org/futurebrand-redisena-la-marca-turistica-de-costa-rica/. Accessed Feb. 27, 2019. See also Jason Torres, "Marca país genera críticas y dudas en varios sectores," *CRHoy*, September 4, 2013, http://www.crhoy.com/marca-pais-desata-criticas-en-el-congreso/.

5. Marca Colombia, 2012, "Colombia presenta su nuevo logo y su nueva imagen," http://www.colombia.co/videos/colombia-presenta-su-logo-y-nueva-imagen.html; "Colombia presenta su nueva marca país," *Revista Summa*, September 10, 2012, http://www.revistasumma.com/29716/; and "Qué país cambia de marca? . . . La respuesta es Colombia," *Brandemia*, n.d., http://www.brandemia.org/que-pais-cambia-de-marca-la-respuesta-es-colombia. In the case of Colombia, Omnicom is the result of temporary alliances between Sancho BBDO and the DDB group, whereas WPP Colombia is the outcome of alliances among JWT, RepGrey, and MEC.

6. "Mincetur invertirá más de US $10 millones en campañas de turismo receptivo," *Gestión*, September 8, 2014. The information is available at http://gestion.pe/economia/mincetur-invertira-mas-us10-millones-campanas-turismo-receptivo-imagen-pais-2107940.

7. Think of the potential for the harvesting of geospatial information from social media feeds as detailed in Anthony Stephanidis et al., "Harvesting ambient geospatial information from social media feeds," *GeoJournal* 78 (2013): 319–338.

8. See the World Bank Group, "International tourism, number of arrivals," *World Bank*, https://data.worldbank.org/indicator/ST.INT.ARVL. Accessed Feb. 27, 2019.

9. See Miniwatts Marketing Group, "Internet Usage and Population in South America," *Internet World Stats*, Feb. 25, 2018, https://www.internetworldstats.com/stats15.htm. Accessed Feb. 27, 2019.

4

(In)Visible Cuba(s)

Digital Conflict, Virtual Diasporas, and Cyber *Mambises*

ANASTASIA VALECCE

At the end of 2014, President Barack Obama announced the re-establishment of diplomatic relations with Cuba. Since then, a series of actions has marked significant changes for the island. Travel and trade restrictions have been eased and, in July 2015, President Obama announced the resumption of diplomatic ties with the island, reopening the US embassy in Havana that month. On November 25, 2016, Fidel Castro died, and with him the last 60 years of Cuban revolutionary history. Since before the death of Castro, as of the beginning of July 2015, several Wi-Fi spots had been activated in different neighborhoods of Havana for 2.00 CUC/hour.[1] These Wi-Fi spots are generally filtered or blocked by the government to prevent viewing of those websites that are considered "dangerous" or "counterrevolutionary." Regardless, access to the internet marked the beginning of a change in Cuba.[2] This shift in governmental policy regarding the use of the internet brought new ways to debate socialist ideology, reformulating strategies to operate, engage dialogue on, and accept any form of criticism of it. In order to understand current and future events, it remains important to analyze the ways in which the uses of the internet in Cuba have shaped national politics, society, and relations between the government and its citizens in the last few decades.

In this chapter, I will explore the role of the internet in Cuba from the perspective of conflict in the virtual space and how it is reshaping the Cuban revolutionary ideal. The study of interactions and conflicts in the Cuban digital space will be analyzed considering three main points. First, I will analyze the activity of the cyber *mambises*.[3] The second point relates to the ways in which these operatives are coordinated, organized, regulated, and how they maintain fluid cyber identities. Here I will bring in the example of Eliécer Ávila, whose digital and ideological identity shifts from being part of the cyber *mambises* to being part of the Cuban blogosphere. Ávila's shift from one position to another creates a visible political and social fluidity that would have been very difficult to express outside of the digital sphere. Finally, I will focus on the dynamics of control in the digital sphere, analyzing two possible outcomes: hypervisibility as a systematic method of intervention to discredit dissident bloggers, and the alternatives used by dissident bloggers to guarantee the circulation of their blogs when they cannot have access to the internet. These strategies create a space of digital conflict that changes the logics and logistics of governmental control and creates a connection with daily non-digital "incidents" (such as unjustified incarcerations, lynchings, public attacks, etc.). I will discuss, as an example, the experience of writer and blogger Orlando Luis Pardo Lazo. Taking into consideration the work of Cuban writer Antonio José Ponte, I will also shed light on how violence is practiced and perceived, and how it changes the interaction between the agent of surveillance and the object of control when the internet is part of the equation.[4]

Thus I will investigate the ways in which cyber *mambises* interact with the Cuba(s) of the (in)visible diasporas in order to control the digital zone in these virtual geographies; I will examine the social and political implications of these cyber activities, and the conflicts generated from them; and I will focus on the methods of control of the digital space and on how control is enacted through a hypervisible presence on the web. Consequently, the virtual interactions between the controller and the controlled change the dynamics of control, adding new layers to the dialogue—or lack of dialogue—and conflict between officials and dissidents on the island. From a theoretical standpoint, I will study the virtual conflict by taking into consideration Alexander Galloway's idea of the internet as a horizontal space of control through protocol in the age of decentralization. This framework will offer a better understanding of the social relations that determine the virtual conflicts among bloggers in Cuba.

Cyber *mambises* are Cuban citizens who work for the government or who are related to it in some way, and who collaborate to maintain the national and revolutionary integrity of any internet activity happening in Cuba. Specifically, the role of the cyber *mambises* is to control the virtual space and make sure that no counterrevolutionary propaganda is disseminated through the web. Dissident propaganda started mainly via blogs, and later developed as a presence in other cyberspaces such as Twitter, Facebook, and YouTube. Internet control happens by censoring webpages such as Google and Yahoo, and certain YouTube videos or specific blogs, because they are considered an implicit or explicit attack on the revolution.

Until at least 2008, cyber *mambises* were an invisible presence that could control internet activity on the island. Their identity was often unknown to internet users, and it was unclear to the general public how control of the cyberspace was organized and regulated. Thus the internet was a malleable space that could be invisibly shaped by governmental blogs. As such, cyber *mambises* throughout the years have developed different censoring strategies. For example, they engage in digital camouflage, using fake names or writing anonymously on "official" or "unofficial" blogs in order to confuse the reading audience, but also to attack and discredit dissidents by presenting dissident bloggers as enemies of the revolution with no moral values. However, cyber *mambises* never make strong counterarguments against the contents of the blogs they target. They also follow a blog or interact on Twitter without disclosing their political position, in order to keep the blogger under surveillance. As time has passed, more and more revolutionary blogs, Twitter and Facebook accounts, and YouTube videos have started populating the internet. Consequently, cyber *mambises* have started explicitly to try to discredit bloggers or digital activists because of their political opinions, using words such as *mercenario, gentucha, enemigos,* and *grupúsculos contrarrevolucionarios* to define them and their activity on the web.[5]

However, if the web allows cyber *mambises* to act anonymously under fake names or official names in order to control virtual activity, the fluidity of the internet also facilitates the (in)visibility of whoever populates the rest of cyberspace. The fragile virtual margin that distinguishes the controller from the controlled makes it difficult to observe any changes and shifts between the position of the controller and the position of the dissident. Such is the case of Eliécer Ávila, who belonged to the revolutionary project of *Operación Verdad* (Operation Truth), and specifically to the "Proyecto de Vigilancia Tecnológica y Política" (Project for the Control of Technology and Politics). Over three hundred students from the Universidad de las Ciencias Informáticas (a computer-science-oriented university) were serving the revolution by being part of *Operación Verdad*. This was a project to control cyberspace and to spread revolutionary ideology on the web. The idea came from the Department of Culture under Abel Prieto after he had held a meeting with the Union of Young Communists of the university.

At the time of Eliécer Ávila's activity in *Operación Verdad*, he was a student in Computer Engineering at the Universidad de las Ciencias Informáticas. On January 19, 2008, a day before the elections of representatives to the Provincial Assembly and to the National Assembly of People's Power, during a closed-door meeting involving students and professors, Ávila questioned the way in which the government handled internet on the island.[6] The interlocutor was the then-Vice President of the National Assembly of People's Power, Ricardo Alarcón. Alarcón was at the meeting to foster and represent Fidel Castro's preferences and facilitate a "united vote" (Ponte 2010, 177–231), probably because several students had questioned the ways in which elections were being handled. Ávila inquired into several issues, among which were the reasons why Yahoo and Google were not accessible in Cuba; however, all Alarcón could say was that he was ignorant about the issues around the internet's prohibitions.

The meeting was supposed to remain private. However, afterward, Ávila declared in different interviews that he had started receiving threats and bureaucratic quibbles from the government that were designed to marginalize him and to limit his participation in any social or political activity. Additionally, he was forced to live on the outskirts of Havana in economically difficult circumstances. In an interview in Miami with Jaime Bayly in 2013, Ávila no longer defined himself as a communist; however, he still very much maintained a socialist political perspective. He declared his disillusion with the revolution, and he explained the evolution that had brought him from the position of cyber *mambí* to that of prominent dissident.[7] Part of this change, he explained, had to do with his exposure to the internet. His participation in the cyber control group granted him access to information that most of his peers did not have, which, in turn, made him think deeply about the limits and the lack of knowledge that most Cubans were condemned to because of internet restrictions—restrictions that, after having been part of the cyber *mambises* for a time, Ávila could not fully accept.

The same year, dissident blogger Yoani Sánchez interviewed Ávila for her blog *14ymedio*.[8] In this dialogue, Ávila explained in detail what *Operación Verdad* was and how it was organized. He also explained to Sánchez the ways in which the cyber *mambises* were directed to censor her, and revealed that they used to receive instructions to discredit Sánchez as a person, rather than by contesting or responding to the topics that Sánchez would present in her blog posts or tweets.

Since the interview, Ávila has collaborated with Sánchez's site. Additionally, he has become active as a journalist and as founder of the movement *Somos +* (We Are More), which aims to create a space in which to debate Cuban society and politics, and he has also created a YouTube show titled "Un cubano más" (One More Cuban), through which he offers his opinions on Cuban political reality.[9] Ávila's main goal in his posts and videos is to invite viewers/listeners to discuss and question current political issues in Cuba, and to call for the right to freedom of expression of ideas not in line with the revolution. Ávila's political and virtual transformation aimed to create opposition from within the system. Ávila's virtual and ideological identity changed from that of a cyber *mambí* to being part of the dissident blogosphere. As he has said in different interviews, his goal is to create a space of dialogue about and critique of the socialist system from a leftist perspective. Consequently, the shift and the visibility of Ávila's position create a new kind of disagreement, which adds a new layer to the virtual conflict from a socialist perspective. Still, his virtual transformations became possible because of a(n in)visible political and social fluidity that constitutes the amorphous nature of the digital sphere. This fluidity makes conceivable new connections in the conflict and creates multi-angled dialogues.

These new forms of dialogue and conflict also require different strategies of control, such as maintaining the hypervisibility of official blogs on the web in an attempt to overshadow dissident voices. However, conflicts in cyberspace are not limited to digital media. Dissidence also spills out of the internet and into a non-virtual space, which is populated by alternatives that overcome cybernetic control and manage to spread blog-gers' voices through USBs, DVDs, and print. Here, digital activists are met with a different series of censorship measures; the materiality of the alternative circulation of information brings daily "incidents" that range from bureaucratic difficulties to verbal and physical violence.

Media hostility in the very first years of the Cuban revolution created a neat line of separation between revolutionary and dissident, a separation later highlighted by Fidel's famous speech: "Dentro de la revolución, todo; fuera de la revolución, nada" (Within the revolution, everything; outside the revolution, nothing).[10] In the twenty-first century, beyond the revolu-tionary need for control that the state has applied since 1959, cybernetic interaction between revolutionaries and dissidents does not allow for the same clear distinction between insiders and outsiders that existed in past decades. There are different kinds of opposition from within the revolu-tionary and socialist wings, a phenomenon that reshapes the conflict and grounds it in a new, less clear, and less recognizable space.

Bloggers are the most visible consequence in Cuba of the presence of non-authorized citizens on the internet, and they offer an alternative source of information from official publications. This alternative journal-ism has given visibility to some of Cuba's overlooked social and political issues to the point where this virtual cohabitation has created a digital conflict. The use of the internet has created, for the first time in decades, an invisible citizenship that exists on the internet through the expression of bloggers' opinions about politics, society, moral values, etc. The cohabi-tation of (in)visible diasporas, (in)visible dissidents, and cyber *mambises* produces a virtual geography where citizenship, conflicts, and dialogues take place in cyberspace, reinventing interactions within visible Cuban society.[11]

The online world allows the coexistence of a variety of perspectives that mark a trajectory in which the rhizomatic movement "in between" becomes more important than the two extremities. The mobility of these subjects creates confusion, but also defines, as in the case of the digital Cuba, a reinvented and virtual Caribbean identity.[12] In the 2000s, the Cu-ban blogosphere offered visibility to local problems, and escaped any tra-ditional form of revolutionary control as it had been implemented from the 1960s onward. Bloggers thus contribute to creating a polyphonic soci-ety far from the monolithic nature of socialist ideology.[13]

Even the criteria for censorship and repression have to change in the borderless online space. As Galloway points out, the internet is a controlled network in a time of decentralization when the center is nowhere and its circumference is everywhere (2004, xiv). In Galloway's opinion, protocol is what allows a horizontal distribution of controlled information on the internet, since protocol is "a set of technical procedures for defining, managing, modulating, and distributing information throughout a flexible yet robust infrastructure" (xv). Understanding protocol is the key to understanding how power functions in societies even when there are resistance and counter-protocol practices, such as the case of hackers, since protocol is always layered, stratified, and hierarchical. Galloway's main question regards where the power has gone with the internet. He argues that protocol defines a space in which "power relations are in the process of being transformed in a way that is resonant with the flexibility and constraints of information technology. The Internet is not simply 'open' or 'closed' but . . . is modulated" (xix). The information flows in a regulated manner; the regulated flow thus determines the politics of technology.

Protocol offers a material understanding of technology, shifting the question of who the technology works for (the user or the provider) in order to clarify the logics of control and power in media (Galloway 2004, xiii). As well, the power relationships happen through an electronic structure that is shifting away from traditional political structures and toward various networks, either biological or electronic. Thus, "non-human" or "in-human" forms share characteristics with near-living things, such as viruses. Similarly, the biopolitics of internet regulations and resistance in Cuba bombard the internet with cyber *mambises* who, as viruses of different kind, create diversity in the blogosphere. Protocol problematizes the revolutionary hierarchical model, creating cultural objects (blogs) and engendering virtual life forms (cyber *mambises*). It also challenges the limits between matter and life, creating a thin line between the revolutionary subject and the revolutionary object, which parallels the shift from virtual to physical attacks and practices of power.

According to Galloway, the digital conflict in this horizontal relation and structural protocol logic can be fought only between networks. Thus, the disruptions practiced by cyber *mambises* and by the blogosphere become the only form of relation and resistance possible among networks. Nevertheless, in the case of the Cuban blogosphere, I believe that the politics of power and control are not based merely on protocol, as Galloway suggests. In fact, as mentioned earlier, the main strategy used by cyber *mambises* to control and discredit counterrevolutionary bloggers is the production of systematic arguments that not only discredit the dissident person, but also overpopulate the web in order to make the dissidence invisible. Dissidents and cyber *mambises* overlap in the digital sphere, making the line between allies and enemies very confusing. The state's goal is to establish a panoptic view through official blogs that constitute a space that is not clearly positioned in the revolutionary logic.[14] Thus the uniqueness of these blogs is eliminated by discounting the value of their critique of Cuban society. Considering Galloway's idea of resistance, the erasure of the blogosphere as a surveillance technique represents a way to resist and exist through non-existence. Cyber *mambises*' hypervisibility renders the blogosphere invisible and more controllable. Whatever the effects of these strategies of control and power, cyberspace redefines the social relations that determine the virtual conflicts among bloggers in Cuba. Virtual debates create a space for new dialogues and disputes in Cuba from a non-hierarchical cyberspace where the boundaries between the traditional ways to perceive a revolutionary and a counterrevolution-ary idea overlap and are flexible. Thus the virtual space as a hypervisible grey zone changes the dynamics of the conflict and creates new strategies of control and violence, virtual coexistence, and digital cohabitation.

As an example of the interaction between virtual and physical violence, I will analyze the case of the dissident blogger, photographer, writer, and activist Orlando Luis Pardo Lazo. This case is not isolated, of course, as many others have had similar experiences.[15] I decided to focus on Pardo Lazo because his is a less-known case at the crossroads of the virtual, digital, and daily confrontation with government. Pardo Lazo's activity as a blogger emerged with a new generation of young intellectuals that decided to use the space of the internet to document their points of view and introduce them into the public domain.

Pardo Lazo was a recognized figure on the island because of his activ-ity as a writer and photographer between 2000 and 2012. Despite the fact that in his writings he always offered a critical view of the contemporary situation in Cuba, it appears the Cuban government only considered him a dissident once he began his activity as a blogger. Pardo Lazo arrived on the internet a little later than others, in 2008, when he started publishing columns of literary criticism on a blog titled *El Fogonero Emergente*, man-aged by another Cuban colleague located in Spain, Jorge Alberto Aguiar

Díaz. Once Pardo Lazo decided to start his own blog at the end of 2008, he named it *Lunes de Post Revolución* (Post-Revolution Mondays), as a message of hope for the future of Cuba after the revolution, but also as a cultural and historical reference to one of the first cultural magazines published in Cuba in the sixties (and very quickly censored), titled *Lunes de Revolución* (Revolution Mondays).

In 2009, after being censored as a writer, he started another blog, *Boring Home Utopics*, as a space in which to represent visually a lost island to the dissidents outside Cuba, in order to tell stories and reconnect Cuban citizens beyond any restriction. This project also aimed to invert the logic of Cuba perceived as a third-world country in need of help. Instead, the objective was to help Cubans outside Cuba to recuperate their memories, and at the same time to depict a contemporary Havana visually, dismantling any kind of romantic memories around it. Thus Pardo Lazo would collect on his blog requests from expatriates all over the world to photograph a certain home, a neighborhood, a specific school, etc. Through his blog, Pardo Lazo made himself a visual witness to and a digital intermediary of the city of Havana. The blog became a way to reconnect and recollect common memories despite geographical borders, creating a new and utopic *cubanía*.[16] This blog was also censored for over a year in Cuba, but still managed to circulate inside and outside the island through proxy technology or flash drives.

His blogs *Lunes de Post Revolución* and *Boring Home Utopics* explored possible futures of "post revolution" realities, and created a space for open discussions about the island, as did all of his following projects, such as his photography blog *País de Pixeles*, his magazine *Voces Cubanas*, and the literary works he began after emigrating to the United States in 2012. All of Pardo Lazo's works are visual critical documents that aim to open debates around the situation in contemporary Cuba. In all of his blogs, projects, and publications, his goal is to discuss the revolutionary administration, criticize its flaws, and open a space of dialogue among Cuban citizens on and outside the island. In several interviews and publications, Pardo Lazo claims his right, as a Cuban citizen, to dissent, to react, and to participate in the decisions of the Cuban government as a citizen. Even when censored, his publications represented an alternative to official news outlets.

An example of the daily restrictions Pardo Lazo had to deal with while on the island is found in his novel *Boring Home*. Officially censored in

Cuba in 2009, and later published in Venezuela, it was awarded the Franz Kafka Drawer Novel Prize, a Czech literary award. After the censorship of the novel, Pardo Lazo experienced all kinds of verbal and physical threats and aggressions. In addition to receiving frequent in-person abuse, Pardo Lazo was the target of pieces published by various government figures who sought to undermine his credibility, creating a lot of "virtual noise" instead of allowing real debate. One example of many is an article by Percy Francisco Alvarado Godoy (2014) on his blog *Descubriendo ver-dades*, titled "La desvergüenza de un mercenario" (The Shamelessness of a Mercenary). The revolutionary blogger refers to Pardo Lazo as a "counter-revolutionary and a sociopath," among other adjectives, and many official articles have used the same kind of rhetoric since the beginning of Pardo Lazo's online presence.[17]

Pardo Lazo's declarations regarding the government's attempts to contain and control the blogosphere, as well as his own production, mainly took place in the virtual space. Consequently, the conflict, censorship, and control mainly happened in virtual territory as well. The cyber *mambises* who worked to discredit him overpopulated the web, and in doing so, they created confusion regarding the validity of his online pieces. However, Pardo Lazo also exposed the non-virtual methods of control, censorship, and violence enacted by the revolution that he had to face in his daily life by reporting on them.

Pardo Lazo's story, as I mentioned, is only one of many examples of bloggers and artists who tell their stories through their blogs, Twitter, or Facebook. As in the case of Pardo Lazo, they all find in the virtual space a place of resistance as well as a place where they can denounce and disagree, and so a place where conflict can happen. As well, the online hypervisibility that the Cuban government uses to monitor, discredit, and create disruption and confusion around these bloggers also exposes officials when they are denounced by bloggers. As Ponte points out, there has been an exposure in media of the violence practiced by the government that coincides with the disappearance of Fidel Castro from the public scene, and with the invisibility of institutions and the impossibility of having a dialogue with them (2010, 177–231). Thus, while the virtual space is overpopulated, the public space is empty and paralyzed when it comes to official answers or freedom of expression.

According to Ponte, there is a performativity to official rituals that includes the practice of verbal and physical violence on a daily basis. Virtual conflict and daily violence run into each other and display their spectacle on the web—for instance, when Pardo Lazo records a public protest or police brutality, or when he visually witnesses Havana's urban decadence (Ponte 2010, 177–231). Cuban vigilance in the virtual era goes beyond the Committees for the Defense of the Revolution, the officers in the streets, or the system of vigilance among neighbors. Havana becomes a space openly controlled in the streets as well as on the web. And it becomes a virtual dispute between the controller and the controlled, between violence practiced by officials and the virtual and digital testimonies of bloggers. The time of creation, as well as the time of punishment, have no temporal limits, boundaries, or official dates. Bloggers, when incarcerated, are deprived of any information on procedure or the time they will spend in jail, nor are they provided the reason for their punishment. Bloggers can then only denounce through their blogs this empty and endless time that paralyzes them in their daily reality.[18] Cyberspace thus becomes the place and moment in which to define the conflict under different terms in which official control is not merely based on protocol but is about the production of content.

Hyperproduction by the Cuban government guarantees a disruption of the messages sent by dissidents. However, this disruption makes the conflict and the dispute possible in a way that it is not in real life, as other dynamics that involve physical violence impede any kind of dialogue around the conflict. There is a close connection between what happens in a police station, at a public event, or in the streets and what is produced online. Physical violence is verbally or visually represented and denounced in the digital space, which often brings to light the real, official, or invented identities of the publishers, enhances the relation between art and politics, and reveals the connection between violence and control. Moreover, even without the internet, bloggers can rely on alternative ways to circulate their writings.[19] For these writers, the internet becomes the invisible space through which they can make themselves visible and acknowledged. The flexibility and the visibility of the internet cross the borders of what can exist within the revolution. The work of these citizens sheds light on issues that were previously invisible. Online dissidents claim their virtual citizenship through their blogs as an alternative to the impossibility of being recognized by their society in their individuality as real citizens. Virtual citizens and cyber *mambises* thus coexist in the same internet society in a relationship of digital conflict. The nature of this conflict challenges and crafts contemporary society both in and outside Cuba, where virtual or physical abuses are one of the consequences faced by dissidents in the violent relationship between the agent of surveillance and the object of control.

In this chapter, I have focused on the virtual conflict in Cuba in order to shed light on the ways in which it challenges and crafts contemporary Cuba. In particular, I explored the role of cyber *mambises* and the ways in which they implement control and censorship; the case of Eliécer Ávila, whose digital and ideological identity shifted from cyber *mambí* to being part of the dissident blogosphere; and the case of blogger Orlando Luis Pardo Lazo as an example of the intersection between virtual conflict and physical abuse. These three examples help to reveal the internet as a place that, as Galloway defines it, functions as a horizontal space of control through protocol. Protocol helps Cuban bloggers to deal with power and control in a digital era. Thus cyberspace is redefining the identities and relationships of both dissidents and official government representatives. The virtual sphere forces all citizens to interact and communicate in virtual debates exploring a social space ignored or repressed in pre-digital Cuba. Virtual conflict becomes necessary in order to reinvent social dialogue and interactions with power. In the attempt to silence and erase information, control sheds light on spaces that are arduous to eliminate even when banned. The virtual identities of revolutionaries and counter-revolutionaries are not so clear anymore, since different points of view that had no space in the binary social discourse of the past have found their spot in heterogeneous online dissidence. The virtual conflict highlights topics that would be more easily censored otherwise. Thus cybernetic space allows the distinguishing of not two poles, but a multiplicity of points of view that inhabit a flexible zone.

These digital clashes represent a new space of debate in Cuba—a non-hierarchical cyberspace where the boundaries between the traditional way to perceive a revolutionary and a counterrevolutionary can overlap and are flexible and, as such, are hard to establish. Consequently, the virtual space becomes a hypervisible grey zone that changes the dynamics of the conflict and creates new strategies of control, virtual coexistence, and digital cohabitation. The virtual Cuba emphasizes movements that create new fluidities that connect the many Cuba(s) of the inside and the outside for the social architecture of a digital future. Digital Cuban citizenship is pushed to its limits, sheds light on non-official/marginal voices that overflow the virtual page, and forces society to react. The Cuban revolution of today has to deal with a different era made of new oppositions, important historical changes, and a cyberspace that in the last decade has transformed the current forms of communication between authorities and (all) present, future, and (in)visible Cuba(s).

Notes

1. Since 2004, US dollars have been banned from Cuba, and two currencies have been introduced: the CUC (Cuban Convertible Peso) and the Cuban peso (Moneda Nacional). One CUC = 25 pesos. However, 2.00 CUC/hour is still a prohibitive cost for many Cubans on the island.

2. As the chapter refers to ongoing contemporary issues regarding the internet in Cuba, there are policies, events, and restrictions that occur on a daily basis that cannot possibly be included in this chapter, since the island is constantly going through many social and political changes.

3. Cyber *mambises* are Cuban citizens not necessarily in the military, but affiliated with the revolutionary cause. On behalf of the government, they control all virtual activity on the island, report counterrevolutionaries' activities, and censor some internet pages when necessary.

4. See Ponte 2010, 177–231.

5. All these words are pejorative terms and refer to people of no value. They are used frequently in blogs or YouTube videos to describe dissident bloggers.

6. The transcription of this conference can be found in Ponte 2010, 177–231. See also *Eliécer Ávila ridiculiza a Ricardo Alarcón*, YouTube video posted by "Faraon Cuba," April 23, 2011, https://www.youtube.com/watch?v=42T0BNNHZA0.

7. *HD Noticias: Jaime Bayly entrevista a Eliecer Avila (Completo) 2013*. YouTube video posted by "72pantalla2," May 14, 2013, https://www.youtube.com/watch?v=YglTusAr0Fw.

8. Yoani Sánchez is a well-known case of blog dissidence in Cuba. She is a pioneer, and was the first to be targeted by cyber *mambises*. Fake identities and websites using forms of her name, such as the posts of Yohandry Fontana and the page www.yoan-islandia.com, attempt to discredit Sánchez by questioning her ability to access to the internet and alluding to the economic support that she supposedly receives from the United States to maintain her digital activity. Both examples here recall the name "Yoani" in order to create a sort of confusion and digital disruption.

9. Cubaencuentro, "Eliecer Ávila estrena en YouTube el espacio de opinión 'Un cubano más,'" n.d., http://www.cubaencuentro.com/multimedia/videos/eliecer-avila-estrena-en-youtube-el-espacio-de-opinion-un-cubano-mas. Accessed on March 2, 2019. See also "Somos +," n.d., http://somosmascuba.com/quienes-somos/. Accessed March 2, 2019.

10. From Fidel Castro's speech *Palabras a los intelectuales* (Words to the Intellectuals), delivered in 1961 at a meeting with artists and intellectuals to define cultural and artistic production following revolutionary ideals. See Fidel Castro Ruz, "Palabras a los

intelectuales," Cuba, 1961, http://www.cuba.cu/gobierno/discursos/1961/esp/f300661e. html. Accessed March 2, 2019.

11. There are many documentaries on the topic of the internet in Cuba that can be found online, such as *Ojos que te miran: entre redes (Eyes that Look at You: Among Networks)* by Rigoberto Senarega (2012); *Off Line* by Yaima Pardo (2013); or *Blog Bang Cuba* by journalist Claudio Peláez Sordo (2014). Additionally, there are many blogs published by both "dissidents" and "revolutionaries" that address issues of race, gender, gay rights, etc., such as *Negra cubana tenía que ser, paquitoeldecuba, chiringadecuba, havanatimes. org, Blogazo por Cuba, Cuba material, Estado de Sats, Octavo Cerco, Espaciodeelaine. wordpress.com,* etc.

12. I am thinking here of Edouard Glissant's theory of the "rhizome" in his work *Poetics of Relation*. According to Glissant, the concept of the rhizome describes the poly-rooted character of Caribbean subjectivity (1997, 11). In a similar way, the opaque space of the Cuban blogosphere determines a new generation of poly-rooted intellectuals who need to be handled in a new way. This phenomenon creates a new Caribbean (virtual) subjectivity similar to the process explained by Glissant.

13. As Ariana Hernandez-Reguant points out in *Cuba in the Special Period*, "the sharp distinction between the official and the unofficial . . . began to wane and alternative expressions (e.g., youth popular culture) challenged the elitism of the art and culture apparatus" (2009, 11).

14. Foucault's idea of the panopticon relates to the traditional strategies of control of the Cuban government. According to the social theory of Panopticism, the architectural structure of the panopticon (thinking of the architecture of a prison) generates a disciplinary mechanism and illustrates the function of discipline as an apparatus of power. The ever-visible inmate is always "the object of information, never a subject in communication" (Foucault, 1995, 200–201). I see similarities to the logic behind the work of cyber *mambises*. The hypervisibility provoked by the overpopulation of blogs establishes an invisible supervision that is everywhere at all times. However, the panopticon view requires a centralized control that is no longer applicable in a decentralized context as conceived by Galloway. Consequently, the (in)visible presence of cyber *mambises* has to operate in a horizontal structure, changing the dynamics of control.

15. Other cases include the well-known case of Yoani Sánchez, Cuban American performer Tania Bruguera, visual artist El Sexto, and the cinematographer and blogger Boris González Arena, to mention a few.

16. The term *cubanía* refers to the sense of feeling like a Cuban citizen.

17. Percy Francisco Alvarado Godoy, "La desvergüenza de un mercenario," June 19, 2014, http://percy-francisco.blogspot.com/2014/06/la-desverguenza-de-un-mercenario. html. Accessed on March 2, 2019.

18. Also see Ponte 2010.

19. The black market for digital writings available to Cubans is explained in an interview with Yoani Sánchez in the Barbara Miller documentary *Forbidden Voices* (2012).

II

Transnational Networks

5

Digital Utopias, Latina/o Mediated Realities

ANGHARAD N. VALDIVIA

Every new telecommunications technology is accompanied by utopian promises of social transformation (Mosco 2004) and an increase of human happiness (Levitas 2010 and 2013), transferred to each new technology. Dating back to the telegraph through to the contemporary digital, dreams and myths promise communication technologies will "transcend time (the end of history), space (the end of geography), and power (the end of politics)" (Mosco 2004, 3). This chapter explores the uses and abuses of the utopian discourse and considers some of the parameters influencing the revolutionary potential of digital technologies for Latinas/os.

The discourse of the technological sublime has been uncannily consistent. Drawing on Harold Innis (2004) and James Carey (1989), Vincent Mosco presents the latest analysis of the myth. Whereas Carey critiques the technological sublime for deflecting attention from the social costs incurred by the introduction of technological innovation into lived communities [Carey 1989, 179] and for foregrounding the transmission aspect of communication [Ibid., 160], Mosco (2004) examines the process of mythification (space, time, and power). The resulting fixation on a digital utopia needs to be examined in relation to the presence of Latinas/os. The twenty-first century digital promised-land hallucinatory discourse, or, as Mosco calls it, "a collective belief that cyberspace was opening a new world" (4), has to be weighed against the lived reality of a highly stratified population. To hold that digital technology and communication are the great flatteners of difference and discrimination relies on "widespread cultural amnesia" (Mosco 2004, 117).

New telecommunication technologies inevitably lead to utopian and dystopian fears and desires. Mentioning caution can get one labeled an anti-utopian, a dystopian, or a Luddite. Critiques situating new discoveries as strengthening capitalism are categorized as anti-dystopian (Levitas 2013). In a historical moment when stratification is rapidly increasing, digital technologies have not ameliorated world poverty, environmental destruction, or marginalization of racialized populations. For example, toxic water in Flint, Michigan is often discussed as if it could only happen in the so-called third world. Similarly, the effects of Hurricane Katrina's devastation were borne primarily by people of color in Louisiana. Finally, #45's election illustrates the deep resentment and disillusionment of a US working class that has seen a huge transfer of wealth affect its present and future ability to survive in a highly competitive economic climate.

Given the changing demographics of the US population, in which the 2000 US Census documented the majority/minority status of Latina/os, it behooves us to disaggregate the discursive terrain for ethnicity and socioeconomic status in relation to the promise of digital communications technology. Squires (2013) reminds us that "Unpacking the large and subtle ways race/ethnicity have shaped our media systems, production, and reception serves to both complicate and complete our view of the past" (126). Digital technologies hold out the promise of increased democracy, unity, creativity, upward mobility, and understanding while becoming incorporated into global structures of profit without social justice goals. They facilitate the upward mobility, or at least the employment security, of a portion of the population while augmenting social and economic segregation (Hargittai 2011; Hargittai and Hinnant 2008; NPR 2015; World Bank 2016).

The aggregated digital utopia discourse circulates many keywords: "digital natives," "knowledge economy," "interactive and participatory democracy," "prosumers," etc. Utopic projections are not necessarily derived from scientific evidence but more from an ideological or popular longing for a better place. Because utopic concepts are mythical does not mean they lack the power to generate policies and politics with implicit inclusive and exclusionary outcomes. Expounding the gains of the internet for the population in the aggregate obscures benefits for some at the expense of others. For example, young, upscale urban users of the internet have more access, bandwidth, and income, while many older rural residents still have difficulty receiving mobile telephony, let alone consistent internet service or electricity. Age, class, and ethnicity contribute to a significant yet shrinking digital divide (Pew Research Center 2015). As the number of digital devices per household varies greatly, public libraries have instituted computer usage rules to manage the flow of the poor at public access locations.

The changing demographics of the US population follow yet another recurring discourse—the Latina/o boom, which repeatedly "discovers" racialized segments of the population (Cepeda 2010; Valdivia 2013). The presence and production of popular culture are treated like Columbus "discovering" America (Cepeda 2001). When the boom subsides, Latinas/os and their cultural production are forgotten, only to be rediscovered as another "boom." Yet a population cannot appear and disappear except in discursive terms. Mainstream media's "discovery" every few decades launches the marketing of food, music, celebrities, and culture to generate profit. The presence, labor, discrimination, and oppression of Latinas/os continues unabated despite the celebratory discovery. The overlap of new technology and boom discourse generates a utopian dream of ascendance and inclusion for Latinas/os through digital technologies that—like all myths of discovery—is only possible through amnesia and denial. Ricky Martin, Junot Díaz, and Jennifer Lopez crossing over into the mainstream following Selena's death was a Latina/o boom. Following an overview of the discourse of new technology or "the myth of the technological sublime" (Mosco 2004), this chapter explores its different "promises" as these relate to the presence of Latinas/os. The Public Interest Standard provided an opening for Latina/o intervention weighed against the tendencies toward concentration and consolidation of conglomerate media, enabling an examination of contemporary and contradictory digital Latina/o utopias.

History

Since the introduction of the telegraph and radio, the discourse of new telecommunications technologies and the forces that mitigate its utopian outcomes have contained recurring elements of unification and inclusion

of previously marginalized groups. Location and geography that subsumed issues of race, class, and ethnicity belied innocently generic terms.
Through cohesion and harmony, the telegraph was supposed to end the
divisions among classes and races brought about by the industrial age
(Mosco 210). Technologies funded by governments for geopolitical reasons were publicly discussed as the cure for social and economic woes.
The US needed sovereignty from the British, whose Atlantic underwater
cables carried sensitive national information and news. Control over and
independence from information technologies and networks represent national ascendance and power. The US, a rising global player, asserted its
status vis-à-vis the UK. The discourse privileged harmony over thornier
issues of geopolitics, focusing on unity rather than postcolonial delinking.

Developments in telecommunications established US broadcast radio
as a commercial medium—with ham operators relegated to the margins
of the electromagnetic spectrum. A bifurcated technology, radio was sold
to consumers as a "receiver" of messages from a major network transmit-
ter (Anderson 2013; Barnouw 1966–1970). This corporate-owned, centralized transmission/sending of messages, interrupted by commercials, was
not the only way for radio to develop, but became a dominant structure
for the future of telecommunications and media in the US. By the 1980s
the US had emerged globally victorious with this corporate pattern of
broadcasting. Returning to broadcast radio reminds us that its original
technological function was truncated for everyone but ham operators
and the military. Radio's utopian public advocacy outcomes seem to be
borne out much more often by Spanish-language radio, which in the US
has huge audiences and influence (Casillas 2014; Castañeda 2008 and
2014), with Latinas/os exhibiting higher radio listenership than the general population and more reliance on radio news. The history of Latina/o
radio includes documentation of efforts to silence it or relegate it to fewer
desirable frequencies and time slots. Dávila and Rivero (2014) reveal that
marketing measures served to miss and misrecognize Latinas/os as components of the radio audience.

Radio broadcasting makes use of the electromagnetic spectrum—a
public good—and thus licenses to commercial radio stations were ostensibly granted to "serve the public interest," reminding us that it was
turned into a commercial technology owned and operated by a govern-
ment-sanctioned oligopoly. FCC guidelines grant and renew broadcasting licenses "to serve the public interest," a standard to be fulfilled at a

local level. Communities with large Latina/o populations ought to have been able to secure licenses for radio stations. However, early operationalization of the "public interest" standard meant transmission interference. The electromagnetic spectrum was parsed out to a small number of license holders, resulting in an oligopolistic network-style broadcasting system, precluding competition and generating great profits. As recently as 2012 the FCC interpreted the public interest standard as promoting "diversity, localism, and competition" (Castañeda 2014, 186); this contemporary neoliberal system, favoring market profit over community benefits, continues the tendency toward centralization and conglomerate ownership and production of media, including radio. In the contemporary digital universe, oligopolistic tendencies have ramifications for racialized populations such as Latinas/os. Reliance on conglomerate-produced media, circulated on digital platforms, results in high barriers to entry, even in internet programming.

Initial government and US taxpayer investment in telecommunications technology, which are turned over to corporations for profit without any remuneration to the taxpayers who originally funded such endeavors, is another pattern in our history of telecommunications, as is the deployment of technological developments for military uses (Difilippo 1990). The digital universe, like radio, was developed with public funds in public universities with government research funds and then capitalized through the private sector for individual and corporate profit. This means that taxpayers pay twice: once for the R&D and then for the public sector purchase and use of the capitalized technologies. Through taxation we all pay for this technology, yet access benefits unequally.

Geography and the Myth

A focus on space remains a salient geographical aspect of the myth: these technologies will unite us across space (Mosco 2004). Lerner (1958) and Rogers (1994) suggest that communication studies became institutionalized in the US academy through their international dimension, an implicit promise of space-time compression. Lerner singles out radio as the "mobility multiplier" whose modern sensibility was supposed to transition populations to modernity, explicitly constructing modernity as masculine and tradition as feminine (Valdivia 1996): international radio news would Westernize/modernize men, yet leave women behind in tradition.

Lerner's myth of the technological sublime posited that radio would lead to the passing of traditional society in the Middle East (the book *The Passing of Traditional Society* was published in 1958), and implicitly, in the entire world. Ironically, in the Middle East, where an intense religious backlash replaced a secular moment, multiple backlashes continue to demonstrate that even digital media can be used to challenge and strengthen religious regimes (Bulut 2016). Within the US sphere of influence, radio deployment also widely targeted Latin America. Following the revolution in 1959, Radio Martí broadcast US propaganda to Cuba. At the Mexican and Canadian borders, radio stations transmit across national boundaries. Latina/o populations in the US, underserved by mainstream radio, rely on border transmissions and the handful of programs from local Latina/o radio. In contrast, Canada resents its population's reliance on US-border broadcasting. Radio transmission challenges national borders.

Unification plays an integral role in the US due to its size. Though the country has become easier to cover with contemporary transportation, it remains huge.[1] Thus the promise of geographical unification is one held out by each new communications technology, as most residents in the US still do not have the resources or will to travel. Ideally, transmission of intelligence would lead to community formation, understanding, and communication at a national level. Given that telecommunications facilitate the mobility of information over that of physical bodies,[2] for diasporic US Latina/o populations to be able to communicate without travel is highly valuable. Some of this promise is fulfilled for Latinas/os by the ability to consume the same media across national boundaries, a strategy for maintaining familial connections and affinities (Vargas 2009).

Geography influences regionality. A country as large as the United States has regions whose distinctions have become less marked. The North, South, East, West, Midwest, and Southwest have distinct characters, populations, foods, and accents whose composition is not static and changes due to economic and migration flows. For instance, the Civil War was fought by the North and the South whose, cultural and economic interests clashed violently. To be from the East or the West coast connotes a range of differences, despite the commonality of the coastal experience. The Northeast and the Southwest represent different styles and approaches to life, not to mention accents and weather. In these comparisons the Midwest, a so-called flyover zone, nearly disappears from the national imaginary. Historically, Latinas/os have concentrated in the

Southwest and Northeast, yet the greatest growth is in the Midwest and Southeast. Latinas/os assert regionality within the US, with Puerto Ricans in the Northeast, Cubans and Caribbeans in Miami, Chicanos in the Southwest, and a heterogeneous group in the Midwest and Southeast. Since the myth of the technological sublime promises regional communication and "coming together," presumably without losing local culture—a form of multiculturalism without the melting pot—does the digital enable Latinas/os to communicate with one another across intra-Latina/o differences, as well as with a range of other populations across regions? Latina/os find a space in community and low-power radio, and network formation designed to share information resurrects the technology's implicit democratic and community formation potential.

Implicit in the geographical and regional promises is communication between urban and rural populations. Though this may have been more salient when the US was primarily rural and agricultural, a contemporary version is US-based Latina/o populations trying to communicate with rurally located families of origin (Jimenez 2016). Contemporary implications of the digital urban/rural divide raise questions for Latina/o agricultural immigrant labor and its communities of origin. Laborers in Onarga, Illinois, and Ventura County, California, work geographically close to large metropoles such as Chicago and Los Angeles, but might as well be on another planet. Community and communication flow with the migrants rather than across space to the urban Latinas/os, who might become a resource and support for the Latina/o migrant workforce.

Implicit in all of the previously mentioned spatial elements of the myth of the technological sublime is the promise of racial and ethnic unity and understanding. While seldom explicitly articulated, this promise has sometimes been seized upon by policymakers and activists. For example, FCC commissioner Newton Minow's 1961 "television is a vast wasteland" warning to commercial broadcasters, while not mentioning race or ethnicity, fueled and inspired activists to form watchdog groups of local stations coming up for license renewal. If these activist groups' research and monitoring revealed that programming content and hiring practices did not represent the local population, this could be interpreted as not serving the public interest. Given that broadcasting licenses had to be renewed regularly and that Minow had warned that renewal would no longer be pro forma, media reform activists hoped to prevent renewal for stations lacking in ethnic representation and therefore to create an opening for new, more representative stations. Civil Rights-era as well as second-wave women's movement politics seized upon this implication and included broadcasting in their activist strategies—protesting license renewal with their data on underrepresentation of the local population in employment and representation (licenses being granted locally). "As part of civil rights activism in the 1960s, people attempted to intervene in the FCC's license renewal process regarding stations that were blatantly racist with their programming and hiring decisions. Initially the FCC resisted the intervention of *any* members of the public in policy proceedings . . . until 1966 when the FCC ruled" that the intervention of members of the public was acceptable (John Anderson, pers. comm.). Previous cases involved black activists in relation to a Jackson, Mississippi, license (Mills 2004a and 2004b). The FCC also intervened in relation to a right-wing preacher, Carl McIntire of WXUR, who lost his license for being a partisan hack (Anderson 2016). While most of the activism related to African American challenges, Castañeda (2008 and 2014) has documented Latina/o, Spanish-language, and English-language efforts to broadcast and affect media policy related to inclusion, especially in the Southwest. In another moment of ethnic inclusivity, or rather of concern about ethnic populations after the Bedford-Stuyvesant riots, in 1971 the Sloan Foundation report on cable TV offered suggestions for using media for social transformation and betterment, including programs to deal with "the Black Man" and even "English instruction for Spanish speaking viewers" (Mosco 2004, 139).

Latinas/os in the Contemporary Digital Environment

It is useful to examine the myth of the technological sublime as it continues to be reiterated in the contemporary digital environment. Whether through facile statements that the internet will solve our economic, social, political, environmental, and cultural issues, or analyses that identify social media as an agent in the social conflict and movements now known as the "Arab Spring," the myth is continuously and uncritically rehashed. The racial and ethnic dimension has been present in all of the previously mentioned components of the myth of the technological sublime. To begin with, the global situation is one that is highly racialized, with migration and population flows being accorded different treatment in relation to the brownness of the skin of those trying to cross national borders due to war and famine. As recently as November 2015, migration flows from Syria, for example, received much global coverage, while ongoing treacherous border crossings from Africa to Greece and Italy, from sub-Saharan Africa to Spain's Moroccan borders in Ceuta and Melilla, and from Latin America to the US border do not figure as predominantly in the global news. The digital sublime appears in the fact that some Syrian refugees travel with their mobile phones, the wealthier ones able to call local taxis to get them to the nearest open border. The hundreds who drown at sea weekly do not appear to have the benefit of digital technology. Their geographical mobility is all too traditionally grounded in their ability to travel physically across treacherous and inhospitable terrain. In the global contemporary situation, many populations still do not benefit from space-time compression.

Within the United States, geographical and regional unity implicitly occupies the mind—note the nineteenth-century struggles of the Mexican American war, which culminated in the 1848 Treaty of Guadalupe Hidalgo, and of the Civil War (1861–1865). The former conflict, when the Southwest became part of the US and in which many Mexicans were crossed by the border, remains a pivotal date for Latinas/os, and the latter resulted in northward migration of recently emancipated blacks. The former redrew national boundaries and the latter generated physical migration. Both followed the establishment of the telegraph for commercial purposes and became part of the backdrop for the discourse of new telecommunications technology. Discussions, acknowledgment, and efforts to unify the country further in the latter part of the nineteenth century implicitly had to include these two racialized populations, so that by the time wireless telegraphy turned into radio, these were two of the (often muffled) voices in the ether.

Unification through communications implicitly incorporates the melting pot metaphor—we will all melt together in the electromagnetic spectrum (Anderson 2016). And indeed, yet one more reason for reviewing early US broadcasting history is that ham radio operators, using radio as a sending and receiving technology, kept being pushed to the outer edges of the usable spectrum because they functioned in a diverse, non-melting-pot way (in addition to the fact that they were interfering with profit-making). To be sure, would-be broadcasters challenging the FCC (included) rogue conservative preachers as well as those advocating for greater racial representation.[3] The existence of a wide range of large, corporate, centralized transmission senders alongside the many rogue and diverse voices remains the case today in the digital sphere, with the former foregrounded and the latter backgrounded.

Thus we get to the contemporary research of Latina/o-mediated realities (Dávila and Rivero 2014; Mirabal and Laó-Montes 2007; and Valdivia 1995 and 2014) exploring the ruptures and continuities as well as limits and possibilities of inclusion for Latinas/os in contemporary mainstream popular culture. In presence and erasure, Latinas/os stand in for the imagined nation. They track the interstices and struggles of the contemporary identity crisis that faces the United States, which formerly thought of itself as homogenously white or binary in composition (that is, black and white). Themes of inclusion and presence cut across popular culture, whether in Latina/o-produced films about Latina/o issues such as *Instructions Not Included* (2013) and *Sleep Dealer* (2008); in a prime-time television show with a primarily Caucasian cast such as *Modern Family* (2009–); in more inclusively Latina/o shows such as *East Los High* (2013–), *Devious Maids* (2013–), and *Jane the Virgin* (2014–); through the careers of spectacular Latinas, that is, Latinas who are foregrounded in celebrity culture as singularly sexy and representing the excess of their embodied ethnicity, such as Jennifer Lopez, Salma Hayek, Eva Longoria, Sofia Vergara, Jessica Alba, Eva Mendes, Selena Gomez, etc. (Molina-Guzmán 2010); or through efforts to include Latinas/os in digital cultures, access, and production. Most Latina representations circulate and reiterate traditional narratives about gender, race, sexuality, and nation that in turn trigger a range of recognizable audience responses and community reactions. Nonetheless, there are moments, characters, plotlines, and social media instances that challenge normalized mainstream Latinidad and contribute to the extension and expansion of presence so that the burden of underrepresentation (Mercer 1994) does not have to congeal the production and presence of Latinas/os. One step toward utopia is getting beyond the burden of underrepresentation. Drawing on a history of representations and discourses of Latinidad, a map of overlapping paradigms of representation of Latinas, the competing discourses that abounded at the end of the last century, and the rise in ambiguous and hybrid representations now appearing in the mainstream, media research suggests an implicit yet unarticulated utopia that guides much of the activism on issues of production, discourse and representation, as well as audience and interpretation in ethnic studies in general and Latina/o media studies in particular (Valdivia 2016).

I briefly turn now to some digital issues. Most of the research on digital utopias implicitly centers the normative subject as white, middle-class, heteronormative, and male (Hartley 2012; Jenkins 2009). The work of Lisa Nakamura stands out as an early voice in troubling the whiteness of this discourse and challenging the assertion that race does not matter in cyberspace (Nakamura 2002 and 2008; Nakamura and Chow-White 2012). However, research into Latinas/os and digital cultures or the internet has been rare indeed (Hacker and Steiner 2002). As is often the case with research in the US, the first set of studies focuses on white populations, the second on African American populations (see, for example, Barron et al. 2014), and then research begins to trickle down to consider Latinas/os, mixed-race, and other populations.

Often digital culture studies single out youth as a category that adopts, uses, and understands the new technology. The myth typically emphasizes young people as bearers of special knowledge and use of the new technology; this is part of the continuity as well as the depoliticization impulses in the discourse (Mosco 2004). Youth is a device to unite—after all, who can be against youth?—and divert from structural factors of inequality. Regarding this, Mosco argues, "But perhaps most important, the story of young computer wizards fits well with the tendency of cyberspace myths to discount many of the traditional sources of division in the world, such as income, wealth, gender, or race, by focusing on the generational divide around technology" (2004, 80). This is a way of denying historical patterns of segregation, such as race, by focusing on a world of harmony and equality—free of the baggage of old divisions. This part of the discourse applies to the global sphere (see, for example, Chan 2014) as well as to the US.

Truth be told, media studies as a field illustrates that youth have always stood for societal concerns about any new technology. They function as the symbol for third-person effect—that is, educators, parents, and politicians are not necessarily worried about the effect on themselves, but they do worry about youth. For example, the Pew Research Center on Internet, Society & Tech reports that

Among Hispanic and African American youth, there is somewhat less access to desktops, compared with white teens. At the same time, African American youth have greater access to smartphones than their Hispanic or white counterparts. Minority youth are much more likely to adopt text messaging apps on their phones than their white counterparts. And while Hispanic youth are equally as likely as white teens to use most of the social media platforms that were queried in the survey, Hispanic teens are more likely to report using Google+ than white youth. African American teens are also substantially more likely than white or Hispanic youth to report playing video games. (Lenhart 2015)

In the absence of socioeconomic factors, the focus on youth overlapping with race effectively depoliticizes digital disparities while providing data suggesting widespread adoption across racialized youth. We might consider whether increased data about youth usage of digital technologies confirms a general sense that youth are more informed and better adopters of new technologies, as Mosco suggests above. In fact, Hargittai (2011) finds that there is no empirical evidence to support the view that youth know more about new technologies, nor that youth are the ones who benefit most from digital media; instead, digital media may be contributing to "increasing social inequality" (236). Research on the digital divide, especially in terms of race and ethnicity, suggests not so much that youth and people in general have less access to computers, but rather that what they do with computers and digital technology differs (Barron et al. 2014; Hacker and Steiner 2002; Hargittai 2011; Hargittai and Hinnant 2008). Factors such as education, income, and parents' professions are a strong indicator of youth sophistication in relation to digital technology. Of course, these three variables are also predictors for socioeconomic status. Digital disparities tend to affect lower-income youth (Singer 2015). In other words, lower income, less education, and lack of professional status on the part of parents affect their access, and more importantly, the time and use that youth get out of technology. The median Latino family has lower income, education levels, and professional attainment than the median white population. So the relevant factors do apply to Latinas/os in general and Latina/o youth in particular.

Nonetheless, considering that the US Latina/o population is young, with a median age of 27 compared to 37 for whites (Pew Research Institute 2012), studying digital issues for Latina/o youth is essential, as the former Chief Technology Officer (CTO) of the United States, Megan Smith, noted. In an interview with the Commonwealth Club (NPR 2015), Smith reported on the government's efforts to tap into diverse youth and to steer them from mundane jobs into releasing creativity and inclusivity in the most productive and lucrative sector—that is, the digital economy. Proposing a measure of "TQ" (like IQ but Tech Q), Smith encouraged major corporations to move a diverse workforce from number 20 to second or third on their priority lists, pointing to Intel, which plans to have a workforce as diverse as the population of the United States by 2020. A number of projects, including summer programs for teachers and students, sought to track youth of color with digital ability into employment in such places as Silicon Valley instead of into the dead-end jobs usually offered by the Post Office or other corporations.

Other efforts to include Latina/o youth are less utopian. In her sophisticated analysis of the crossover of reggaetón music from Puerto Rico to the US and into global culture, Rivera (2014) studies chat rooms frequented by antifans and how the US armed forces recruit Latinas/os in collusion with reggaetón and Daddy Yankee, who freely uses military iconography in his songs, his performances, and the art accompanying his musical releases. The message is further reinforced by the presence of the US military giving away swag that can only be obtained if concertgoers "volunteer" their details online, creatively recruiting Latinas/os and African Americans in the absence of a mandatory draft. Whereas CTO Megan Smith was trying to divert diverse youth into the heart of innovation and productivity of the digital economy (with an emphasis on entrepreneurship), the Armed Forces are using digital technology to build a database to recruit racialized youth into entry-level military employment. These career paths demonstrate the complex digital utopia promised to Latinas/os and other working-class racialized youth.

Sleep Dealer (2008) presents a second dystopic moment of digital Latinidad.[4] The futurist motion picture, cowritten and directed by Alex Rivera, focuses on a young Mexican man forced to sell his labor across the border, resulting in a transnational Latino alliance with his metaphorical counterpart, a US Latino soldier. (Early in the film, his Mexican supervisor tells him, "This is the American dream—we give the US what they have always wanted—all the labor without the workers.") Both men operate in a cyborgian hybrid world of technologized bodies whose labor is virtually transported across borders to accomplish geopolitical and economic goals. Distributed on the film festival circuit, this film deserves wider circulation for the novel and trenchant manner in which it treats themes of exploitation of the Global South labor and natural resources;

border crossing; incorporation of technology into work and into the human body; and the quotidian militarization of space. Produced and populated by Latina/o and Latin American creative labor, the film represents potential abuses of digital technology for Latinas/os in the near future/present. The presence of military drones, surveillance, and the ever-increasing privatization of natural resources, such as water by Coca-Cola in India, locate *Sleep Dealer* within the present experience of millions and not just the fantasy world of independent film.

Finally, Flores-Yeffal, Vidales, and Plemons (2015) offer a careful account of the construction of cyber-moral panics about Latinas/os through an online anti-immigrant movement that demonizes Latinas/os and encourages a call to action from its followers that sometimes results in the deaths of innocent Latinas/os and contributes to a hostile climate against them. Through use of fictitious data, including wrongly referencing the *Los Angeles Times*, these anti-immigrant groups make use of the public sphere through the online environment to incite aggression toward Latinas/os. Abuse of the digital environment circulates misinformation that prevents unity and understanding and endangers the lives of millions of law-abiding people.

Conclusion

Mosco (2004) argues that when technologies "cease to be sublime icons of mythology and enter the prosaic world of banality—when they lose their role as sources of utopian visions—they become important sources for social and economic change" (6). Myths obscure power and continuities—especially in power (83). The rediscovery of Latinas/os lays bare these continuities. Mosco (84) quotes Baudrillard's critique of Fukuyama's *The End of History*—"the leftovers—the Church, communism, ethnic groups, conflicts, ideologies—are indefinitely recyclable" (1992, 27). Including "ethnic groups" within the architecture of modernism challenges the myth. Similarly, Ohmae in Mosco divines that the end of geography will lead "to a social convergence[, and that] divisions in income, education, race, ethnicity, and gender will ultimately give way to the power of the new technology to accelerate exposure to a global way of life" (Mosco 2004, 90), ignoring the fact that these new technologies accentuate these divisions. Locating "bonds of family, race, and religion" in the primordial (99), Ohmae restages Lerner's *The Passing of Traditional Society*. Amnesia does not apply just to cultural memory but to academic memory in that we begin to forget foundational research.

There is relatively little research on Latinas/os and digital utopias. What research does exist strongly suggests that the so-called digital revolution not only cannot dissolve stratification but may actually contribute to it. Utopian promises held out to all are enjoyed by few. For example, as Megan Smith noted, despite education in IT, youth of color generally end up in dead-end coding jobs rather than in creative and generative positions. As Rivera documents, military employment is surreptitiously offered to Latina/o youth via their fandom of reggaetón and Daddy Yankee. Social scientists find that although access to computers and digital technology in the US is nearly universal, the time, quality, and uses that that technology is put to differ widely based on socioeconomic metrics with widely differing outcomes of income and professional attainment. Latina/o studies scholars have long noted that communications technology allows Latina/o culture to circulate globally while simultaneously stopping or inspecting Latinas/os at the border (Fusco 1995; Lugo 2000 and 2012). The same technology that records, tracks, and polices borders is used to circulate Latina/o popular culture for the profit of major media corporations. While this technology is useful for Latinas/os communicating across space, especially when separated by economic and war-fueled migration, we have to ask whether utopian promises benefit the population in a democratic manner—and at this time, the answer continues to be "no."

Acknowledgments

The author wants to thank the editors of this volume as well as John Anderson, Cameron McCarthy, and John Nerone for providing feedback and contributions as this manuscript was prepared.

Notes

1. It took me almost all day to get to the "Digital Utopias" conference in Atlanta from San Francisco—the trip included two planes, a taxi, and a car ride to the conference hotel. This involved getting up early on the West Coast, as I lost three hours flying to the East Coast. So my early morning departure ended in a late evening arrival.

2. Until the advent of telecommunications, transportation and communications traveled together. This is why German had just one word for transportation and

communication (Bettig and Guback 1987): information could not travel any faster than human transportation.

3. See John Nathan Anderson, *A Can of Worms: Public Intransigence on the Public Airwaves*, master's thesis, University of Wisconsin-Madison, 2004, 60–61 (Carl McIntire), 80–81 (Rick Strawcutter), 85 (Lonnie Kobres); see also John Anderson, "Right-Wing Pirates: Hateful but Rare," *DIYmedia.net*, August 28, 2017, https://www.diymedia.net/right-wing-pirates-hateful-but-rare/.

4. The film has been the subject of many scholarly analyses, focusing on issues of transnationalism, migration, NAFTA, and dystopia (see, for example, Jeffries 2015; and Villazana 2014).

6

The Politics of Participation

La Bloga, Latina/o Cultural Politics,
and the Limits of Digital Participatory Culture

JENNIFER LOZANO

In this essay, I turn to what may seem to be an unlikely archive—the Latina/o literature and culture blog *La Bloga*—to analyze a largely overlooked sphere of Latina/o cultural politics and digital media production. In doing so, I emphasize a legacy of cultural politics that emerged from the Chicana/o movement and that has influenced new realms of Latina/o cultural production, such as online content creation. That Latina/os are exceptionally active online (Negrón-Muntaner et al. 2014), however, has been strategically overlooked by scholars in ways that perpetuate stereotypes of digital illiteracy (Ramírez 2008; Everett 2008; Nakamura 2002). By examining the blog's history, I first discuss how literary and artistic culture, as well as racial politics, prompted its creation and online involvement; I then interpret the blog's operation and content in light of scholarship on digital media use, participatory culture, and its democratic political value. As Donald Matheson notes, digital media studies still largely emphasize comparisons to Jürgen Habermas's notion of the ideal public sphere (see Matheson 2009; Barlow 2008; Jenkins 2006; Byrne 2008; and Papacharissi 2002) or to traditional journalism (see Papacharissi 2007;

Robinson 2009)—both ideally understood to mediate between the inter-est of the state and personal interests on behalf of "civil society."[1] These theorizations, Matheson argues, emerge from liberal assumptions about democracy and the individual, even though blogs do not always adhere to these assumptions (2009). Following this line of thinking, I argue that through its very emphasis on Latina/o culture and cultural politics, *La Bloga* offers a different approach to participatory culture and political in-volvement that critically negotiates both Latina/o identity and creative media production.

A Word on Method and Scholarly Framework

This study employs textual analyses and interpretation as its primary methodological approach. In doing this, I provide an analysis of the litera-ture surrounding digital participatory culture, followed by analyses of the blog's history and production culled from interview responses from blog-gers, and, finally, an analysis of layout and content. With regard to con-tent analysis, I follow thematic threads that emerged organically during interviews with the blog's creators (including literary culture and politics, racial identity and affirmation, and writing communities). Since *La Bloga* has posted almost daily for over 12 years, the content I select for analysis is not intended to be comprehensive, but instead provides examples of the way the blog attempts to fulfill its stated mission. Additionally, although *La Bloga* is among the most active sites at the intersection of Latina/o literature, culture, and blogging, it still receives only a modest amount of web traffic and would likely be a blip on a quantitative research report.[2] Textual analysis allows for close consideration of histories and details that would otherwise be lost. As I explain in the following section, Latina/os are rarely studied as producers of digital content, which is often the result of gendered and racialized methodological practices that set exclusionary parameters for what counts as participatory culture.

Participatory Culture and Politics

Participatory culture references a shift in media production, wherein on-line users or consumers are enabled and compelled to create and circu-late new content (Jenkins 2006, 331). Under this paradigm, most notably theorized by digital media scholar Henry Jenkins, individuals or groups produce content online while also facilitating the consumption of the on-line platform and, more often than not, advertisements. Hence, users are both producers and consumers or "prosumers" (Jenkins 2006). In the case of *La Bloga*, bloggers' posts produce literary and cultural discourse, while consuming the Blogger platform through their online activity and by linking to and participating in other blogs. The concept of a "prosumer" is useful in that it highlights the overlay of grassroots and capitalist en-terprise within contemporary digital media production. As I will show, however, it can also downplay the ways in which participatory culture can be overly mediated by mass culture and the demands of for-profit produc-tion (Jenkins 2006, 18).

Conversely, a central tenant of participatory culture, especially as theo-rized by Jenkins, is the potential liberating effect of digital media literacy and participation. Following the theories of Pierre Lévy, Jenkins explores participatory culture's "knowledge communities," or "voluntary, tempo-rary and tactical affiliations" generated through similar intellectual and emotional investments, as "central to the task of restoring democratic citi-zenship" (2006, 27–29). Jenkins emphasizes participatory culture's ability to influence "entrenched institutions" such as the mainstream media and the entertainment industry to generate more of what consumers want, whether it is more representative journalism or a better game series. In regard to blogging, Jenkins highlights the technology's ability to reframe dominant news narratives, the ability to link to various perspectives on a story, and the ability to contribute to and pool individual knowledge with a larger group—what Lévy calls "collective intelligence." Although Jenkins rarely explicitly invokes the "public sphere" in his research on participa-tory culture (2002; 2006; 2008; 2009), he privileges many of its attributes, such as debate and discussion, collaboration that brackets individual his-tories and differences (such as private interests), and the triumph of rea-son and rationality. For Jenkins, these newer forms of collaboration and participation online, specifically those enacted through popular culture, can provide practice for skills needed to bring about social change (2006). Similarly, Habermas refers to the "literary public sphere" as a "training ground" for the eventual emergence of a political public sphere (1991, 29).

Since digital media studies first became a field of inquiry, however, it has been criticized for not considering race in its analyses (Everett 2008; Nakamura 2002; Jenkins 2008; Daniels 2012). Likewise, digital media studies has paid minimal attention to the blog medium, and within the scholarship that does exist, adult male blogs are privileged, despite the rise in young female bloggers. These two phenomena are related in that the number of blogs that are minority-identified has grown exponentially, but scholarship tends to pass over this type of blog. Blog scholarship also favors filter-style blogs, which draw content from external sources, as opposed to journal-style blogs that draw primarily from internal, personal knowledge and that are most associated with women and people of color (Herring et al. 2004). Thus the numbers of blogs scholars feel obliged to study are fewer, which in turn helps to devalue the genre as a whole.

My analysis of *La Bloga* considers Jenkins's insights into the potential of participatory media beyond the typical communities and users he and other scholars frequently study—"early adopters" of technology who are "disproportionately white, male, middle-class and college educated" (Jenkins 2006, 23). His studies also focus on online users whose "productions," unlike *La Bloga*, are dependent on and facilitate the consumption of large, for-profit media products. Additionally, the most recent scholarship on participatory media has focused on Twitter and social networking sites (SNS) (Papacharissi and de Fatima Oliveira 2012; Gerbaudo 2012; Lee et al. 2013), and the scholarship that does exist on blogs does not emphasize their use by people of color (Daniels 2012). Focusing on *La Bloga* thus provides an example of participatory media that is not directly mediated by large corporate ventures and that is organized loosely around identity, literature, and culture. By looking closely at how *La Bloga* has deviated from the dominant model of participatory culture, I highlight how expanding our theoretical purview to include the influence of cultural politics might involve more people of color in studies of digital media content creation, as well as demonstrate innovative ways to generate content that negotiates both identity and media production.

Cultural Politics 2.0: From the Chicano Movement to the Blogosphere

La Bloga began in 2004 when Chicano writers Manuel Ramos, Rudy García, and Michael Sedano started using the Blogger platform to facilitate camaraderie and conversation about Latina/o literature and culture. Ramos explains that they were always interested in writing about political topics on the blog, and wanted *La Bloga* to be a place for Latina/o "news and reviews" (Ramos 2011). Prior to starting *La Bloga*, the three founders had participated in the developing array of text-based internet platforms that enabled people to connect with one another and build relationships. Through their online engagement, *La Bloga*'s would-be creators sought to provide support and companionship for each other—a consideration that has largely faded from critical conversations about the internet (Yuan 2012). The earliest of these technologies was Usenet, "a global electronic bulletin board" consisting of "newsgroups" devoted to a specific topic of interest (Burkhalter 1999, 63). As Sedano explains, "Topics flowed down a screen that [was] populated with useful congress . . . Usenet was social media before such a term existed." Joining soc.culture.mexico and then soc.culture.mexican.american (SCMA), two Usenet groups organized around a specific culture, he recalls "talking about books with anyone who would read." The "desultory conversations, unbridled flame wars," and "racist trolls," however, soon made SCMA an unwelcoming online space (Sedano 2011).

This early experience with the internet and prejudice highlights an aspect of interactive technology that still plagues internet users and especially women, people of color, and LGBTQIA people. The impact of these "hate" experiences contributes to the creation of smaller, ethnic-identified digital spaces such as *La Bloga*. As Dara Byrne's study of dedicated ethnic social networking sites (SNS) shows, the ability to express and to be exposed to expressions of racial identity, especially for youth of color, is crucial to being able to resist the negative effects of racism (2008). Similarly, Sedano recounts maintaining a desire to connect with "people like him," Latina/o and interested in books and literary culture. After Usenet, he joined "CHICLE" (Chicano Literature Interest Group), a Listserv mailing list that discussed folklore, literature, research, and other topics related to Chicano culture up until it shut down in 1999. It was through this digital venue that the three cofounders met and eventually collaborated on what would become *La Bloga* (Sedano 2011).

Although the idea of support for one another online is now less central in current conversations about the internet, it is indeed a political concern and one that is crucial for the psychological and physical well-being of users of color. For Latina/os, the Chicano/a and Puerto Rican movements were among the most visible expressions of this type of socially affirmative and political organizing. Moreover, as some scholars have now critiqued, literary and artistic culture was central to these movements for expressing grievances, solidarity, and alternate visions of the future (Lopez 2010). Thus, *La Bloga* can readily be seen as an online descendent of Chicano/a and Latina/o cultural politics.

Given the centrality of public sphere–oriented politics to scholarly debates about the internet, however, Latina/o digital content like *La Bloga* tends to disappear from the purview of noteworthy online production. To compound matters, the most recent study on Latina/o media presence reports that Latina/os are grossly absent from creative production roles offline as well. For instance, Latina/os are underrepresented in contemporary television and film production (including news), which leads to fewer stories from diverse Latina/o perspectives. Specifically, the number of writers, directors, and producers has "proportionally declined or not kept pace with population growth" (Negrón-Muntaner et al. 6). Within the production realm of traditional print publishing, Latina/os fare no better (Grecco, Rodríguez, and Wharton 2007). As I explore in the next section, in addition to *La Bloga*'s socially affirmative impetus, its operational emphasis on making creative work accessible and providing alternative, cost-free outlets for producing, promoting, and circulating Latina/o identified stories is also political and relevant to the contemporary media moment.

Online Cuentos: *La Bloga*'s Production, Promotion, and Storytelling

Perhaps taking a lesson from critiques of the Chicano/a movement's narrow, often sexist and heterosexist terms for Chicano identity, *La Bloga* takes a more capacious approach to Latina/o identity (Torres 2003; Blackwell 2011). Although meeting and communicating with like-minded individuals were Sedano, Ramos, and Garcia's original purposes for the blog, the site expanded beyond the needs of Chicano writers and readers. In fact, while Ramos and García at first intended to create "an Internet magazine devoted to Chicana and Chicano literature," they quickly decided to broaden their scope to include "all Latino culture—movies, poetry, music, etc., but always with a focus on literature" (Ramos 2011). Today, *La Bloga* still features the writing of the original three founders, but has expanded its contributors to include a total of 11 Latina/o voices from across the US, including several Latinas (Sedano 2012). The writers alternate the days they post, providing a plurality of perspectives and accommodating the labor required to maintain an active, not-for-profit blog. While the contributors I interviewed are all college-educated and many are writers by profession, others have backgrounds in the military, law, and teaching. *La Bloga* contributors also identify as Puerto Rican, Mexican American, and other mixed ethnic affiliations, and represent several generations (Ramos 2014). As one female blogger explains, *La Bloga* "attempts to show all things Chicano and Latino" and "fearlessly takes on issues of identity" (Palacios 2011).

In line with this ethos, *La Bloga* relies solely on its bloggers to determine the topics that the blog covers. Talking to Ramos about the creation and operation of the blog, he relates that *La Bloga* is rather "anarchistic" in its approach to content generation. There is no set writing schedule for bloggers to follow, nor is there a "beat" or general topic assigned to them (Ramos 2014). Instead, they write on topics that they find relevant and that they anticipate readers will also be interested in. With its diverse, 11-member cast of contributors, this approach tends to avoid the demand to capture a unified Latina/o brand and audience that other large media outlets such as NBCLatino.com and CNN Latino have desired but failed to attain.[3]

Without the corporate demand to pin down a "Latina/o" identity and audience, *La Bloga* is in the unique position of creating for itself the terms and ideas relevant to Latina/os. For instance, when few media outlets provided coverage of the "librotraficante" activist response to Arizona's HB 2281, which banned ethnic literature texts from the Tucson Unified School District, *La Bloga* posted weekly updates about its activism, legal developments, and similar legislative efforts.[4] Moreover, the bloggers curate, promote, and circulate the work of a wide array of both unknown and well-known Latina/o writers. This blogger-centered approach is distinctive from other iterations of participatory media studied by Jenkins in which prosumers' participation is directly mediated by a large brand or media company (think the Harry Potter series, CBS's *Survivor*) and the content created by the prosumer is secondary. While Blogger.com hosts *La Bloga*, since the latter does not run third-party advertisements, the blog generates no profit from its operation and production (Ramos 2011). The bloggers contribute their time and effort free of charge, but benefit from an accessible outlet on which to write about Latina/o culture and news, as well as to promote their own creative writing. To that end,

La Bloga maintains an always-growing list of authors whose work has been featured on the blog, and provides links to the authors' websites. Currently, the list contains 152 authors (49 of whom I am familiar with), which is consistent with the blog's commitment to providing exposure to emerging as well as established writers.[5]

La Bloga also acts as an informal learning environment by deconstructing and demystifying the creative and media industries through a lens of racial identity. As Randy Ontiveros explains in his book on the cultural politics of the Chicano movement, although we are currently more enmeshed in forms of cultural production than ever before, "there are far too few educational spaces, formal or informal, where people can learn how to think critically about the culture they consume, or how to produce and circulate their own content" (Ontiveros 2014, 33). Although *La Bloga* is unrestrictive in the topics it covers, certain topics have organically accrued prevalence on the blog, such as the challenges of writing and cultural production for Latina/os (Ramos 2014). In this way, *La Bloga* acts as an informal learning environment that departs from Jenkins's and education scholar James Gee's understanding of such a space as necessarily blind to differences of race, gender, age, disability, or social class (Gee 2004, 85; Jenkins 2009, 9).[6]

One such example of its work as an informal learning environment can be seen in a March 2, 2011, post titled "*The Cazuela that the Farm Maiden Stirred*—Virtual Book Tour and Giveaway." In this post, Reneé Colato Láinez demystifies and politicizes creative work by explicitly linking the production and reception of Samantha Vamos's children's book to the racial identity of the creative team and the book's readers. While studies show that most mainstream cultural production—even when featuring Latina/o artists—continues to be aimed at a "neutral," white audience (Dávila 2012; Negrón-Muntaner 2014), the author of the blog post, along with children's book illustrator Rafael Lopez, highlight how such production and reception are anything but "neutral" and emphasize the power of racialized cultural expression. Lopez begins by explaining to a young audience the great length of time it takes for a book such as Vamos's to make it to print. In just a few paragraphs, he touches on the relationship between the printer and artist, as well as among the printer, artist, author, publishing house, and art director, that help bring forth the "azuline blue of a Mexican tile" or "the right radiant shade of amarillo-oro [yellow-gold]" (Láinez 2011). In a sense, the collaborative process Lopez describes is akin to Jenkins's concept of collective intelligence, whereby everyone contributes their expertise toward solving a problem; however, Lopez's expertise is deeply connected to his racial identity and cannot be bracketed within his creative work. He explains that "color is an expression of my identity, my heritage, and I believe it is the most direct route to the emotions of children and families who will turn the pages of my books" (Láinez 2011). The reader is thus factored into the production and reception process, and although the colors Lopez carefully select represent his own identity, they are also conjured with a larger, raced audience in mind. Imagining this audience, he explains that "you feel like celebrating when recognizing a familiar hue that resonates for you" (Láinez 2011). Lopez's post makes the often-elusive work of cultural production seem accessible to Latina/o youth (Negrón-Muntaner et al. 2014) and takes a different approach to Jenkins's emphasis on a blog's ability to reframe dominant news narratives. For *La Bloga*, the idea of reframing ethnic self-knowledge through positive articulations of Latina/o literature and culture is equally powerful.[7]

La Bloga ultimately recoups the literary as a deconstructive and reconstructive agent in mainstream media industries and storytelling. Olga Echeverría's post, "Flores for Brisenia," also written in March 2011, brings this quality into focus and further undermines a "public sphere" understanding of blog culture.[8] The post is a four-paragraph memorial for Brisenia Flores, an undocumented 10-year-old girl who was killed along with her father in Arizona by anti-immigration vigilantes (McKinley 2009). At the time of the post, the murder suspect was on trial with no major media coverage of the story (Coscarelli 2011), which confirms the understanding of Jenkins and other scholars of blogs as more democratic in their coverage and circulation than the mainstream press (Jenkins 2002; Rettberg 2008; Robinson 2009). As a memorial, however, Echeverría's post provides a different type of coverage and addresses an audience already familiar with the event and its circumstances. *La Bloga* assumes its readers are invested in matters of racial justice, immigration, and education in addition to Latina/o literature and culture. This amounts to the blog's "shared knowledge." For Jenkins, shared knowledge—another concept drawn from Lévy—references a shared understanding or premise that makes participation in a discourse community feasible (Jenkins 2006, 27).

Thus, part of the blog's shared knowledge is that racial discrimination and violence are real and have harmful systemic effects. One of these effects, of course, is the lack of outlets for Latina/o-oriented storytelling, online and off.

As a result of its shared knowledge, "Flores for Brisenia" uses emotion in a strikingly different context than has been theorized by digital media scholars in recent years. Unlike studies that focus on social media use and effect during times of heightened social crisis such as the 2011 Egyptian Revolution (Gerbaudo 2012; Papacharissi and de Fatima Oliveira 2012), the aftermath of Hurricane Katrina in New Orleans (Robinson 2009), or even a national presidential campaign (Jenkins 2006), Echeverría's post attests to and documents everyday violence committed against people of color that too often goes unnoticed. The objective of the post is not to reach the largest audience or to incite a revolution so much as to reach and connect with *an* audience that mainstream media outlets still do not believe exists—a literate, culturally aware, creative, and political online Latina/o constituency (Negrón-Muntaner 2014; Dávila 2012).

To attend to the desires and emotions that characterize this post and reflect the blog's "shared knowledge" and political engagement, I find Sara Ahmed's theories on the political viability of emotions instructive and worthy of elaboration before turning to the post. For Ahmed, emotions do not just exist in bodies or in objects or occur as a direct result of an object infringing on the body. Rather, emotions are constantly produced by the effect of one surface upon another (both object surfaces and body surfaces); however, since emotions are performative and involve speech acts, through repetition, norms of emotions become "stuck" together (such as familial "love" as positive)—an adhesion that can conceal other histories (Ahmed 2004).

Following Ahmed's theory, Echeverría's memorial post uses poetic writing and the emotions attached to her word choices to reveal the wide history of racial violence in which Brisenia's death is situated, but that dominant news coverage often omits. In the post's second paragraph, she writes, "I'm laying her [Brisenia's] name down on this page. Right next to 14-year-old Emmett Till. Remember Till? And his mother's persistent will to keep open the casket of her murdered son? For the world to see what arrogance and hate destroyed" (Echeverría 2011).

In this passage, Echeverría takes the subject that has been "stuck" with the emotions attached to "illegal alien" and that is associated with "criminal" and "stranger," and connects it instead to victims of acknowledged racial violence such as Emmett Till. In the third paragraph, she also recalls by name the "four little black girls blown away in a Birmingham church. . . . Addie Mae Collins. Cynthia Wesley. Carole Robertson. Denise McNair" (Echeverría 2011). Both paragraphs function as a meta-commentary on Echeverría's act of memorializing ("on this page") and connect the writing of forgotten names to the brave act of Till's mother, who refused to placate white guilt. Both are everyday resistances embedded in rituals of memorial that take control of the narrative of racial violence and recuperate the lives of people of color as worth mourning.

Speaking to the lack of this type of public memorializing for non-white victims of violence, blog reader JBV comments on the post, saying, "Thank you for this lovely memorial. Reading this I'm reminded that I watch CNN every morning and never heard this story covered!! We all must keep our eyes open and our memories fresh" (Echeverría 2011). Here, *La Bloga* again acts as an informal learning environment for its readers, one that emphasizes the role of writing in accessing an embodied, historically situated way of knowing that is needed for social and political awareness and action. This is especially poignant in JBV's mention of different modes of apprehension—"our eyes" and "our memories." If "our eyes" emphasize a neutral biological tool for seeing, the necessity of "our memories"—the personal record of a life as it is lived socially, in connection with others—emphasizes the importance of lived experiences to making our perceptions "fresh" or useful.

Jenkins's premise of shared knowledge is, of course, also informed by emotion. Yet the emotions behind Jenkins's prosumers are notably different and are largely driven by competition or the pleasure of "besting" another, emotions typically gendered as masculine and recognized for business and physical success.[9] This gendered hierarchy of emotion affects scholars' perception of which digital media creations are considered "political" and relevant. While my analysis of Echeverría's post highlights some of the democratic features of the blog, such as her coverage of Brisenia's murder, that otherwise had minimal media attention, and her ability to reframe the dominant news narrative of the tragedy, its rhetoric does not perform in a manner that would make it legible to Jenkins and other digital media scholars' emphasis on externally oriented, democratic, and rational "practice" for political participation (Barlow 2008; Jenkins 2006).

For as many ways as *La Bloga* operates like Jenkins's examples of participatory culture, there are even more that diverge from his model. For instance, there are no links to other sources on Echeverría's post so that readers can pool disparate knowledge ("collective intelligence"), and no debate in the comment section regarding the story's coverage. I suggest that these differences actually indicate the political quality of *La Bloga*. In a media environment still largely inaccessible to Latina/o voices, the political value of debate and discussion decreases substantially. As Byrne argues about race-dedicated SNS, these minority-produced sites challenge the centrality of a "public" that needs to be stripped of private interests in order to think rationally about collective issues (2008). What is striking about Echeverría's post is its poetic esthetic that evokes concentrated images and feelings that can unite multiple readers, unlike the competitive emotion described earlier. In the fourth paragraph, for instance, "Flores for Brisenia" rapidly narrates geographically disparate events in a compressed fashion that is less typical of news stories and more typical of poetry: "He shot her in the face. And the world has yet to weep. There's so much going on, you see. Birds falling from the sky. Fish washing up dead along the shores. Black gold spills. Pink-slip layoffs. Budget cuts. Gas prices rising. Food prices rising. Cost of living rising, everything rising . . . And her name, her name keeps coming down like endless rain—Brisenia."

In this paragraph, many events are channeled through one narrative voice that speaks in choppy fragments and highlights the anxiety (not liberal distance) of the events and the inability of language to register their full connection. Moreover, Echeverría catalogues the events and their impact on one person, Brisenia, and many persons. In light of the decontextualization that often occurs via mainstream media and particularly the internet (Dean 2010), this poetic writing style forces us to consider connections where they are otherwise obscured. Racial violence is presented as a part of environmental damage, which is also a part of economic downturn and poverty. The post shows the power of writing to deconstruct media obfuscations, expand the concerns of Latina/o identity, and reconstruct typical news narratives. The connection to the poetic also draws on a legacy of Chicana/o and Latina/o activism, and especially that of Chicana feminists who used a similar poetic aesthetic in their political activism.[10]

Addressing the viability of pain or grievance for political organizing, Ahmed argues that pain, as "the sociality of bodily surfaces that 'surface' in relationship to each other," can be used politically as long as the injury is not fetishized to the point of being detached from history or, as seen in Chicano movement politics, it assumes an equivalence to injury (2004, 31–33). While the blog's history, operation, and content work to facilitate readers' and writers' connection over Latina/o literature and culture, the deeper desire is to document and respond to the critical and artistic issues of Latina/os over time—a significant political act. *La Bloga* is interested in the social and historical contextualization of artistic production and identity, as well as in generating a political response in this form of online content creation and interaction.

Conclusion

According to *The Latino Media Gap*, Latina/os over-index in online content creation and yet, as this essay shows, their online contributions are often undervalued (Negrón-Muntaner et al., 2014, 1). Small blogs like *La Bloga* that deviate from what is considered noteworthy, however, are useful to study precisely because their deviance provides us with alternative ways to think about and do participatory culture. While only time will tell if this prosumer-centered approach to participatory culture will remain a viable strategy for Latina/o online producers, it is crucial to document this history and counteract the erasure of Latina/os online. Moreover, studies of Latina/o-based, grassroots digital media can provide an opportunity to analyze how non-"early adopters" handle the differences and contradictions of identity—a political topic on its own. For *La Bloga*, the contradictions of Latinidad become fodder for the blog without the expectation that a rational conclusion or consensus must emerge. Since Latina/o identity and experiences are central to the blog's very existence, the next day's post will emerge and continue the conversation. Latina/o identity is not a problem to be solved, a game to be improved upon, or a product to be developed, and there is no unified Latina/o voice to discover. This, of course, is also a lesson of the Chicano/a movement. As the US continues to grow in its diversity, more attention needs to be given to the cultural politics of sites like *La Bloga* and the way they intersect with mainstream media industries and the circulation and promotion of Latina/o cultural expression. The continued comparison of blogs to the public sphere does not adequately register the convergence of digital media and Latina/o cultural politics. We should consider not only how participatory media (in tactical, temporary bursts) can lead to political change, but also the way in which long-standing blogs and digital media sites such as *La Bloga* are already being used politically.

Notes

1. The public sphere was first theorized by Jürgen Habermas through a study of developments in eighteenth-century Europe and defined as a space between the private and the public, in which "private people" came "together as a public" to engage "in a debate over the general rules governing relations in the basically privatized but publicly relevant sphere of commodity exchange and social labor" (Habermas 1991, 27). For digital media scholars, the important aspect of Habermas's idea is his emphasis on a space for rational-critical debate regarding issues of public importance. Habermas, however, has expressed doubt about the potential of the internet to create a comparable public sphere (Habermas 2006).

2. *La Bloga* has consistently held a top spot in Google Blog and regular Google searches for relevant search terms between the years 2011 and 2016. Search engines index blogs by the number of inbound links a blog has, thereby correlating the number of links a site has to internet users' approval of that site for relevant search terms (Rettberg 2008). A website's search engine ranking thus indicates its visibility to potential readers and also its engagement with other blogs and websites.

3. In November 2013 NBCLatino.com announced the closing of its operations after only 16 months, and in February 2014, CNN Latino, a Spanish-language syndicated network, followed suit after only a year in existence (Treviño 2014, "NBC Latino").

4. Started by author and activist Tony Díaz, librotraficante organized people and resources to educate the public about the bill and to collect and distribute donated books from the banned list to designated "underground" libraries in Houston, San Antonio, Albuquerque, and Tucson (Díaz 2013).

5. Authors who are featured on *La Bloga*, Ramos explains, are sometimes suggested by a blogger, reader or the author themselves. *La Bloga* will then verify that these authors have been published in some manner and that they have web pages with "meaningful material" to which *La Bloga* can link.

6. Gee's and Jenkins's emphasis on the temporary, flexible, and experimental nature of affinity spaces that capture users' attention more effectively than a top-down approach to learning offered by traditional education systems is insightful and promising. For this reason I am cautious about the notion that identity differences become largely inconsequential in these spaces.

7. Maggie Rivas-Rodriguez's study *Brown Eyes on the Web: Unique Perspectives of an Alternative U.S. Latino Online Newspaper* provides a relevant precedent of this type of identity-oriented storytelling by analyzing and comparing the development of online editions of two San Diego newspapers—an alternative Latina/o newspaper and a mainstream newspaper—in 1998 (2003, 22, 81–84).

8. The posts I examine in this essay were first posted during 2011–2012, which is the same time frame in which I conducted interviews with the bloggers.

9. Exceptions to Jenkins's competitively driven examples of prosumers are the youthful creators of online *Harry Potter* fanfiction (2006).

10. For two canonical examples of a Chicana lesbian, feminist poetic and political aesthetic, see Gloria Anzaldúa's *Borderlands/La Frontera: The New Mestiza* (2007) and Cherríe Moraga's *Loving in the War Years: Lo Que Nunca Pasó por sus Labios* (2000).

7

Afrolatin@ Digital Humanities or Rethinking Inclusion in the Digital Humanities

EDUARD ARRIAGA

The digital humanities (DH from here on) and the study of Afrolatin@ communities and their cultural productions are two fields that have experienced a boom in the last two decades. Both are becoming increasingly important in creating networks of interest and communities of practice that go beyond national boundaries.[1] The digital humanities have been presented as sets of marginal academic practices that are currently claiming and occupying a central position in what are considered the scholarly practices of the twenty-first century. Such centrality and prominence may be seen as a consequence of the increasing importance of digital technology and the influential role of software industries in our daily life (Manovich 2013). Likewise, Afrolatin@ representations acquire more academic attention due to their connections not only with artistic manifestations but also with activist movements worldwide (Jiménez Román and Flores 2), as well as increasing and permanent migrations.

The relationship between the two fields seemed to be nonexistent or at least little heard of until recently. The DH have embarked on efforts and debates to bridge the gap between digital projects and the inclusion of difference.[2] Afrolatin@ studies, on the other hand, is interested in highlighting African-descendant communities—from an interdisciplinary perspective—in the offline world and especially in the historical connections between Africa and the Americas.[3] Another point of divergence and possible separation between the two is the attention paid to art, literature and, in general, artistic representations as objects of study. While the DH have been constantly engaged in creating collections, digitizing and codifying canonic literary and historical texts, visual traditions, etc., Afrolatin@ studies have tried to make visible the existence of what Kwame Dixon and John Burdick call "hemispheric blackness" (2012, iv). Despite the apparent disagreement and lack of convergence between the two fields, this essay will argue that it is precisely the digital world and its possibilities that have galvanized new ways of being and identifying as Afrolatin@ in the Americas, through the emergence of new images, imaginations, and practices of representation. Further, I will argue that such relationships will render the complexity required to bridge the gap announced by some DH practitioners, making both fields inclusive and connected to current ways to communicate and produce knowledge.

Digital Humanities: Race, Diversity, and Inclusion

The definition of the DH as a field has been widely debated. As Terras, Nyhan, and Vanhoutte have shown (2013), the conversation has been going on since the sixties, bringing in diverse perspectives. As a field that evolved from other academic practices such as "humanities computing, humanist informatics, literary and linguistic computing, and digital resources in the humanities, to name but a few" (Terras, Nyhan, and Vanhoutte 2013, 2), DH has usually been presented as an emergent field excluded by traditional disciplines in the humanities and especially by well-established humanists, who saw computational methods as foreign practice to their fields of study (Rockwell 2011).[4] Based on this foundational narrative, specialists such as Rockwell propose that inclusion in the field has to do with interdisciplinarity as a value that allows practitioners to work with both academics and "alternative academics without faculty jobs"—namely librarians, computing staff, students, and faculty (ibid.)—opposing the traditional organization of academia. The kernel of such encounters, however, is the common interest in "applications of computing" (ibid.) becoming the exclusive mark of what can be seen as an "inclusive" excluded field. Further, Rockwell argues that it is precisely this common interest that is the essence of what is now considered DH and that it shall continue to be that way, to the benefit of both the field and its practitioners. Rockwell, however, qualifies this by saying that "it would be a shame if the digital humanities ceases to be such [a] space in order to accommodate other forms of difference" (ibid.). So what kinds of inclusion are we talking about when in DH the inclusionary spectrum is limited by refusing to accommodate "other forms of difference" as proposed by Rockwell? What "other forms of difference" is he referring to here? Are race, gender, ethnicity, language, physical and mental conditions, as well as sexual orientations, etc., some of the differences that are not welcome to the "big tent"[5] if their participation proposes changes to the common interest that holds the community together? What happens when such "other differences" come to the field or become interested in the way computing has been applied, used, and considered from "the zero-point hubris" (Castro-Gómez 2006) that has represented or underrepresented them? In any case, it is precisely these interventions by diverse perspectives and differences that really enrich a field of discursive practice.[6]

As an indirect response to such a debate, Tara McPherson asks in an eponymous article, "Why are the Digital Humanities so white?" McPherson argues that the digital and the humanities/social sciences (as two ways of inquiry) needed desperately to bridge the gap that exists between them in order to consolidate productive and critical projects. She sees such a gap as "an effect of the very design of our technological systems" (2012b, 140) represented not only by the visual end of computation but overall by the code that is at the back end. To instantiate her proposal, she carries out an analysis that correlates the creation of a computational system such as MULTIC/UNIX and the impact she deems it had on the sociracial organization of the United States. For McPherson, modularity and efficiency were two values at the core of such software that would later affect the organization, representation, and existence of race. In that light, "the organization of information and capital in the 1960s powerfully responds—across many registers—to the struggles for racial justice and democracy that so categorized the United States at the time" (149). Her analysis also sets up the grounds to question the role of contemporary scholarly fields such as DH in addressing concrete sociocultural issues embedded in our "common sense."

McPherson's argument would later be used to feed more debates and, specifically, to produce divergent initiatives in the DH community. One of the most interesting is the debate around theory vs. practice(-making).[7]

In 2012 Adeline Koh published "More Hack, Less Yack? Modularity, Theory and Habitus in the Digital Humanities," a blog post addressing such a discussion. In both the post and its comments, Koh builds on the concept of "common sense"—used in McPherson's article—to criticize the making and "making-happen" dynamics of DH. She sees such a concept as an issue excluding not only theoretical (yack) discussions in the field, but also alternative approaches and initiatives that do not necessarily share such a "common sense." As a closing remark on her post, Koh proposes that "As Digital Humanists, we have the responsibility to interrogate and to understand what kind of world, and what kind of civilization, our computational languages and forms create for us." Therefore, it is clear that Koh, based on the aperture created and addressed by McPherson, among others, opens the door for the development of a digital scholarship that would go beyond mere interest in computational applications. Koh, like others, is concerned with the dead end of inclusiveness to which DH come by presenting the field as inclusive without knowing how or being willing to accommodate "other differences." When criticizing and evaluating it, Koh then proposes a reaccommodation through both action and dialogue that would allow the field to advance by situating its position in complex sociosymbolic systems of knowledge production and transmission.

Although these initiatives discuss the inclusion of differences—in a broad sense—in the DH, they do not focus on the cultural production of a particular group, ethnicity, or racial community. By studying programming and code as textual/cultural production with socioracial and cultural implications, or spotting the colonial conceptions and actions of digital scholarship, these debates open up the space in both DH and the humanities at large to undertake projects that would allow us to understand the relationship among digital, textual, and difference. It is in this space where emergent combinations, connections, and interests can take place, questioning traditional and "common sense" conceptions to actually try to understand the way our world (on a human scale) works. In that sense, DH would benefit from going beyond collecting canonical humanities content (Earhart 2012) to start thinking critically about such content, exploring and creating spaces for diverse cultures, races, ethnicities, epistemologies, etc.[8] Such practices and approaches would enable both the humanities and those affected by humanistic inquiry to create tools and forms of representation in order to showcase their own images and discursive positions. Some related questions that arise are: Can we talk about DH as a set of practices that really question humanistic content and allow other perspectives to enter into the conversation? Is there room in these fields for approaches that would question the status of what is considered human? These and other questions have been addressed from diverse perspectives in the last nine or ten years; however, there is still work to do.

Afrolatin@ Digital Humanities?

The immediate response to the question that serves as the title for this section is "No, there is not currently something we can call Afrolatin@ DH." If we take a look at some of the most important existing associations in the field,[9] it is clear that there is no particular initiative or project concerned with the cultural digital production of Afrolatin@ communities.[10] This means that, at an institutional level, we cannot talk about Afrolatin@ DH as a sub-field concerned with and interested in connecting the study of Afrolatin@ communities to the issues and possibilities brought about by digital tools, methodologies, and approaches.[11] Nevertheless, the lack of presence at an institutional level does not mean such projects do not exist. In fact, thanks to the connections brought about by digital communication technologies, now it is easier to find and interconnect diverse and complex images of Afrolatin@ and Afro-descendant communities emerging at several levels—personal, group, national, regional, continental, and transcontinental. It seems to be precisely the digital world and its possibilities that have galvanized the emergence of complex identifications of Afrolatin@s in the Americas, influencing the creation of images from individual to group.[12] If the productive connection between computing and humanities helps us think "how we know what we know" (McCarty 2012), what some Afrolatin@ communities and individuals have been doing is investigating not only how they know what they know but also how others know what they know about them, and the way they have been represented, in order to construct their own representations/counter-representations through digital means.

The formation and emergence of black Latin@ communities (later termed Afrolatin@ or Afro-Latin American), both in their homeland and in adopting nations such as the United States, may be seen as a complex process of constant interaction among diverse ethnic communities, as well as constant a process of identification (self-identification and negotiation with other identities). Being Afrolatin@, whether in the US, the Caribbean, or Latin America, is a state that is "performed" and, as Peter Wade has argued, "lived as an everyday experience" (2005, 239). In that sense, Afrolatin@ emerges as sets of complex identities that have been imagined, adapted, and adopted in different ways at different locations and in different historical moments. However, it was not until the end of the twentieth and the beginning of the twenty-first centuries that the notion of Afrolatin@ emerged and gained currency at both national and post-national levels.[13] Such emergence took place due to the confluence of interests and political endeavors, and the prominence of race- and ethnicity-related topics in global agendas. People who had been left out of or neglected by national, regional, or transnational conversations due to racial issues now resort not only to the power of traditional communication media but also to the increasing importance of new digital technologies to question existing representations of blacks in the Americas and create new self-representations. Afrolatin@ then became a category that gained currency thanks not only to the recognition—or not—of black Latin Americans as an important constituency in diverse locations across the globe, but also to the impact of digital devices and digital communication practices in disseminating those reinvented, resignified, and remediated images and representations (Wabgou et al. 2012).

In the last decade, a surge of personal, institutional, and community-driven projects has emerged from the relationship between Afrolatin@ individuals and the dynamics of digital tools. Although they have different objectives and interests, all of them manage to interconnect archival, performative, and communicative practices in order to construct contemporary digital images and conceptions of Afrolatin@ identities. These projects make Afrolatin@ and Afro-Latin American representations even more complex than those that were at stake during the preceding decades, becoming space for connectivity and communication for communities that did not have access or voice when the production of discourse was mediated by traditional practices of writing.

Some of the most interesting projects that combine computing applications with the study and representation of Afrolatin@ communities are, among others, Proyecto Afrolatino/Afrolatin@ Project, Afrolatin@ Forum, CanAfro, and AfroCROWD, located in North America, as well as Museu Afro Digital/Afro Digital Museum and Library of Afro Colombian Literature in Latin America, PretaLab, and Olabi.[14] With diverse scopes, objectives, and types of datasets collected, curated, and analyzed, these projects look not only to the conservation of aesthetic or historical memories about Afrolatin@s, but also to the reconstruction and sometimes construction of a past that has been neglected, erased, or imposed, of a present that is continuously changing, and of a future that seems to be their ultimate goal. As opposed to other initiatives, these endeavors, rather than showcasing a canon that may not always exist, manage to link current practices and identifications both within and outside the digital world.[15]

CanAfro[16] is one of the first digital projects that, adopting a hemispheric scope, tries to identify—through textual collections and databases—what has been and what is becoming understood as "Afro" in the Americas. With the sponsorship of the Canadian Foundation for the Americas (FOCAL), this project, developed by a multidisciplinary group, consists of a collection of legal documents and of sociological, anthropological, and critical essays on African descendants in the region, their legacy, and their current conditions. Although the database has not been updated since 2009, it is still up and running, and can be consulted freely. Given its structure and appearance, this project might be classified as a Web 1.0 initiative that serves as a collection to be consulted but not as a platform for collaboration or community participation.

The site has collections of links to websites, images, and documents that show Afrolatin@s and Afro-Latin Americans as groups located in both the Americas and the Caribbean and, in addition, as groups that are and have been underrepresented and underdeveloped. The project, then, stands up as the place where Afrolatin@ historical traditions may be studied and reviewed to help those communities become visible. From postcolonial readings by Frantz Fanon to pictures of Haitian workers in the Dominican Republic, the initiative seems to aim for the articulation of discursive information and social action. It is as if the statement guiding the process of information collection would be that knowing history, current conditions, and "objective" conceptions of Afrolatin@s would help to change both discourses and realities.

Projects like CanAfro seem to be some of the first initiatives in connecting computational media and storage with Afrolatin@ representation. In the case of this particular website, it is noteworthy to say that such a connection is not coordinated through a bottom-up dynamic in which the communities become organized to use those tools, but rather through a top-down process in which governmental agencies coordinate the connection. FOCAL as well as the Inter-Agency Coalition for Race in the Americas (World Bank, Inter-American Dialogue, and Inter-American Foundation) are two of the main actors in funding this project, and therefore central nodes in the representations of race and ethnicity in connection with digital tools. Such connection deserves to be further investigated in future projects, but for now it reveals a point of origin that will later diverge toward more community-based initiatives with different objectives and achievements.

Afrolatin@ Forum[17] is a similar project, but its scope is more centered on the recognition of Afrolatin@ as a trans-national racial, ethnic, and cultural constituency within the US. In contrast to CanAfro, this project intends to become a forum in which community members and other interested individuals can discuss both the formation and current conditions of Afrolatin@s as a "minority" in the Americas and, overall, in the USA. With the power of Web 2.0 digital tools, members of the forum engage in blogging, discussing as well as collecting experiences from the community about what it is like to be Afrolatin@ in a society with some-times-reductive conceptions of race and ethnicity (Jiménez Román and Flores 2010, 20).

Afrolatin@ Forum could be seen as a more community-driven type of project that seeks to question discursive trends of racial and ethnic classification within the context of the Americas. With the aid of digital technologies, the Forum intends both to connect and to make visible several instances and ways to be black and of Latin American background in North America—particularly the United States. In pursuing such an objective, the project manages to consider not only written and academic material, but also oral, performative, and artistic forms of history that encompass diverse ethnicities from the Caribbean, Central, and South America coming together under the umbrella of Afrolatin@ as complex denominator. Unlike CanAfro, the Forum intends to prepare the political ground through complex connection with community-mediated actions. In this case, tools such as video, blogs, podcasts, and digital writing serve as channels through which to achieve political presence not only at a cultural general level, but also at a concrete level based on figures from national censuses. This ultimate goal is an instance of the complex connection among local, national, and transnational endeavors, even more so in an age in which information is growing at exponential rates due to digital innovations.

Although Proyecto Afrolatin@, or The Afrolatin@ Project, and Afro-CROWD are also interested in the identification, recognition, and collection of oral histories about Afrolatin@ communities through digital means, these projects adopt a position in which working with code and pursuing methodological innovation become two of their main objectives. The former has the purpose of "Facilitating awareness about and promoting the digital curation of the Afrolatin@/Afrodescendant experience" and the idea of using digital tools to support and preserve histories of the struggle of Afro-descendant people in the Americas.[18] The latter seeks to "increase the number of people of African descent who actively partake in the Wikimedia and free knowledge, culture, and software movements."[19] These two projects strive to enable people from Afrolatin@ communities to take part in the creation, evaluation, and dissemination of knowledge.[20] To carry out such an objective, both projects offer workshops in which the individuals self-identified as Afro-descendants become acquainted with code structures and digital tools to showcase their own knowledge production. Although these projects are developed in the US, their interests and actions reach communities in both the Caribbean and the Americas at large.

The case of both projects (Afrolatin@ Project and AfroCROWD) becomes an instance in which the digital is seen as space that minority groups and communities must appropriate in order to claim rights and modify historic symbolic representations. As history has been told from particular perspectives silencing the past (Trouillot), these initiatives seem to look at the digital as having the possibility both to make visible what has been invisible (the silenced past) and to transmit new knowledge(s) to new generations. It is precisely what resides at the core of activities such as Edit-a-thon[21] or Conversemos Afro,[22] in which members of the Afrolatin@ community come together to tell their stories from perspectives never heard from before. By storing and turning those identity accounts into digital information, these projects are trying to remix and intervene in the digital archive. However, such an aim raises questions: Who will eventually own those stories, images, and representations, and that digital information? What is the role of grassroots community members in keeping and programming digital tools for their stories' collection? How do they avoid turning memory (stories and representations) into commodities that could be used for different purposes by different agents with different interests? These questions make us reconsider a kind of invisible politics of place (Taylor) to which we trust our personal belongings, both material and spiritual. Likewise, it is paradoxical that one of the alternatives for turning objects, stories, and people that have been considered invisible to visible is transforming them into objects ruled by invisibility as a value of the online/virtual world. These initiatives thus put on the table the discussion about the real possibility of intervening in the so-called digital archive and at the same time getting the most out of it in the offline world, where people continue to be discriminated against, executed, and excluded due to their skin color, origin, or social status. These projects take advantage of the digital and can be considered unorthodox digital humanities practices, but they also make us think about the role of the digital in disseminating desired messages as well as the control over the digital world held by so-called prosumers (Jenkins).

In Latin America, it is possible to find other projects interested in the intersection I have been highlighting. One of the most important projects[23] that attempts not only to explore connections between the digital and the racial/ethnic but also to propose a rearticulation of knowledge production through digital tools is the Afro-Digital Museum[24] (Museu Afro-Digital). According to Livio Sansone, one of the project's coordinators, the museum is "a concrete intervention in the geopolitics of knowledge, an attempt to reverse the division of the world into places where there is production of knowledge and others where such knowledge is just a product that must be consumed" (2013, 345). Such intervention occurs at several levels and always takes into consideration that knowledge construction, art, and culture should be collaborative and networked processes that do not belong to one individual, one culture, or one nation. In this light, the project is featured as a museum without owners, as a space of democratization, self-representation, and creative use of digital tools to break down fixed cultural positions and fulfill new demands of citizenship (new sensitivities, conceptions of political representation, of authorship, and so on).

The museum creates a network of collaboration made up of community members and institutions—universities, NGOs, and local cultural organizations—that mirror, store, and transmit cultural representations and memories of blackness and Afro-Brazilian culture. According to Sansone, these types of initiatives might be seen as a third stage of re-invention and appropriation of the Afro-Brazilian discourse, which has traditionally been used in nationalistic and populist projects, but that to-day is connected and interconnected to transnational, trans-hemispheric, and global initiatives of cultural creation and identification (2013, 350). In that sense, the museum defies traditional conceptions of culture, memory, and preservation by placing, at the same level, historical documentation with cultural manifestations by contemporary members of the community who claim their right to create, preserve, and disseminate self-representations and images. Such interactions make this project a concrete example of the coordination and coexistence between embodied, archival knowledge and the digital pointed out by Diana Taylor ("Save as"). But additionally, this project shows interesting processes of interaction among art, technology, and ethnicity that seem to address the importance of art and creativity in attaining social goals and objectives.

These and other endeavors are concrete examples of the productive interaction between concerns of racial/ethnic representation and the digital as a discursive and concrete practice with significant currency in today's world. Further on, these projects propose methodological innovations in using computing applications to solve, understand, and explain human issues, and, at the same time, they question universal conceptions of humanity, knowledge production, transmission, and dissemination. Users of these projects would have the opportunity to engage in diverse forms of reading, consuming and, even more important, producing their own content at the same time they question the organization of a symbolic world that has misrepresented them because of their racial and ethnic connections. Some strategies employed by the users/producers of such projects include relational reading through documents and written information stored in databases such as CanAfro; creation of audiovisual content (usually published through platforms such as YouTube or Vimeo) geared toward the representation of diverse forms of identification, representation, and performance as Afro-Latino, Afro-descendant, and black in the region, as in the case of Afrolatin@ Project, Afrolatin@ Forum, and AfroCROWD; digital writing and production to intervene in, mix, and modify existing accounts of Afrolatin@ communities through code writing, sound, and visual recording, in the case of Afrolatin@ Project and AfroCROWD; and preservation of memory and rearticulation of canonical literary and cultural representations in order to influence social policy and real lives, as in the case of the Library of Afro-Colombian Literature, as well as the Brazilian Afro-Digital Museum. In summary, we are looking at something we could term the Afrolatin@ DH, a type of critical approach to the field from racial and ethnic perspectives that try to question universal conceptions of both the human and the humanities by underscoring values such as diversity, complexity, and coexistence.

Projections and Future Plans

As we have seen, Afrolatin@ DH may exist if we consider them as a set of approaches interested in questioning the interaction between ethnicity/race and current digital technologies. In Latin America and the Americas at large, the digital is no longer an option, but rather a necessary path that is becoming a governmental strategy,[25] an alternative channel for communities, and a cultural reality that is affecting and changing the way we behave, think, and act. The inclusion of "other differences" in DH and other fields of research opens up the door to thinking and rethinking what we understand as human, and the way human beings interact with their symbolic systems.

However, the future of such interactions raises questions including: What are the real effects of the digital images produced by Afrolatin@ communities in both the digital world and in scholarly fields? Are Afrolatin@ communities having a real impact as coders, entrepreneurs, digital curators, digital language creators, etc.? How can we understand ethnosocial proposals and ethnocultural productions in an age of both extreme individualism and complex forms of collaboration? What would be the real influence of Afrolatin@ digital projects in attaining social goals not only for their particular groups but also for other historically excluded groups? How are Afrolatin@s negotiating notions of access, surveillance, and control over their digital production? These and other questions deserve to be investigated, analyzed, and confronted from several perspectives in order to understand the way our world functions on diverse scales. In the meantime, the interaction between humans and the digital realm becomes increasingly complex, and we need to think and rethink the types of questions we want to ask, as well as the methodologies we want to use to respond to them.

Notes

1. The digital humanities (DH) are experiencing a boom represented by the growing interest of universities, cultural, and social institutions as well as by the creation of specialized centers to develop, assist and create projects using digital methodologies to respond to questions pertaining to the humanities. Likewise, the emergence of local, regional, and international organizations such as GO::DH and associations in Brazil, Argentina, Mexico, Australia, etc., are examples of the global dynamics of the field. Afrolatin@ studies, in turn, through diverse projects aim to study and help to "repair" the historical harms inflicted upon African and African-descendant communities due to slavery. In this light, transnational agencies such as the United Nations (UN) as well as the Organization of American States (OAS) promulgated the International Decade for People of African Descent that runs from 2014 to 2024. In addition, constant migration, as well as continuing actions for advocacy and self-determination by artists, writers and activists who consider themselves Latin Americans of African descent, are some of the elements that have prepared the soil for Afrolatin@ studies or approaches to emerge and gain currency in the Americas at large.

2. See Mathew K. Gold, *Debates in the Digital Humanities* (Minnesota: University of Minnesota Press, 2012). Pay particular attention to Part III.

3. See Kwame Dixon and John Burdick, eds., *Comparative Perspectives on Afro-Latin America* (Gainesville: University Press of Florida, 2012).

4. See also Kirschenbaum 2009.

5. This was the title of the conference of the Alliance of Digital Humanities Organizations held at Stanford University in June of 2011. Things have changed to the point where recent instances of the conference have been devoted to themes such as access (2017) and bridges (2018).

6. These and other questions are part of ongoing debates in the field. However, some of them are being addressed from perspectives of inclusion through concrete projects such as "The Human Touch" (2007) by Martha Nell Smith; Storify of Race in the Digital Humanities (https://storify.com/adelinekoh/race-and-the-digital-humanities) by Adeline Koh; Around DH in 80 days (http://arounddh.org); and some others that are exploring inclusion and expansion of the field. That being said, the criticism of DH is based on a perspective from which the digital euphoria obscures the vision of DH practitioners to develop critical humanistic approaches.

7. See the digital humanities' debates around "making" vs. "theory" in blog posts such as Adeline Koh, "More Hack, Less Yack? Modularity, Theory and Habitus in the Digital Humanities," 2012, http://www.adelinekoh.org/blog/2012/05/21/more-hack-less-yack-modularity-theory-and-habitus-in-the-digital-humanities/; and Bethany Nowviskie, "On the Origin of 'hack' and 'yack,'" 2014, http://nowviskie.org/2014/on-the-origin-of-hack-and-yack/.

8. Such space would ideally be open to epistemologies, either affiliated with the academy or not.

9. Some of the most important associations are under the umbrella of the Alliance of Digital Humanities Organizations (ADHO), which gathers together associations in

diverse countries. None of them, however, proposes race or ethnicity as a central variable in carrying out activities.

10. Kim Gallon (2016) makes the case for what she calls "Black Digital Humanities," a perspective that has been in the works for more than a decade now. In that case, however, she speaks about black communities in general, but with a clear African American perspective.

11. There have been several efforts toward the development of Black DH in the North American academy, with some initiatives covering global blackness. See projects such as the African American History, Culture and Digital Humanities developed by the Maryland Institute of Technology, University of Maryland (http://mith.umd.edu/research/aadhum/).

12. Afro-descendant traditions, existing for centuries in diverse locations, have become more interconnected, initially thanks to the influx of media outlets such as television, radio, and news, and later, digital communication technologies that managed to remediate and make new images emerge from complex relationships.

13. See Anani Dzidzienyo and Suzanne Oboler, *Neither Enemies nor Friends: Latinos, Blacks, Afro-Latinos* (New York: Palgrave MacMillan, 2005).

14. These are just some of the projects and initiatives going on in the region. Many more are not listed here due to lack of space.

15. These projects use several strategies to create new images and question previous cultural and historic production in African-descendant communities (including blurring gender divisions, parodic representations, etc.). These strategies, however, differ from those used by postcolonial literature, as the new communicative dynamics blur the lines of action and representation.

16. The website was accessible at http://canafro.iglooprojects.org/ until 2018. At the time of publication of this article, the site seems to be down.

17. See the afrolatin@ forum at http://www.afrolatinoforum.org/.

18. *The Afrolatin@ Project*, accessed May 12, 2015, http://afrolatinoproject.org/.

19. *AfroCROWD*, accessed May 12, 2015, http://www.afrocrowd.org/.

20. The discussion of free knowledge and access to information is fundamental to this point. See Kim Christen, "Does Information Really Want to Be Free? Indigenous Knowledge Systems and the Question of Openness," *International Journal of Communication* 6 (2012): 2870.

21. This is an activity carried out periodically by members of AfroCROWD in which participants edit Wikipedia for Afro-centered content.

22. *Conversemos Afro* is a digital space created by Proyecto Afrolatin@.

23. Some projects from Afro-Latin American communities that deserve to be mentioned include: The Library of Afro Colombian Literature (http://www.banrepcultural.org/blaavirtual/biblioteca-afrocolombiana); "Memorias del Río Atrato" (Atrato River Memories) (http://memoriasdelatrato.org/); and Observatorio Afroperuano (Afro-Peruvian Observatory) (http://www.lundu.org.pe/observatorio.html).

24. The Museum is an initiative that has been embraced by several regions in the nation, giving birth to at least three branches representing diverse ways to be and represent Afro-descendants in Brazil: Rio de Janeiro (http://museuafrodigitalrio.org/s2/); Mato

Grosso (http://200.129.241.116/mafro/); and Maranhão (http://www.museuafro.ufma.br/site/).

25. Brazil (Cultural Hotspots and the Open Access movement) and Colombia (Create Digital) are two examples of Latin American governments using the digital as a discursive and economic strategy for development.

8

Modularity, Mimesis, and the Informatic Ideal

On Intersectional Struggles for Digital Human(itie)s
in Latin America

ANITA SAY CHAN

In late December 2014, the website of Peru's Supreme Court was quietly taken over by AnonOpsPeru, the Peruvian node of the global cyberactivist network Anonymous, whose new message on the site read: "The Government will try to silence us. The press will keep things hidden. But we will raise our voices and show the world reality. Together we will fight for a fair Peru." The virtual takeover—and spectacle—followed weeks of some of the largest urban manifestations to capture Peru's capital city of Lima in decades. Tens of thousands of citizens from a diverse range of backgrounds filled the streets—and social media networks—in wave after wave of protests against Peru's controversial new labor law, known popularly as Ley Pulpín. Seen as a concession to big business, the law created a new category of cheap labor by allowing employers to cut benefits for employees between the ages of 18 and 24—including social security, life insurance, bonuses, and holiday benefits. And while targeting youth most directly, the law, protesters argued, would be used segment worker alliances and fire older employees, who could be replaced with cheaper options.

Most of Anonymous's most visible and notorious actions have been in protest against state and corporate actions seen as limiting conventionally recognized digital rights—on issues from copyright and privacy to freedom of expression, government transparency, and open access. I want to suggest, however, that the actions of AnonOpsPeru—alongside other digital activists in the region—mean to contest emergent tactics and policies being adopted around the digital (often experimentally) as means of both managing populations and economizing governance in the information age.

In this text, I explore these tactics as expressive of what I call here a growing digital age "informatic ideal." More than simply extending an "industrial ideal," which historian of technology Deborah Fitzgerald argued was used to promote efficiency in and amplification of production *outputs* through modern machinery (2010) in the nineteenth and twentieth centuries, contemporary state tactics, including Peru's new labor law, increasingly exemplify an embrace of what digital studies scholars point to as an information age idealization of modularity that, I stress, concerns itself more with input "compliance" than with output amplification. Derived from programmer practices in code design that grew from the 1960s onward, the modular principle stressed the value of making individual input elements of large coded systems deliberately detachable, non-interdependent, segregate-able, and even invisible to other parts (McPherson 2012). In that way, those units deemed "problematic" and "buggy" would be easy to detach and replace "with a completely different implementation without disturbing" (Raymond 2003, 15), or even being noticed by, the others. Programs like the UNIX operating system later came to be considered and celebrated as the design project that epitomized the Modular Principle in practice. Quoting the prominent open-source coder Eric Raymond, feminist digital studies scholar Tara McPherson elaborates that modularity in software design was meant to decrease "global complexity" and cleanly separate one "neighbor" from another (Raymond 2003, 85). It thus enabled rapid program growth while economizing on resources otherwise needed to manage code development closely, maintain functionality, and integrate or disintegrate program parts.

Yet if the modular principle is meant to ensure that no part of the system will register an interruption elsewhere in the system, and is designed to keep overall program functions normal, then diverse intersectional and multi-mediated visibilization tactics—as well as their reverberations through varied web- and street-based spectacles—demonstrate Latin American citizens' work to interrupt state and neoliberalized applications of the informatic ideal. Emphasizing diverse intersectional participation, global inclusivity, and collaboration for social change as goals, instead of continuity, citizen tactics propose the possibility of developing other informatic ideals that might instead stress human interdependence and coalition as defining principles over modularity's stress on detachability, segregation, and non-interdependence. Their efforts, I suggest, echo the calls of feminist, postcolonial, and Latin American digital humanities scholars for more dedicated efforts to cultivate stronger intersectional participation and global inclusions within digital humanities (Galina 2013; Liu 2012; McPherson 2012)—not only as a means to merely underscore the value of multi-disciplinary social collaboration, but as a tactic to contend with modularization and the growing risks of neoliberalization within academic and education-oriented projects themselves (McPherson 2012).

Modularity in EdTech

Without doubt, one of the policy arenas in which the design influence of elite global engineers, technology designers, and digital entrepreneurs has had greatest impact over the past decade is that of new education programming. Across Latin America, new IT-based solutions—along with their associated discursive framings—have fundamentally transformed the design and deployment of national education policies. Educational technology analysts note the expansion of ICT (Information and Communication Technology) for Education (ICT4E) initiatives worldwide that claim to prepare diverse learner populations for a competitive, twenty-first-century information-centered economy by extending new digital technologies (Bajak 2012; Cristia 2012; Cristia et al. 2012; Oppenheimer 2012; Severin and Capota 2011; Trucano 2012). A range of nations—17 documented in Latin America alone as of 2011, and 20 others in African, Asian, and Eastern European countries—have launched large-scale ICT4E programs that generally claim to extend digital "inclusion," connect the nation, and enhance future productivity by drawing presumably "disconnected" learning sectors—particularly at-risk, minority, indigenous, and economically marginalized populations—into global circuits of exchange (Oppenheimer 2012; Severin and Capota 2011). Tech industry analysts, too, note how new developments in low-cost, student-centered computing products were spurred on, with an IT firm like Intel adding some seven million of its own student-tailored Classmate PCs to schools across the Americas (Cristia 2012; Severin and Capota 2011).

In Peru, such policy influence was evident in the rapid adoption and growth of the One Laptop per Child (OLPC) initiative. Between 2007, when Peru first launched its partnership with the MIT-launched OLPC program, and 2012, the initiative experienced rapid and continual national expansions. Despite the stark lack of evidence supporting pedagogical efficacy and without either large-scale instructor or public enthusiasm for the program, within that period OLPC in Peru grew from a pilot program of fewer than 2,000 laptops to a nationally scaled project distributing over 900,000 XOs by late 2011. Such hefty expansions and investments demonstrate—even beyond Peru—how the techno-enthusiastic framings of engineering and design circles were able to gain purchase and rapidly transform national policy before debate among key sectors of the public and stakeholder populations could take place. As IDB policy analyst Julián Cristia wrote, it was evident that OLPC was "just the tip of the iceberg" (2012) in the global spread of ICTs as twenty-first-century "learning solutions."

There is little doubt that growing investments in new digital education projects continue—at rates that defy critical findings from recent studies and despite scholarly arguments for more balanced approaches. Moreover, the uptake of such programs can exceed existing infrastructures for producing research. Indeed, their enthusiastic, often-incautious adoption seems to operate more on the accelerated timescales of commercial IT developers than on the deliberative pace of academic researchers. These programs often betray policymakers' uncritical buy-in into the technological framings of elite engineers and IT designers. Indeed, state policies and tactics expressive of the modular principle—whether OLPC or Ley Pulpín—see its application as necessarily working to transform the bases of national economic competition in a time of digital change. And while their extension via promotions of an informatic ideal has been critiqued for curtailing shared collective rights, they are indeed often devised *alongside* and in explicit alliance with prominent actors in the global technology industry—in the name of realizing a nation's full innovative potential.

The 2014 Virtual Educa Conference, hosted in Lima, Peru, for instance, was organized by the Organization of American States in collaboration with regional government ministries and a notable array of transnational corporate sponsors, including Intel, HP, Google, Microsoft, Telefónica, and Oracle. The event was held at Peru's Ministry of Culture, and for a week filled the multistory building with elaborate demo areas and tech industry showcases featuring the latest in their lineup of education-oriented products. Everything from digital tablets to Google's Classrooms in the Cloud was on display, along with other corridors featuring robot kit vendors, digital encyclopedias, and row after row of interactive touchscreen blackboards.

The most striking presence, however, at the Virtual Educa event were the literally *thousands* of public-school teachers invited to attend, and who had been brought in from the rural provinces of Peru—including from regions in the remote jungle and high Andes—to be treated to the amenities and affordances that the conference's alliances brought forth, as well as to attend talks given by other corporate sponsors, government officials, and international policymakers in attendance. One talk, given by Matias of Silicon Valley's Hewlett Packard to a literally standing-room-only audience of Peruvian public-school teachers, for instance, explained the company's view on the contemporary challenges facing educators and their role in fostering innovation in the digital age. He said, "We've worked in many countries . . . and one of the challenges we've seen is that the education system in which we all participate today, in our opinion is a system that's now obsolete. It is not a system that generates talent, nor is it a system for personalized education. . . . But here's the news I am here to deliver: we are here to help you . . . HP turns 75 this year, as one of the world's leading technology [companies], and all this experience we bring and make available to you, to change lives and today, to prepare for a better future. So count on us in this transformation!" (pers. comm.).

This was not the first time I had witnessed such a perplexing approach to public relations from tech-sector actors—who not only seemed untroubled by their direct pronouncements to audiences of working professionals that those people were obsolete and working against generating a society of future talent, but who actually seemed certain that there was a virtue in doing so. It was, in other words, a thoroughly unabashed pronouncement of the informatic ideal and modularity—and the instant disposability and extractability of work histories and practices now deemed "obsolete"—as a design principle. But here, it was applied not only toward the alleged end of optimizing the design of a previously constructed technology, but also for the optimization of the design of the very social and professional system that surrounded it.

When Matias did switch over to a more conventional form of public relations address, to reassure and assuage his audience, he did so by telling them that even if the current education system they participated in was one that had become obsolete, there was at least one resource educators could count on to avert risk: HP and its 75-year-long history of "experience" as one of Silicon Valley's oldest corporate exemplars. Here, Silicon Valley was summoned as an existing material model whose own presumably self-evident success record was assumed to require little explanation. But Matias's framing of HP did not turn on high modernist framings (Scott 1999) of the company as manifesting a preserved system of high order and rationality, or even on its ability to leverage such value toward new wealth creation. Rather, this narrative turned more on the notion of HP having managed to cultivate a record of survival and growth in the Valley's highly competitive and rapidly changing ecology of technologically paced growth and death, and of sudden market popularity and as-sudden market irrelevance, for nearly a century.

Here, in other words, Matias placed his emphasis on the company's long (and unparalleled among Silicon Valley's technology companies) record of proven self-optimization—of a responsiveness to conditions of rapid market change and uncertainty—and its ability to self-improve by not only investing in likely winning innovations, but also presumably choosing to unplug less-optimal ones. Its ability to become and remain a market leader throughout the sudden market changes of the twentieth century, and its ability to manage the uncertainties of the computing industry for nearly a century, it was suggested, were what made it an unparalleled ally with whom to confront dynamic market and technological changes already manifesting in the twenty-first century's digital economy.

One has only to replace HP with a Global Fortune 500 company from another product sector—from, say, the banking or energy or consumer goods and services industries (speaking of other clear industry giants whose growth over the past century had made them household names worldwide)—to appreciate the distinctiveness of HP's reception. For whatever symbolic power and global capital is surely shored up in the unique market dominance and recognizability of any Fortune 500 player, it is rather hard to imagine the same accusations coming from any corporate actor other than HP without it being met with at least some degree of indignation or distrust from audiences. IT sector actors today somehow prove an exception, and HP met instead with a roomful of applause.

Universalizing Modular Models

Decades earlier, in the mid-twentieth century, computer programmers were just beginning to appreciate the utility—and design elegance—of limiting and even foreclosing on information exchange to enable better management of complex systems. Underscoring the benefits of applying "modularity" as a key principle of design, Carliss Baldwin and Kim Clark advocated an embrace of principles of information hiding and detachability in program designs as a means to reduce system interdependencies among coded parts. In *Design Rules, Vol. 1: The Power of Modularity*, Baldwin and Clark argued that while computers from 1940 to 1960 had "complex, interdependent designs," in an era they call the "premodular" phase of computing (149), computer engineers had increasingly begun to adopt modularity for hardware design from the early 1950s onward—with UNIX finally emerging in the 1970s as the first coded operating system to adhere fully to the modular rule. Its design innovation determined that program modules would stop "promiscuously shar(ing) global data" within the whole, which would allow problems in the system to stay "local" (84–85), and, as open-source coder Eric Raymond described it, avoid "a tendency to involve programs with each other's internals. . . . It should [thus] be easy to replace one end with a completely different implementation without disturbing the other" (Raymond 2003, 15).

Baldwin and Clark in particular are keen to underscore that while computing system designers might have embraced the benefits of modularity as a design rule decades prior to the 1980s, growing complexity and uncertainty in the heated post-'80s computing market incentivized new reforms that valorized modularity as a means to manage work practices more generally. As they elaborate in the preface to the 2005 edition of the Chinese translation of *Design Rules: The Power of Modularity*, "[B]etween 1970 and 1980, the greater computer industry changed from a highly concentrated and vertically integrated oligopoly dominated by IBM to a fragmented and vertically disintegrated *modular cluster* of independent firms." Emerging from this was a new "post-1980 industrial order" (Baldwin and Clark 2005, 8) in computing marked by new degrees of market competition as defining developments.

Computing scholars like Chris Kelty have noted that modular design innovations in UNIX afforded the organizational innovations that accommodated multitasking, portability, and dynamic design, and fostered UNIX's rapid uptake and spread among researchers and engineers in the 1970s (and it remains a beloved and hallowed objects for many OS design professionals and students to this day) (Kelty 2008). In contrast to code production under monolithic organizational structures, UNIX's modularized system design accommodated rapid change and continual evolution based upon the diverse contributions of independent work units; and unlike with monolithic operating systems (like Windows, for instance) that tend toward conservative, proprietary organizational structures and design logics, here new projects could be rapidly incorporated—or rapidly disincorporated—as modules to optimize the overall operating system's functionality. For digital studies scholars like Tara McPherson, such accommodations in technological design worked against former corporate production structures that dedicated resources to tightly coordinating and controlling all production parts of the system as a means to retain internal structure and knowledge. But she writes that it also unexpectedly worked in parallel with distinct affordances that post-industrial transformations looked for. As she writes, such traits were surprisingly compatible with the core tenets of post-Fordism: "a mode of production that begins to remake industrial-era notions of standardization in the 1960s: time-space compression, transformability, customization, a public/private blur, and so on" (McPherson 2012).

Today, such design logics have indeed been noticed for generating what can often seem like contradictory conditions of precarity among workers of even Silicon Valley's most elite, leading internet companies—all of which visibly build upon modularized API and free software structures as their development model. While Google, Amazon, and Mosaic all fell into the top-five ranked US companies for highest turnover rates (average worker tenure was a year at each company) in a 2013 survey of IT worker retention rates, Microsoft surprisingly ranked higher in worker security, with an average of seven years for employee retention (Giang 2013). Such digital production sectors have not been the only ones to feel the impact of modularized communication. McPherson, for instance, has noted a growing tendency toward the segmentation and segregation of knowledge production within academia, noting the difficulty of generating and sustaining genuinely interdisciplinary interfaces (especially, for her, around questions of race) even in young fields like digital studies. While a growing body of critical race scholars has begun to engage expanding digital studies-generated critiques of race-based representations in new media and greater explorations of social access to media and the digital divide, she notes that these efforts rarely come into contact with the most widely cited scholarship in digital studies, which privileges analyses of the form and phenomenology of computation and the digital over questions of political segmentation and exclusion. As McPherson notes, "Important works emerged from both 'camps,' but the camps rarely intersected" (143).

Her concerns extend beyond the academic separability of critical race and digital studies to questions of the separability of "discrete" knowledge sectors based on claims of expertise. As she asks:

> What if this very incompatibility [between scholarly camps] is itself part and parcel of the organization of knowledge production that [modular] operating systems like UNIX helped to disseminate around the world? Might we ask whether there is not something particular to the very forms of electronic culture that seems to encourage just such a movement, a movement that partitions [social issues like] race off from the specificity of media forms? Put differently, might we argue that the very structures of digital computation develop at least in part to cordon off [issues of the social] and to contain [them]? [And] might we come to understand that our own critical methodologies are the heirs to this epistemological shift? (McPherson 2012a, 24)

And indeed, McPherson notes how modularity's impact today reverberates through even the most routine activities of recognizing the boundaries of academic knowledge work when she explores the problem of "why it seemed so hard," as someone working in an interdisciplinary field like the digital humanities, "to hold together my long-standing academic interests in race and gender . . . [with the] world of digital production and design" (2012, 140). As she writes, by the mid-twentieth century, the modular principle had clearly "taken hold not only in computation but also in the increasingly niched and regimented production of knowledge in the university after World War II" (2012, 149). She cites the rise of a new "relentless formalism" in humanities and social science–based methodologies that amounted to a "logical corollary" to academic "depoliticization" in spaces of higher learning (2012, 150). McPherson notes, moreover, a rise in "patterned isolation" among humanities and social science disciplines that allowed a "cut out and separate" mentality to reach a new crescendo on campuses after World War II. She thus challenges her audience with the imperative that new forms of scholarship must move beyond conventional disciplinary boxes, writing that

> the digital humanities and code studies [indeed] must also take up the questions of culture and meaning that animate so many scholars of race in fields like the new American studies. But likewise, scholars of race must analyze, use, and produce digital forms and not smugly assume that to engage the digital directly is to be complicit with the forces of capitalism. The lack of intellectual generosity across our fields and departments only reinforces the divide-and-conquer mentality that the most dangerous aspects of modularity underwrite. We must develop common languages that link the study of code and culture. (McPherson 2012, 153)

But against the spread of an informatic ideal that would seek to modularize communication and foreclose much-needed cross-disciplinary, cross-cultural dialogues, we have actually seen varied collectives across the Global South—spanning indigenous and urban youth-based movements alike—struggle for dialogic spaces over the last decade, very frequently through efforts undertaken around digital media. And in multiple contexts in the Global South, we see indigenous groups working around online tactics specifically to build social intersections, interfaces, and coalitions across difference that press for spaces and tactics of dialogue—to work against a future of monologic digitality and modularism as a human digital ideal.

On Mimesis and Dialogic Space

A scene from Puno, Peru's southernmost province—known more as a center of indigenous culture than as a center of high-tech developments—illustrates the above. On a day in mid-April 2011, a team of a dozen or so transnational activists of native languages, media arts, and free software turned Puno's municipal meeting room into a digital workshop for an indigenous language project. Among the participants were self-identified geeks and hackers from Barcelona, La Paz, and Lima; media artists from Córdoba and Quito; language activists from across the Andes; and rural teachers from Puno's local towns. These were actors working across differences in day-to-day geographic locales, as well as in their identified disciplines. But they were all gathered together—traveling from across the continents—to work on translating software into Quechua and Aymara, the two largest indigenous languages in Peru, so that software could then be installed in the one million XOs that had been distributed to rural and urban schools nationwide, as part of a new national digital education partnership with the OLPC project.

The organizers called this event a Translation Hackathon, and as with many global hackathons, this event was marked by participants' use of a number of portable technologies. Multiple laptop cases covered with free software stickers and slogans were visible, along with several models of OLPC's green and white XO laptops, wireless USB routers, portable projectors, and chargers, and digital cameras were scattered around the table's collective stock of gadgets. The event thus shared some commonalities with what is conventionally recognized within Western engineering circles as hackathon events that organize temporalities of concentrated coding among student or professional IT designers—and that a number of science studies scholars and ethnographers have written about as being as much about an intensity of producing and performing "hacker" identity as producing code (Coleman 2010 and 2013; Irani 2015). Feminist science studies scholar Lilly Irani, for instance, has written about how hackathons function in dominant geek imaginaries as a celebration of geek competition, engineering prowess, and a showcase of the power of individual genius and authorship, which are all central to performing the mastery of dynamic design. It is here, however, that Puno's hackathon seems to have broken away significantly from conventional framings.

When I arrived, for instance, things were just getting under way, with participants settling in around a shared table. No sooner had laptop screens begun to open, however, when one of the participants, Francisco Ancco Rodríguez, himself a native Aymara speaker and retired public school teacher from the nearby town of Acora, called for the group's attention. Drawing out a round bundle of cloth, he unfolded it on the table's surface, and spread out the dried coca leaves clustered at its center. Selecting three, he arranged them into a small fan formation, and began leading a short prayer in Aymara, holding the fan of leaves—a k'intu—firmly in front of him. Just before placing the portion into his mouth, he waved the fan before him and blew a breath of air over them—and then invited the group to draw their shares from the pile.

The ritual, a ceremonial offering known in the Andes as a *despacho*, is one that the language activists participating in the group had seen before—although not one that most of the technology activists were accustomed to paying deference to. Long performed in Andean communities on auspicious occasions, the despacho is still understood as a means of communicating with the natural world's spirits. In its most simplified version, it is framed as an offering to the Apu mountain spirits or the Pachamama—the female cosmic energy often translated as Mother Nature, but in the Andean world associated as much with death as with birth and life. In whatever instantiation, however, it is practiced as a means of entering into a careful dialogue with ambivalent forces not fully controlled by man. Such powerful energy is read as running through varied objects in the Andean world, encompassing, as anthropologist Olivia Harris explains, "a whole spectrum of sacred beings: the mountains, the dead; untamed places such as gullies and waterfalls. . . . The defining character of these [energies] is not so much evil or malice as abundance, chaos, and hunger. . . . [They] are the source of both fertility and wealth, and of sickness, misfortune, and death" (Harris 1995, 312).

This kind of worldview around nature and living spirits is a form of relating that informs orientations around the sacred, as well as the mundane—that can be taken, that is, as simply a living, present feature of an environment with which people are already in dialogue. But in the context of a hackathon, it is called upon to do other kinds of work: to decenter a staging of human ingenuity and dominance over nature and technological design alike, and to underscore another kind of moral subjectivity. An organizer of the hackathon, Irma Álvarez, herself a native Quechua speaker, explained what the despacho represents in the context of the translation hackathons she has organized: "It's an offering to begin any important work, a thanks to the Pachamama and the Apus to give our recognition to the coca leaf that's sacred to us as Aymaras and Quechuas. So that when we start any important work, we always ask for permission from our gods and Apus so that they give us strength and energy to continue our work" (pers. comm.).

For Álvarez, work, labor, and even the act of making an offering must necessarily be understood as collective and inclusive; no one and no contribution is read as either discrete, dispensable or measured against another to determine optimal compatibility with the system's higher design. It thus extends one means of making technology and the informatic both cross-culturally legible and dialogic, clearly conscious of its role in channeling multiple logics—moral, civic, and cosmological—and in speaking to and for diverse subjects with varied modes of listening and expressing, and bringing them into interface with one another through a practice of technological "cocreating."

She further reads these practices as linked to a history of other translation practices represented by other indigenist educators and vanguard movements that stretch back more than a century in Peru. These include work represented in the indigenist journal *Amauta*, edited by one of Latin America's most renowned Marxists, Peruvian José Carlos Mariátegui, and work by figures like Manuel Z. Camacho, who led a movement for clandestine schools in Puno to make classes available in Aymara to Aymara populations, and had to teach by candlelight for fear of being jailed in 1904. Such indigenous movements issued ardent critiques of assimilationist models of education. And their efforts, at times bloody, sustained throughout the nineteenth and twentieth centuries, issued varied critical discourses—and experiments and innovations in education—that urged broader national reforms.

The hybrid aesthetics and literacies contemporary digital movements from the Andes promote are indeed ones that echo past vanguard experiments in technology, literacy, and education. Such local practices, emerging from both urban and rural sites across Peru, explicitly challenged the Peruvian state's turn-of-the-century vision of modernization, and the roles educational and literacy technologies were projected to play therein. Works by Vicky Unruh (1994), Cynthia Vich (2000), Juan Zevallos Aguilar (2002), Guissela González Fernández (2005), and Jose Garambel (2010) stress how, in the early twentieth century, Puno was recognized as one of the most fervent areas for indigenist literary movements in the region. Between 1900 and 1940, diverse artists and intellectuals seeking to reframe the nation's relationship to indigenous culture wrote and published numerous works that defended indigenous populations, condemned elite landowners' usurpation of lands, and insisted on new models for education and creative production that better reflected local cultural concerns and visions for the future. Literary circles like Puno's Orkopata group thus pushed for new forms of literary expression that blended indigenous languages and narrative conventions with *castellano* through the vanguard publication *Boletín Titikaka* (1926–30) (González Fernández 2005; Unruh 1994; Vich 2002; Zevallos 2002).

Between the late teens and mid-1930s, in fact, vanguard literary activity was emerging throughout Latin America (Unruh 1994). Much as was the case for those outside the continent, their activity included several forms: the emergence of small groups of writers committed to creative innovation; the affirmation and dissemination of critical and aesthetic positions through written manifestos; experimentation with multiple literary and artistic genres to cut across generic boundaries; the publication of magazines as outlets for both artistic experiments and cultural debates; and the organization of study groups that generally fought against modernity's push for cultural homogenization. What many participants noted was unique to Latin American vanguard circles, however, was their embeddedness within local contexts of deep cultural heterogeneity, and the relative proximity they then had to enable engagements and investigations into local language, folklore, and cultural history (Unruh 1994). Puno's *Boletín Titikaka* thus came to be known as one of the most lasting vanguardist magazines coming from Latin America's own peripheral zones—and from outside major cities (González Fernández 2005; Vich 2002; Zevallos 2002). It grew, in fact, to have a readership not only across Peru, but across Latin America and globally—reaching as far as Lima's best-known vanguard publication, *Amauta*. It was known for articles on "aesthetic Indoamericanism," and the *Boletín*'s editor, the surrealist writer Gamaliel Churata, devoted extensive attention to linguistic investigations in essays and bilingual poetry using vernacular verse.

Other Punenan indigenists of the era worked specifically through educational models to challenge what they saw as the state's problematic application of literary technologies and educational models as a means to reform indigenous populations. At the beginning of the twentieth century, the Puno educator and intellectual Jose Antonio Encinas issued some of the earliest national proposals for a model of indigenous education rooted within native culture (Garambel 2010). He thus criticized the imposition of a system that, he wrote, operated on the principle that "everything native should be forgotten," and worked to push forth new state policy—the first on bilingual education—in the 1940s to enable Peru's two largest indigenous languages, Quechua and Aymara, to be used in class instruction. Encinas's work, alongside that of the artists and educators of Puno's vanguard movements of the early twentieth century, influenced the founding of one of the Warisata schools just outside Puno's borders, in the Bolivian town by the same name (Gustafson 2009; Pérez 1962; Salazar 1997 and

2005). Founded in 1931 as a collaborative project between local Aymara community leaders and progressive Andean educators, it saw itself as a radical experiment in indigenous education and education through collective uses of technology. Education at Warisata was seen as a key means of recuperating indigenous territory and expressing collective rights. Thus, the school did not adopt Western or Limenan models, but aimed to translate indigenous community structures into pedagogic spaces, with a council of Aymara elders—the *Parlamento Amauta*—that helped to oversee it and technologies that were applied for both educational and communal purposes.

And while such developments may indeed be a rather far cry from the showcase of geek engineering prowess and creative genius Western hackathons are known to channel, their consistent invocation and references in conversation with Andean hackathon participants allow them to translate to new actors and audiences (including Western and urban engineers collaborating in Andean hackathons, who similarly perform deference to nature's "unknown forces" in its presence). It is arguably as expressive of what STS and design studies scholars—Paul Dourish, Lilly Irani, and Kavita Phillips—describe as postcolonial approaches to computing. And they write of it as cultivating "a way of asking questions, a mode of investigating and a form of conversation. It is not a theory of ends—it does not imply the historical end of colonialism, the end of exploitation, the end of history, nor is it a road map to egalitarianism, communitarianism, or democracy as philosophical ends. Postcolonial computing is an approach to familiar areas of research that could too easily slip into simple, rigid patterns, achieving closure and canonicity at the expense of discovery" (2012, 21). Such approaches are significant in being distinct from those taken by either scholars or engineers in fields like ICT4D and HCI—who have tried to resolve problems in intercultural collaboration and design by using a "taxonomic model that sees culture as something that is inherently stable enough to be fixed as an invariant," rather than something dynamic, living, and constantly in flux across global and local space (Philip, Irani, and Dourish 2012, 12).

Conclusion

One other means of redirecting and hacking an informatic ideal around modularization is still playing out elsewhere in Peru—around the historically visible actions, organization, and responses to Peru's Ley Pulpín that opened this paper. Even as tens of thousands of citizens took to the streets on the 18th of December 2015, quickly organizing to protest Peru's new labor law just days after its passage by the Peruvian Congress, members of President Humala's administration remained stalwart in defending the necessity of the law to bolster the overall competitiveness of the Peruvian economy. Against protestors' chants underscoring the devaluation and neoliberalization of labor, the phenomenon of worker segregation, and the selectivity of labor law protections, the state reiterated that the new law would function to encourage the formalization of Peru's youth labor market—and insisted that the law need not be popular or populist in the short run to be beneficial in the long run.

The state further dismissed critiques it framed as asserted only by a select class of "pampered" middle-class youth who were seeking elite worker protections—hence the references to Pulpín, a name designating a wholesome beverage for children—instead of recognizing (as the state supposedly did) the problems of working-class youth. Without the economic incentives granted by Ley Pulpín to large companies, working-class youth, who disproportionately remained in the informal labor sector, could never hope to gain formal employment. Behind the scenes at the first major protest, #18D, however, youth across the city were building an organizational structure that aimed to cut across such attempts at segmentation. Clustering into 14 urban zones—structured geographically around Lima's existing neighborhoods—demonstrators created parallel media channels, using social media networks, alternative press outlets, blogs, satire sites, and memes, around which urban neighbors could organize, exchange spontaneous individual messages, and visualize representation in other urban zones.

In the midst of this, AnonOps launched a first and then second media attack on government websites. While logics of modularization underscored the replaceability of labor, and the supreme ability of the system universally to assess, process, and incorporate any manner of material or informatic resource necessary, here came messages that simply resisted system processing. "The Government will try to silence us. The press will keep things hidden. But we will raise our voices and show the world reality. Together we will fight for a fair Peru." The message acknowledged that it might aspire to contribute to any tangible material change. But the simple act of replacing the government's content with a new message demonstrated the potential to alter, as well as the symbolic power of maintaining, authorized message streams. And showing how even a bit of temporary information-based noise in that stream could be considered somehow abhorrently offensive clearly struck a collective nerve. And from then on, Anonymous's infamous Guy Fawkes personae and masks became regular fixtures among protestors.

Seemingly out of nowhere, waves of weekly protests emerged—each of which continued to be attended by tens of thousands—and kept the city embroiled in collective dissent. And, to the surprise of many of Lima's social scientists, who noted the city for the broadly diverse but stratified social and racial populations and provincial populations it brought together, the protests seemed to have done the impossible: bringing together wildly diverse and typically segregated segments of the city—from the polite, middle-class neighborhoods of Miraflores, to the rugged working-class zones of Lince and Callao, to the spans of new settlement zones growing at the edges of the city from rural migrations from the provinces and indigenous communities in San Juan de Lurigancho and Villa El Salvador. And it brought them into side-by-side coalition. Social media hashtags proliferated with each subsequent protest—#18D, 26E—and from the numbers turning out, it was clear no one seemed tired of the urban antics or the spontaneous visibilities and spectacle they were creating.

Days before the fifth organized protest, Congress finally called an emergency session to pose another vote around Ley Pulpín on January 26. By 3 pm that day, the law had been officially repealed, and the youth *pulpines,* to the surprise of many, declared victorious by official news channels in altering the determined decisions of the state and raising its accountability to the public. Articles proliferated around the use of social media and memes as technologies to bolster democratic dissent and participation. Less-frequently mentioned, however, were the protestors' approaches to using the city as social infrastructure and *technology*—one that could be used to build coalitions and unite and interface distinct urban sectors, rather than reinforce social divisions across class or geographic divides, if simply deployed differently.

These tactics, I would argue, defend a right to dialogue by and between diverse civic actors, who bridge worlds and communities of practice between hackers and indigenous activists. Such dialogic spaces require new forged understandings and cultural interfaces in order to be made "legible." Bridging generations, connecting urban with rural imaginaries, indigenous leaders with global hackers, and ethics that push toward the future with others remembering an obligation to honor the past, then, such encounters might be read as moments of "awkward engagement," in anthropologist Anna Tsing's framing of the term (2004). They signal a space where distinct forces and interests meet in a "zone of cultural friction"—and where the dissolution of difference cannot be taken for granted. But they also represent another strategy that draws from what anthropologists and critical theorists have framed as a "mimetic function" of communication. Michael Taussig, drawing from Walter Benjamin, writes not only of "the power of the copy to influence what it is a copy of" (1992, 250) for instance, but further describes mimesis in human contexts as fundamentally built upon the tendency toward a "radical displacement of self." This, he argues is generative of positive possibilities for the present—so that "no proposition could be more fundamental to understanding the visceral bond connecting perceiver to perceived in the operation of mimesis" than the notion that "Sentience takes us outside of ourselves. . . . The fundamental move of the mimetic faculty tak[es] us bodily into alterity" (40). He reminds his audiences, in other words, how it may be that through the act of mimesis, and through what appear to be processes of copying the original, something new can be generated that enables another space and possibility of inclusion against a modularized informatics ideal to come forth.

III

Digital Aesthetics
and Practices

~~~~~~~~

9

Cuban Digital Pedagogies and the Question of the Interface in Yaima Pardo's *Offline*

JUAN CARLOS RODRÍGUEZ

In the credit section of her documentary *Offline* (2013), Cuban filmmaker Yaima Pardo uses the Facebook profile format to represent her identity and the identities of the rest of the film crew. According to Pardo, she created a self-reflexive digital screen presence to highlight how, in today's internet era, real identities, even of Cuban subjects with limited access to the internet, are constructed as digital identities. It should not be a surprise that Pardo used Facebook to commemorate the fourth anniversary of *Offline*, a documentary about the internet debate in Cuba. In a Facebook post from May 20, 2017, she wrote: "Remembering *Offline* from 2013 to 2017, tell me how my connection is doing?" (Pardo's Facebook wall; all translations are mine). After questioning the poor quality and high price of internet connection in Cuba (2.50 CUC per hour, in a country where the average wage is between 25 and 30 CUC per month), she concludes her post with the following demand: "We would like to connect more comfortably from home and in a massive way" (Pardo's Facebook wall).

Pardo's insistence that things continue to be the same four years after *Offline*'s premiere seems a bit awkward, considering the dramatic changes experienced in Cuba since 2013. In December of 2014, President Obama normalized relations with Cuba, opening a new political chapter in

US-Cuban relations. On November 26, 2016, Fidel Castro, the main leader of the Cuban revolution, passed away, eight years after leaving Cuba under the authority of his brother Raúl Castro, who left his post as president in 2018 (though he remains First Secretary of the Communist Party). At the time, without a public succession plan, the Castro family's long-expected political retirement was still a transition process filled with uncertainty. To add more uncertainty to Cuba's future, President Donald Trump announced in 2017 that he was cancelling President Obama's agreements with Cuba, a measure that may involve the tightening of travel and business restrictions between the two countries. Although many things have changed, and even if wireless spots are now more widely available in Cuban cities compared to 2013, some things remain the same: many Cubans like Yaima Pardo are still demanding less-restricted access to internet networks in Cuba, which are still tightly controlled by the Cuban state.

Yaima Pardo's *Offline* is a documentary that discusses the situation of the internet in Cuba in 2013, presenting two diagnoses: that Cubans are confronting a new kind of illiteracy, technological illiteracy, because most of them do not have access to the internet; and that this technological illiteracy could be detrimental to the civic and economic development of the island. These diagnoses echo a debate on technological illiteracy first introduced in Cuba in 2011 by film critic Juan Antonio García Borrero (García Borrero 2013, 15–33). Pardo's documentary follows the path of Borrero's intervention, which has the merit of reframing the debate about the internet in Cuba as a question of knowledge rather than politics. After questioning the media war between the Cuban state, eager to control internet access and content, and some Cuban bloggers, who defended their right to freedom of expression, García Borrero redefined technological illiteracy as an issue of educational policy with civic and economic ramifications.

Through interviews that echo García Borrero's call for a second literacy campaign focusing on technological literacy, *Offline* promotes the massification of internet access in a country where connectivity to digital networks is highly restricted and has generally been limited to tourists and institutional agents. The group of subjects interviewed by Pardo, which includes intellectuals, educators, and web activists who run digital platforms in Cuba, consider the lack of internet access in the country a disadvantage for its citizens, a way of falling behind in comparison to the rest of the world. Although some of these perspectives can be associated with a developmentalist ideology, Pardo makes clear that the goal of Cubans is not to achieve digital education and information literacy through a technocratic project, but instead, as two subjects interviewed point out, through a critical distance that can be fostered by "educación desconectada" (unwired education). *Offline* can help us rethink not only the social consequences of limited access to the internet in Cuba but also what it means to make a documentary about digital networks in a world in which the internet, as Alex Gil points out, is "quickly becoming the dominant image of our cultural heritage" (Gil and Priego 2013, n.p.). The very idea of framing the debate of internet access in Cuba as a question of digital education and information literacy is itself an attempt to use the cultural heritage of the 1961 revolutionary literacy program, a form of "educación desconectada" that inspired García Borrero's arguments, in order to validate the internet as a new source of cultural heritage.

In the last decade, Cuban digital dilemmas have circulated on multiple screens, taking the shape of e-mails, blogs, webpages, and documentaries (Venegas 2010a). According to Cristina Venegas, "debate about digital technologies in Cuba carries extra weight during a unique transition to a global system of relations and greater exposure of Cuba to international political currents" (33). The increasing number of documentaries about the internet in Cuba suggests the important role of visible evidence and testimonies as rhetorical tools that provide a framework for articulating individual and collective demands for the democratization of the internet on the island. In Cuba, where internet access cannot be taken for granted and digital activists are frequently regarded as dissidents and counterrevolutionaries, documentary has served to reframe the image of the internet as a legitimate source of cultural heritage, in part because, as a media discourse associated with critical distance and social authority, it is itself considered a legitimate format through which to transmit and debate cultural heritage.

In this chapter, I will analyze Yaima Pardo's *Offline* to explore how the cross-fertilization of documentary and digital conventions can be used to reconstruct web navigation as an immersive experience that offers itself as a pedagogical intervention and critical interrogation of internet infrastructures and practices in Cuba. My main argument is that *Offline* offers a critical and affective pedagogy of digital networks in Cuba that operates not only at the level of content but also at the level of the digital interfaces it displays, where the convergence of documentary and digital conventions takes place. *Offline* can be described as a non-interactive database documentary that combines interviews with video clips, reconstructions of Human Computer Interface (HCI), and projection mapping to create dense and image-saturated views of the contemporary Cuban mediascape. When digital interfaces are incorporated by documentary as part of its strategies of nonfictional representation, they become moving images. In *Offline*, computer interfaces function as documentary reconstructions that serve to display digital interactions as graphic spectacle and visible evidence.

In Pardo's documentary, the nonfictional pro-filmic space (the space filmed) takes the shape of an informational, multilayered, and navigational space, a "spatial montage" made of live-action footage, multiple windows, superimposed computer graphics, and projection mapping. This hybrid window into Cuban cyberspace, created in *Offline* by the nonfictional treatment of digital interfaces, reframes the tension created by new media between immersion and information control. According to Lev Manovich, "A computer image is situated between two opposing poles—an illusionistic window into a fictional universe and a tool for computer control. Visually, this conceptual opposition translates into the opposition between depth and surface, between a window into a fictional universe and a control panel" (2001, 290).

Instead of creating a window into a fictional world that is opposed to a control panel, *Offline* creates a window into the sociohistorical world in which the depth of live-action testimonies and the surface of computer simulations and control panels become part of the reality under scrutiny. In *Offline*, the immersive dimension of nonfictional representation (live-action footage, interviews, and database video images) and the operational dimension of digital interfaces (reading e-mails, clicking web links, navigating multiple windows, downloading data, but also witnessing machine errors produced by internet access restrictions or limitations in data transmission capacity) contaminate each other and produce a tense convergence of cinematic conventions and data processes. It is through this tense convergence of national and global database images, functional and dysfunctional interfaces, and the nonfictional remixing of pro-filmic spaces and cyberspaces that *Offline* comes to represent some of the polemics and disputes, as well as some contradictory and ambivalent aspects, that form part of the internet debate in Cuba.

In the following pages, I will discuss various strategies used by Yaima

Pardo in *Offline* to lay out this tense convergence of documentary conventions and digital operations, such as the use of projection mapping in talking head interviews, the remixing of database images, the juxtaposition of computer graphics and urban images, and the representation of functional and dysfunctional interfaces as cinematic images. The saturated projection of Cuban digital dilemmas in *Offline* is the result of an interface that articulates the interactions between documentary and digital conventions, creating a "documentary display" of web navigation "in which the visual realm" of human-computer interactions "is maximised as the field of exhibitionistic, expressionistic, and excessive attractions" (Beatie 2008, 4). While the interviews with experts and internet practitioners in *Offline* appeal to "the intellect and cognitive faculty," in which "logic seems to prevail over affect," the graphic design of Pardo's documentary constitutes a "documentary display" of digital interfaces that produces "a sensuous and affective knowledge—a knowledge that is produced via the senses . . . and draws on relations between sight and imagination" (Beattie 2008, 16).

Offline constitutes an affective pedagogy of the internet in Cuba because its documentary display of digital interfaces serves to show Cubans what the World Wide Web looks like and how it feels to navigate it from Cuba, with all its content possibilities but also its system restrictions and limitations. Pardo's affective pedagogy is motivated by the fact that many Cubans have never used a computer to navigate the web. That is why her documentary reproduces the interactive experience of navigating the web. Through reconstructions of digital interfaces, *Offline* suggests that the internet can play an important part in the interactions between Cuba and the rest of the world by opening the world of information to Cubans.

In this documentary display of digital interfaces, however, the spatial tension between immersion and information control, manifested through the remixing of documentary conventions and data processes, produces a tension between two forms of knowledge. While *Offline* is a documentary display of the internet that functions as an affective pedagogy that appeals to the senses, it is also a critical pedagogy due to the fact that the interviews with experts serve as informed comments that create the critical distance necessary to contextualize the operations of the internet in Cuba. It is precisely through the constant reframing of testimonies and digital environments that these two modes of knowledge emerge as effects of the tense convergence of documentary and data. While the overwhelming documentary display of digital interfaces may produce the complacent pleasures of a visual spectacle, the testimonies of the subjects interviewed remind us that the internet represented in *Offline* is not simply entertainment, but also operates as visible evidence of a dysfunctional system that needs to change in order to be turned into an intellectual and cognitive tool.

The Interview in Cyberspace: New Ways of Sharing Authority

In *Offline*, Yaima Pardo combines street and studio interviews. Most interviews conducted in the street are testimonies to the lack of internet access in Cuba. Most studio interviews, in contrast, are comments and opinions delivered by expert academics and internet practitioners who have developed digital projects in Cuba. The spatial distribution of testimonies suggests a division of roles between Cuban intellectuals speaking from a virtual space with limited access to the internet and "cubanos de a pie," ordinary Cubans, speaking from a low-tech urban environment in which internet connection is too expensive.

One of the participants in the street interviews, speaking in front of an internet café in Havana, complains about the fact that children are not allowed to enter internet cafes, a policy that limits the educational potential of digital networks. He argues that instead of promoting jobs in the tourist sector, the government should improve digital networks in Cuba to promote knowledge-based entrepreneurship that would contribute to the new Cuban economy, which combines self-employment with foreign investment. The exclusion of Cubans from digital networks is also denounced with irony by some participants interviewed in the street who wear t-shirts with messages such as "WiFi 8 CUC por hora" (WiFi 8 CUC per hour) and "Cuba Zona Libre de Internet" (Cuba Internet Free Zone), the latter a parody of neoliberal jargon (Free Trade Zone) that underscores the contradictions of Cuban socialist capitalism. Later, Pardo will use computer graphics to compare the price of the internet in Cuba (4.50 CUC per hour) with the average monthly salary of Cubans (18.50 CUC), to underscore that many Cubans cannot pay for an hour of internet, as it equates to 25 percent of their average monthly salary.

Studio interviews include conversations with film critic Gustavo Arcos, visual artist Mauricio Abad, social activist Dmitri Prieto Samsonov, magazine editors Daniel Díaz Mantilla and Alien García Agüero, and historian Josefina Toledo Benedit. These participants form a diverse inter-disciplinary group and offer different perspectives on the role of the inter-net in Cuba. In studio interviews, Abad, Arcos, Prieto, and Díaz Mantilla denounce the unilateral and uniform perspectives provided by official Cuban media with a presence on digital networks. According to them, it does not make sense to compare the information provided by *Granma* and *Juventud Rebelde* because they simply duplicate the same point of view, one given from a position of power. In contrast, Prieto character-izes the internet as a decentralized paradigm of information, and later he adds that the internet could play an important role in the future of Cuban democracy because it can facilitate the socialization of decision-making. Díaz Mantilla insists on the power of web 2.0 because it allows users to generate and share information, while García Agüero argues that not to exist on the internet in 2012 is not to exist at all.

In studio interviews, Pardo uses multiple cameras to frame the bod-ies and faces of the interviewed subjects from different angles to evoke an immersive tridimensional spatiality. The nonfictional performance of the subjects interviewed in the studio is juxtaposed with database images superimposed on the screen and projection-mapping images that appear in the background and on the very bodies of the participants. The pro-jection-mapping images circulate in loops and represent digital images, texts, and iconography. Projection mapping allows for a new relationship between the body and the screen that results in a screen incarnation in which the body of the interviewed subject becomes a corporal and mobile screen. Viewed as a documentary display of digital interfaces, the face of the interviewed subject functions as an interface mediating two experi-ences: human presence and digital embodiment.

Pardo projects digital interfaces over the bodies of the experts inter-viewed to simulate these participants inhabiting the interface between the immersive and informational dimensions of cyberspace. The immersive and screen-embodiment experience of the interviewed subjects is made possible by creating a virtual interview setting composed of projection-mapping images. In this realm of multiple windows and screens, the in-terviewed subject is inside a screen (creating the illusion of depth and immersion), while a screen is also inside the subject's body (creating the illusion of a flat control panel). The interplay of the body's immersion and flatness created by projection mapping operates as a documentary display of digital interfaces that turns the interview into a cyber-spatial visual spectacle. While the visual spectacle of the internet serves as a commentary on the opinions of the experts, the verbal testimony of experts serves as a commentary on the video jockey's (VJ's) representation of the internet as a visual spectacle.

Although the verbal testimony of the interview subjects corresponds to ideas and opinions that contribute to establishing a critical distance from which to evaluate the possibilities of the internet, the very act of evaluating the internet takes place in a simulated cyberspace, within the very immersive and informational context that is under scrutiny. The representation of experts' bodies as digital screens suggests that a critical pedagogy of the internet cannot take place outside, but only within, the realm of digital interfaces. Even if *Offline* does not admit a critical outside, it does not annul the possibility of a critical distance. In the documentary, this critical distance is represented as the interaction between that which is said in the verbal performance of the interviewed subjects and that which is made visible by the VJ's digital performance of projection mapping. Pardo creates a documentary display of digital interfaces that is at once a critical and affective pedagogy because it depends on the interactive production of intellectual (experts) and sensuous (projection mapping) knowledge. The representation of cyberspace in *Offline* depends on the tense convergence of immersion and flatness, of witnessing and visual spectacle, of informed explanations and random image sequences, which also manifest a tension between two modes of knowledge production: cognitive and affective.

Documentary filmmakers generally use the interview format as a vehicle to share authority with nonfictional performers who play their own roles as real people for the camera (Spence and Navarro, 2010). During the production of the documentary, Pardo encouraged this collaborative process of authorship by telling subjects interviewed in the studio to act as if they were located in cyberspace, "in a sort of mental country" (Pardo, Avelle and Rodríguez, n.p.). According to Pardo, documentary participants were even allowed to smoke in cyberspace. In the multilayered reality of *Offline*, the interviewed subject's nonfictional performance is complemented by the VJ's creative performance of projection mapping. The operation of digital interfaces through projection-mapped images also becomes a form of nonfictional performance that highlights the role of human-computer interaction as an instance of documentary reconstruction. In *Offline*, Pardo shares her authority not only with the interviewed subjects but also with the VJ projecting images and the artists whose works are exhibited over the course of the documentary. The VJ's role as art director, set designer, gaffer (lighting designer), and nonfictional performer emblematizes Pardo's collaborative, participatory, heterogeneous, and interdisciplinary conception of the production design.

The only opinions missing in *Offline* are the opinions of revolutionary state officials. Although Pardo made an effort to interview the Cuban minister of communications, it did not take place. In order to document the bureaucratic process of requesting an interview with a Cuban revolutionary official, Pardo re-creates the interview request as a graphic montage using the same documents submitted to Cuban authorities. This montage of official documents serves as an illustration of the opinions of Gustavo Arcos, who denounces that "when a journalist . . . wants to investigate a phenomenon, some obstacles begin to appear, there is no access to information, ministers do not grant interviews, it is very difficult to offset information through other avenues." And then Arcos adds: "There is no dialogue through news and information. There is no investigative reporting in Cuba." This segment ends when the interview request form is stamped with a text that reads, "interview application on hold." The interview request on hold is an official document that serves to make evident that bureaucracy is itself a dysfunctional interface; rather than facilitating communication between the Cuban state and its people, bureaucracy serves as an obstacle that blocks any attempts at dialogue between Cubans and the state. Through this official documentation, Pardo invokes the absent perspective of the Cuban state and its bureaucratic system. She includes her failed efforts to address the Cuban state as evidence of her interest in incorporating the perspective of revolutionary institutions in the context of the Cuban internet debate, but also as evidence of the Cuban state's indifference to interpellations coming from Cuban citizens interested in discussing Cuban policies. By exhibiting the silence of the Cuban state on matters of digital networks, *Offline* underscores the arrogance of Cuban bureaucrats who are not willing to participate in or contribute to the debate about the potential role of the internet in Cuban techno-literacy and education policies.

Various participants in *Offline* denounce the ineffective use of digital networks by Cuban official media as well as the restrictive media policies of the Cuban state, particularly its centralized control of internet access and digital networks. The explicit critique of Cuban authorities is also included by Pardo in a series of cartoons, received as e-mail attachments and created by Cuban artist Lázaro Saavedra. These e-mail attachments represent another participatory practice developed by the filmmaker and her collaborators that allows them to share creative and social authority. Due to the low speed of internet connections in Cuba, the most common file sharing practice is not attaching documents to e-mails, but transferring files using USB flash drives. If we focus on their role as digital model of information transmission, these e-mail attachments could be interpreted as a social satire of file-sharing practices in Cuba. If we look at their content, they serve as satiric comments that illustrate the critique of Cuban authorities expressed by some Cuban experts interviewed in the documentary.

The pencil-drawn cartoons are digitized handmade creations that evoke the collaborative process made possible by media convergence and system compatibility. They represent various satiric vignettes in which Saavedra makes fun of the authoritarian and repressive reactions of Cuban bureaucrats to the use or expansion of digital networks. The Cuban debate over the internet is represented in Saavedra's digital cartoons as a violent conflict motivated by technophobia. In the second cartoon, a Cuban bureaucrat with internet at home wakes up after having a nightmare: he dreams that one day, almost all will have access to the internet. In the third cartoon, the fear assumes the sinister character of a dismemberment fantasy: a monstrous figure screams to a group of mutilated figures without arms, "Internet is shit. All those who want to have internet, raise their hands." Through this cartoon, Saavedra denounces two issues—the repression of freedom of speech in Cuba, and state violence against internet activists—while representing the lack of internet access as a symbolic mutilation of the Cuban people that, in turn, eliminates opportunities for civic engagement.

The first attached cartoon illustrates the idea, expressed by one of the Cuban experts, that the TV panel show *Mesa Redonda* operates as a panel of oligarchs who have access to the internet. Saavedra's drawing represents the institutional control of digital networks in Cuba with the figure of a privileged computer user, dressed as a Spanish conquistador, who tells some Cuban indigenous subjects, "You tell me and I will look for it." The punchline of the joke comes in the internal conversation that takes place among the Cuban indigenous subjects, a reaction to the comment made by the computer user: "Tell him to look for Hatuey, to check if it was true." Hatuey, a rebellious Taino who confronted Spanish colonial forces in Cuba, represents a Cuban desire for emancipation that condenses a rejection of institutional and foreign control. But the rebellious Taino symbol appears in the context of a passive reaction that represents the attitude of institutional dependency promoted by the Cuban state's paternalistic relationship with the Cuban people. The figure of the Spanish conqueror symbolizes the Eurocentric and colonial roots of the Cuban revolution's state-sponsored paternalism, but also the ubiquitous influence of Spanish tourists and touristic industries in Cuba.

Negotiating Cultural Heritage and Social Authority by Remixing Database Images

Offline is a remix of database images that exposes the role of national history and global culture as sources of cultural heritage and social authority in Cuba. After denouncing the lack of investigative reporting in Cuba, Gustavo Arcos mentions that many people in Cuba admire American filmmaker Michael Moore for his documentaries against media and corporate power in the United States. He adds that he would like to see a Michael Moore in Cuba, a Cuban media-maker who would go to a province, ministry, or place of power like the Central Committee to look at the other side of an issue, a different version of reality. Difference, Arcos warns viewers, is frequently confused in Cuba with dissidence, which in turn is typically equated with counterrevolutionary activities. Pardo juxtaposes Arcos's interview performance with database video images of Michael Moore's documentary *Capitalism: A Love Story*. The incorporation of database videos of Moore's documentary serves as a tribute to a style of investigative reporting that is applauded but not practiced in Cuba. Although *Offline* is stylistically different from Moore's documentaries, Pardo aligns her project with Moore's inquisitive reporting in order to invest her project with the social authority and legitimacy of a progressive global icon. In doing so, Pardo also demonstrates that database images available in digital networks could become a new source of cultural heritage.

The strategic use of database images for the purpose of presenting the internet as a source of cultural heritage becomes more evident later in the documentary, when the issue of lack of technological literacy is discussed. While experts and people in the street complain about the lack of access to and lack of knowledge about the internet, Pardo includes database video images of the Cuban revolutionary literacy campaign of 1961. By juxtaposing testimonies and visible evidence in a poetic montage that inspires the creation of meaning by association, she evokes the images of the 1961 literacy campaign as an affective memory, as an inspiring and iconic episode of Cuban revolutionary history. This poetic association of images not only underscores the contrast with the current state of affairs, but also provides a legitimate frame for the need to develop a second literacy campaign in Cuba that would focus on technological literacy. This strategy of identifying a project with the same goals as the revolution is similar to the one used by many Cuban hip-hop artists, which, according to Geoffrey Baker, opens the space for constructive criticism: "Many interpret constructive criticism as the right to demand that state representatives strive to achieve the goals of the revolution, as praising its ideals but criticizing its practices" (2011, loc. 612, Kindle). While *Offline* includes a strong critique of Cuban digital networks, it also pays tribute to the ideal visions of the revolution presented by Cuban documentary in the 1960s. These nonfictional images of the early 1960s come to play the role of a media legacy whose social authority and affective meaning serve to legitimize Pardo's techno-literacy project while also inspiring her documentary critique of the shortcomings of Cuban digital networks.

Videos of the 1960s national literacy campaign are followed by videos of people around the world practicing sports such as skateboarding, surfing, and snowboarding. These are remixed with images of natural landscapes, web ads, digital platforms, and images of war, all of them cut at a fast pace to suggest the speed of the massive amounts of information that circulate on the internet. Pardo uses these images to illustrate the opinions of Dmitri Prieto Samsonov and Daniel Díaz Mantilla regarding the need for a digital literacy project that would be non-technocratic and allow for critical distance. According to Díaz Mantilla, access to more information involves the great responsibility of developing critical distance among internet users. Prieto Samsonov adds that this critical potential will allow internet users to distinguish truth from falsehood. In this sequence, global culture is represented as a fast and excessive mediascape that opens many possibilities for pleasure and entertainment but also for confusion and misinformation. While the graphic design of *Offline* seems to equate and neutralize all database images in a digital remixing of global culture, Cuban experts remind us that the cultural consumption of digital networks and images is never neutral.

After presenting the internet through database images of global culture, Pardo reframes once more the discussion of the internet with database images coming from Cuban national culture. Images of Cuban films made in the 1960s that represent the Cuban War of Independence of 1895 appear on-screen along with a projection-mapped image of José Martí, the leader of the Cuban anticolonial struggle, who also promoted in his writings the use of new technologies. In her interview, historian Josefina Toledo Benedit suggests that a technology like the internet would have been of great use to Martí in organizing the war. By commemorating the figure of Martí while praising the capacity of the internet, Pardo performs a symbolic digitization of the national hero and social innovator. Pardo's documentary display of José Martí as a digital figure constitutes an affective pedagogy because it seeks to touch and move the audience by appealing to its members' admiration and respect for the national hero. Martí's social authority appears as an archival remixing of literary and database images, serving also to legitimize Pardo's digital pedagogy as a national multimedia project. Martí's symbolic digitization in *Offline* evokes the idea that documentaries can play an important role as cinematic interfaces for the development of digital humanities practices in countries where internet connection and access to digital interfaces cannot be taken for granted, countries in which, nevertheless, a porous border exists between online and offline digital practices, such as storing, exchanging, sharing, and consuming internet contents and computer software with the use of portable USB flash memory drives.

Martí's symbolic digitization not only serves a commemorative function that honors the national hero's defense of new technologies, it also serves to legitimize the criticism against the restrictive internet access policies imposed by revolutionary authorities. A subject interviewed by Pardo in the street questions why, if Cubans, from Martí to the revolution, gave their lives in anticolonial struggles—first against Spain, and then, against US hegemony—the only people with access to the internet in Cuba are Spanish and American tourists. He adds that Cuban nationality has become an obstacle to having access to "connections with the rest of the world," and his words are juxtaposed with database images of Fidel Castro and his forces, first entering Havana after the revolutionary victory, and then fighting in the battle of Girón. The participant invokes the revolutionary goals of national freedom, represented by the database images of military activity, to underscore the contradiction that exists in

Cuba between the idealistic defense of national culture and the practical restrictions imposed by the Cuban state on those with Cuban nationality.

Later in this sequence, Josefina Toledo reads a passage in which Martí expresses his technophile views on portable machines, and the quote is followed by images of mobile phones. Martí's quote serves to introduce a discussion of the role of mobile phones in digital culture. Far from simply constituting a passive consumption of global culture, access to digital technologies involves an active remixing and constant renegotiation of the meanings of national and global culture. By remixing database images, Pardo's project works as a documentary display of the potential links between Cuban and world information networks. The remixing of national and global database images evokes Manovich's idea that "a computer database becomes a new metaphor that we use to conceptualize individual and collective cultural memory" (2001, 214). Pardo creates a visually saturated representation of the internet, in which national history and global culture recontextualize each other, in order to present an alternative image of cultural memory that differs from the pervasive monotony of the official information networks that populate the Cuban mediascape.

At the end of *Offline*, the representation of the database takes a self-reflexive twist: the credits of songs appear as individual digital files, while all the materials and videos used appear in a list inside a window that includes the entire contents of a digital folder. Pardo reminds us that, when we watch her documentary, we are really watching a remixing of database images that, in a way, is also a tribute to offline data transmission practices in Cuba, which include the use of portable USB flash memory drives. All the images used in *Offline*, even those corresponding to interactive digital interfaces, are prerecorded images and videos; these digital files are part of a database whose diversity comes to symbolize the different perspectives on the Cuban internet debate, but also its current and future possibilities. By remixing national and global culture in *Offline*'s database, Pardo creates a geopolitical cultural memory of the internet debate in Cuba that appeals to a transnational imaginary in order to question Cuban nationalist views on technology. Pardo reminds us that, even if civic and corporate global forces seem to go beyond, run parallel to or are disconnected from Cuban digital networks, they do have an impact on the development of the internet in Cuba.

Digital Interfaces as Moving Images: Cuban Digital Dilemmas as a Tension between the Real and the Virtual

The Human Computer Interface is a disputed site that reveals the conflict among different views of technology. In his book *Interface*, Branden Hookway argues that this technological conflict is associated with the cultural tension between the real and the virtual:

> If such a cultural tension is granted to exist between the virtual and the real, then the figure of the interface, both as a concept and as a collection of ways in which human beings singly and socially interact with and through machines, delimits the site of that tension, the arena within which the human and the machinic contest one another with respect to both the simulated and the real. . . . As a site of encounter, the interface demonstrates that no encountering of technology may be ultimately viewed as siteless or atopic; in this sense the interface is also the end of singularity, the end of augmentation, the threshold across which the contestants are fully separated in order to begin the struggle anew. (2014, loc 2399, Kindle)

In *Offline*, the tension between the real and the virtual is represented as a documentary display of digital interfaces created by the dynamic recombination of live-action footage, projection mapping, database images, and digital infographics. In studio interviews, projection-mapping simulations complement the live-action footage of interviews to suggest that the interviews are real events that take place in the virtual arena of cyberspace. In the case of database images, Cuba's national hero, José Martí, and Cuba's revolutionary events, such as the triumph of the revolution or the 1961 literacy campaign, represent national history as a cultural legacy whose real preservation depends on digitization and whose real transmission is subject to the virtuality of digital archives.

But *Offline* evokes the tension of the real and virtual in various other ways. Pardo uses live-action footage of Cubans using computers and mobile phones and playing video games to situate the virtuality of digital practices in the real space of Cuban homes. She also includes footage of Cuban musicians and DJs using computers to remix music to document the role of digital technologies as a tool in the context of Cuban cultural work. Cultural work as digital work is also represented by a collage of downloaded database images that illustrate the diversity of digital projects that are part of Cuba's alternative cultural circuits, such as BAK (Proyecto de Cultura Informática), Festival Rotilla, the ISA Students' Digital Magazine, and the Puños Arriba Hip Hop competition. At the end of the film, each subject interviewed presents him- or herself to the camera, and Pardo adds graphics that show the digital platforms in which they participate and perform their digital identities. Different voices and digital platforms stand for the diverse perspectives of the Cuban internet debate.

Pardo also superimposes web news and message threads about the fiber optic cable that would bring internet connection from Venezuela to Cuba on live-action footage of Havana's Malecón, an emblem of urban life in Cuba. The depth of field of the landscape, when contrasted with the flatness of the information transmitted, recalls the tension between immersion and the control panel explained by Manovich, suggesting that urban life and digital networks are inextricably connected and create a multilayered experience composed of real and virtual realms in conflict. When Pardo combines images of Havana's urban landscape with web news about the fiber optic cable, she reminds us that the virtuality of digital networks cannot be detached from the local realities of digital infrastructures. And when she adds the digital commentary thread that includes the views of some Cubans as they react to the news about the fiber optic cable, she reminds us that virtual technologies can play an important role in the examination of Cuban realities. The virtuality of digital identities included in this sequence refers to a participatory process that generates authentic questions and objections in response to the real contradictions of Cuban digital policies.

Later in the documentary, she once again juxtaposes images of Havana's urban landscape with some infographics that compare the price of internet connection in Cuba with Cuban average salaries, revealing the economic disparities that separate real Cuba from virtual Cuba. The digital interface that reveals the cost of digital services is superimposed over live-action images of the streets of Havana, of people traveling the city inside old American cars or using other old technologies. The contrast between old and new technologies symbolizes the technological gaps that exist between lo-tech Havana and hi-tech Havana. Pardo superimposes digital infographics on images of the streets of Havana to make visible the complex layers of the Cuban digital divide, a form of social inequality created by economic disparities, political disputes, bureaucratic authoritarianism, and technological incompatibility.

Further symbolization of the Cuban digital divide that plays with the contrast between lo-tech and hi-tech products is the images of a wooden computer created by Cuban artist Abel Barroso. Barroso's wooden digital devices (computer, iPhone, and robot) refer ironically to a primitivist imaginary. Pardo includes Barroso's wooden computers and robots, but not simply as comic relief; she also uses them to illustrate Alien García's warning that if Cuba does not embrace new technologies, Cubans run the risk of becoming "Neanderthals." In the discourse of some participants, not having internet is equivalent to backwardness. Pardo also refers to slow internet connections as a sign of technological backwardness. Through an associative montage of images and sound, Pardo links the slowness of data transmission with the slow pace of Cuban life. In an interview at her home, Yani Monzón expresses that the internet is something that "estamos pidiendo a gritos" ("we are crying for"). The image is followed by the internet connection sound of a telephone modem, an ambivalent sign that comes to symbolize both the urgent cries of those who claim their right to the internet and also the slowness of modem connections in Cuba. Immediately, Gustavo Arcos argues that life in Cuba is very slow and people "waste a lot of time in everything, because Cuba continues to have an analogic life." Later, Pardo includes some images of old cars and wheelbarrows crossing Havana as a reminder of the slow pace of life in the lo-tech streets of the Cuban capital. The social evolutionary connotations of these sequences are very problematic because they seem to frame the Cuban internet debate within the highly questionable dichotomy of civilized vs. primitive. This frame contradicts the call, made by other participants, for a non-technocratic digital literacy that will include critical distance as well as offline practices ("educación desconectada").

In *Offline*, Pardo uses the slowness of digital interfaces to suggest that the Cuban digital divide can be explained as a case of technological underdevelopment. In contrast, she includes many representations of dysfunctional digital interfaces in the form of error messages (of pages that cannot be displayed, of videos that are not available, of downloads that cannot be executed) as evidence of state restrictions on internet use in Cuba. In a sequence in which some participants discuss the potential of the internet to expand civic participation in Cuba, word searches for "evolución" (evolution), "pensamiento" (thought), and "sociedad" (society) are executed in the Google search engine, resulting in a message error indicating that a server has not been found. *Offline* reminds us that while the aspiration is to use the internet as a civic tool, state control over digital networks in Cuba is a reality that can be evoked by clicking on a search engine and finding out that network interaction is dysfunctional, leading to dead links.

Offline's dysfunctional interfaces highlight the degree to which digital control can become a reality under scrutiny for documentary. When digital interfaces become moving images, they are no longer active control panels conducting processes in real time, but instead they become part of a cinematic visual spectacle. In *Offline*, the internet is made accessible to Cubans, but only as a loop of images and not as a fully operational interface. *Offline*'s dysfunctional interfaces serve as an ambivalent yet self-reflexive reminder that invites us to question the contradictions of a non-interactive internet that is only available as prerecorded data, but also to denounce the reality of digital interfaces displaying the virtual spectacle of state control.

Years before the production of *Offline*, Yoani Sánchez and other internet activists had used video to document how Cuban hotels exercised control over internet access in Cuba. In a series of videos, Sánchez and her husband try to connect to the internet at a Cuban hotel, but a hotel agent denies them access to the hotel computers. The intention of the video is to serve as evidence of the exclusion of Cubans from digital networks, a form of censorship executed by the Cuban tourism industry in complicity with the Cuban state. Sánchez also documented the use of physical violence by Cuban state agents (dressed as civilians) against Cuban internet activists in order to dramatize how the media war between the Cuban state and those defending internet use and freedom of expression was moving from cyberspace to Cuban streets. Praising the use of video by internet activists like Sánchez to document the violence of state retaliation against Cuban dissidents, Antonio José Ponte, in his book *Villa Marista en plata*, declares that those images, which circulated globally, "ended state violence without witnesses in Cuba" (2010, 221).

In *Offline*, Pardo avoided any explicit reference to Yoani Sánchez. When I asked her why she did not interview Sánchez or other internet activists from Cuba, she said that Sánchez perhaps deserved her own documentary; but she also explained that she wanted to frame her project away from the media war imaginary surrounding Sánchez's activism against the Cuban state. That is why Pardo decided not to include Sánchez and to focus her efforts instead on getting an interview with a government official to explore the internet as a policy issue having to do with digital education and technological literacy rather than freedom of speech. If she included Sánchez, she knew that the possibility of interviewing government officials was going to vanish as soon as they found out about Sánchez's participation.

Instead of exposing state control over the internet as a violent clash of forces in the street, Pardo offers an alternative view of Cuba's digital dilemmas that is more consistent with her own pedagogic framework: she exposes the Cuban state as an impenetrable and dysfunctional interface that makes communication impossible. On the one hand, Pardo reveals how the state wants to contain the internet debate in Cuba by ignoring it, by using bureaucracy as a barrier, as an obstacle, rather than as an effective interface for communication between the Cuban state and its citizens. On the other hand, state control over the internet takes the shape of a message error in a dysfunctional interface that exposes the systemic dysfunctionality of Cuban digital networks. In this second case, visible evidence is still at the service of denouncing state control over technology, but it no longer exposes the violence of human acts taking place in the streets; instead, it delivers the silent and anonymous testimony of operational failures in the realm of virtual systems. As revealed in *Offline*, the state control of digital networks in Cuba works better when systems become extremely inoperative.

Although Pardo was not interested in framing her project within the context of the media war, she did provide an ironic comment on the complicity of the Cuban state with the Cuban tourism industry. At the beginning of *Offline*, the login page of the Hotel Nacional appears on the screen, someone types in her/his login information, and an error message appears on-screen indicating that the video requested is not available. On the one hand, by representing Cubans' lack of access to the internet from Cuban hotels as an unavailable video, Pardo not only questions hotel restrictions and state censorship, but also hints at the difficulty of documenting such practices. On the other hand, this error message seems to camouflage one of Pardo's production strategies: the use of Hotel Nacional's computers and internet network to record most of the database images and videos simulating the interactive operation of digital interfaces. One of the great ironies of *Offline* is that Pardo insinuates complicity between the Cuban state and the Cuban tourism industry at the same time as she camouflages her documentary's very condition of possibility:

the unintended complicity of Cuban tourism with the critique of Cuban digital networks. The fact that *Offline* was able to put on display so many digital practices and so many system failures, as they were witnessed from a hotel computer in Havana, is a testimony to the fact that state control over the internet in Cuba is an imperfect, questionable system.

Acknowledgments

The author would like to thank Ernesto Sánchez Valdés for his contribution to this research.

10

Carnival, Hybridity, and Latin American Digital Humor

The Ecuadorian Case of *Enchufe.tv*

PAUL ALONSO

Enchufe.tv, an Ecuadorian comedy series, has become the most popular online TV show in the country and a regional phenomenon in Latin America, with millions of YouTube views per episode. The online show questions cultural stereotypes and social norms, while adapting and parodying transnational audiovisual formats and entertainment genres. The creators—young filmmakers from Quito—have stated that one of their goals is to "reinvent Ecuador's audiovisual culture" while maintaining the web as their main platform for developing critical humor.

This article analyzes *Enchufe.tv* as a case study of Latin American digital humor, an increasingly relevant and carnivalesque scene from which to negotiate local, national, and regional identities discursively. In a cultural dialogue with the social and political context of the nation, digital humor and satire have become a prevalent site for questioning cultural values and traditional practices while developing a postmodern reappropriation of transnational media languages and entertainment formats. The case of *Enchufe.tv* reveals not only the challenges and opportunities of the digital medium for independent audiovisual projects, but also how the limits of critical humor are negotiated in cultural, political, and commercial terms. In this sense, *Enchufe.tv* has also become a paradigmatic

example of today's global digital media: a hybrid, glocal product success-
fully received in the region due to its cultural proximity.

Enchufe.tv: Hollywood at the Service of Ecuadorian Idiosyncrasies

Enchufe.tv was created in 2011 by a group of young Ecuadorian filmmakers (Leonardo Robalino, Christian Moya, Martín Domínguez, and Jorge
Ulloa) who were critical of the country's audiovisual production and were
seeking to renovate Ecuadorian audiovisual culture. Produced by Touché
Films in Quito, Ecuador, the humorous and satiric skits feature Ecuadorian idiosyncrasies, and, according to the creators and producers, are
based on personal experiences, popular sayings, Ecuadorian traditions,
and family and romantic relationships, among other topics that are relat-
able to their young audiences.

From the beginning of their project, they decided that the internet
would be the primary medium for *Enchufe.tv*, because they would enjoy fewer restrictions there (such as the use of colloquial language, swear
words, slang, and controversial topics) than in traditional media outlets.
On November 13, 2011, the first sketch (*El peor casting*)[1] was uploaded
to their newly created YouTube channel. During their first season, four-
to-five-minutes sketches were uploaded every Sunday; shorts lasting less
than a minute and known as "microYAPA"[2] were uploaded on Tuesdays.
On Thursdays, a preview or "Promo" of the upcoming sketch was released. After a few months, their videos went viral, drawing millions of
visitors to their YouTube channel. Some of the most popular videos of this
initial period were *Visión carnaval, Me gusta,* and *Compra condones.* The
last remains *Enchufe*'s most popular video, with 22 million views. By July
2012, *Enchufe.tv* was ranked as the most popular Ecuadorian YouTube
channel on the web. Viewership came primarily from Ecuador, but soon
Mexico became its main market, comprising around 30 percent of viewers and subscriptions to the YouTube channel. Colombia, Ecuador, Peru,
and the United States are the other principal markets for *Enchufe*'s content
(Andrés Centeno, pers. comm.).

In September 2013, *Enchufe.tv* released a compilation of their first-
season videos on Ecuavisa, a national television station. In a country
where TV penetration is 97 percent and internet penetration is 57 percent
(2013a), national TV allowed them to reach broader national audiences.
With the resulting massive success, routines of production have evolved

and their processes have been consolidated. The weekly content demand, however, creates an inevitable tension between constant production and maintaining quality standards. Now the producers try to generate all the content (which has increased) during the first half of the year and have them ready for upload by the beginning of the new season (Martín Domínguez, pers. comm.). Since the web remains *Enchufe*'s main platform, the social media routines have become more complex.

Enchufe.tv's business model is an interesting example of entrepreneurship used to make an independent web project sustainable: a production company (Touché Films) produces a comedy series of high audiovisual quality as a showcase for its talent and potential in order to find new advertising clients. The production company funds the project until it becomes sustainable through sponsors and advertising, which for *Enchufe. tv* happened in its third year. By 2015, the company employed more than 30 people in diverse areas (creative team, production, postproduction, actors, digital and multimedia operations, and management). Their projection for 2015 was to produce a feature film, and to shoot their content in international locations, countries in which they not only have large audiences but also new business partners. In 2013, they were ranked globally as the 49th most subscribed-to channel on YouTube. That same year, *Enchufe.tv* received a Golden Play Award, awarded to YouTube channels with over 1 million subscribers. In 2014, *Enchufe.tv* won the Show of the Year award at the Streamy Awards (the so-called Oscars of the web). By February 2015, its YouTube channel had reached almost eight million subscribers, and its videos had accumulated more than one and a half billion views. Its Facebook page has almost seven million likes, and on Twitter it has around 700,000 followers. With all this local and regional popularity, for many observers *Enchufe.tv* has become a breaking point in audiovisual culture in Ecuador, a country where the media operate in a tense political climate.

Ecuadorian Media and Satire under Correa's Government

After a period of political instability in which Ecuador had seven presidents in ten years, Rafael Correa's leftist government was inaugurated in 2007 and reelected for a third term in 2013. A popular president (his approval ratings have remained above 50 percent), he changed the constitution, increased the government's public spending, defaulted on foreign loans, and clashed with the United States on several issues. According to the World Bank, between 2006 and 2013 poverty levels in Ecuador dropped from 38 percent to 29 percent (BBC 2013b). While many considered him a progressive, Correa, who described himself as part of a "Christian Left," was opposed to abortion (even in cases of rape), and called gay marriage "barbarism" (Miroff 2014).

The relationship between the media and Correa's government was tense. The president referred to the private media as his "greatest enemy." While he protected WikiLeaks founder Julian Assange in Ecuador's Embassy in London for several years, Correa also took several steps against his country's private media outlets. His administration was characterized by the use of defamation laws to sue and convict journalists who were publicly critical of the government. Correa also made use of a law that required the independent media to carry long official messages that interfered with their programming. At the same time, he also used his weekly radio and TV show as a platform from which to attack the opposition and critical media. Ramos (2012 and 2013) considers Correa's measures against the media and the press to have been part of what she calls "state activism," a set of policies designed to reduce the traditional privileges that private media have enjoyed in the country and to put them at the service of citizens. In doing so, Correa created the "largest media empire in Latin America in the hands of government" (Lara 2013). Many international organizations warned against his attacks on freedom of expression. The Committee to Protect Journalists accused him of turning Ecuador into one of the most restrictive countries for the press in the Western hemisphere (Taal 2013).

In June 2013, a controversial new Organic Law on Communications was approved in Ecuador. President Correa considered the law an initiative to democratize media, strengthen freedom of expression, and promote "a good press" in the country (Martinez 2013). However, several private media outlets in Ecuador and international organizations considered it an attempt to silence the media and punish any criticism of the government. The law created state-mandated ethical guidelines and defined social communication as a "public service," making it susceptible to state regulation. As a result, with 174 documented aggressions against media outlets, journalists, and citizens, 2013 became the most violent year against freedom of expression in Ecuador (Fundamedios 2014a).[3]

Correa's repressive measures against the media have been compared to those of Chávez in Venezuela. Both presidents, for example, repeatedly harassed the private media, accusing them of serving conservative elites, used government advertising and economic incentives to induce positive reporting, imposed legal sanctions and other forms of "soft censorship" to limit press scrutiny, expanded state-run broadcasting, and became media figures with their own airtime on national television (Kellam and Stein 2016; Boas 2012; Frajman 2014). In Latin American countries such as Ecuador and Venezuela, where media ownership has been described as oligarchic, mostly privately owned by a small number of rich, conservative families, recent leftist presidents such as Correa and Chávez fostered increased ideological antagonism with the media (Boas 2012). As noted by Kellam and Stein (2016), "in a context where the president's ideology differs from the dominant ideology expressed in the press, presidents without viable electoral opponents vilify opposition media to portray them as their political opponent" (41).

The government's attacks against freedom of expression in Ecuador also targeted satire and political humor. Political cartoonist Xavier Bonilla (also known as "Bonil"), from the newspaper *El Universo*, was sanctioned twice for his satirical work during Correa's tenure. In 2014, the Superintendent of Information and Communication (Supercom) sanctioned Bonil and the newspaper through a process initiated by President Correa for the publication of a cartoon in 2013 that referred to police breaking into an opposition politician's home. On that occasion, Supercom fined *El Universo* two percent of its average earnings for the previous quarter for failing to prevent the publication of the cartoon, while Bonil was required to correct the vignette within 72 hours. The second time, the same entity imposed administrative sanctions against the newspaper and Bonil for alleged discrimination against a pro-government congressman in a satirical cartoon published in 2014. These accusations and sentences were perceived as a strategy by the government to restrict freedom of expression and as part of "a systematic plan by Rafael Correa to control the press in the country" (Freedom House 2015). Similarly, Correa also targeted digital and social media. In 2013, the Ecuadorian government proposed penalizing individuals who expressed opinions on social media that could be considered defamatory (Fundamedios 2013). At the same time, the president recruited "trolls" from among his followers to fight critical and satirical voices against him and his government online (Constante 2015; Higuera 2015).

This is the political context in which *Enchufe.tv* appeared and evolved. When it became a popular and massive success, the project interested not only new advertising clients (big companies such as Supermaxi, Movistar, and, later, Claro[4]), but also the government. According to the magazine *Soho*, "existe un documento de la Presidencia de la República que evidencia un contrato de 11 mil dólares, por servicios de comunicación social, con Touché Films. Está fechado en diciembre de 2012. Esto trajo muchos problemas en su momento y las acusaciones de haberse vendido al Gobierno se multiplicaron por redes sociales" (Varas 2014).[5] Andrés Centeno, executive producer of Touché Films, conceded that they had two government ministries among their clients (Varas 2014).[6] According to Centeno, they developed three products for these entities, but it was as Touché Films and not *Enchufe.tv*. Criticism increased in 2012 when a video by *EnchafoTV* (a parody of *Enchufe.tv*) appeared, mocking Guillermo Lasso, an opposition presidential candidate. Some former members of Touché Films participated in the production of the video. After these tensions, the creators and producers of *Enchufe.tv* tried to clarify that they do not make political humor.

Carnival, Satire, and *Enchufe.tv's Mundo al revés*

Ecuador's sociopolitical tensions might explain why the producers of *Enchufe.tv* claim that their humor is independent from the political sphere. By distancing themselves from explicit sociopolitical critique and focusing on the esthetic and commercial aspects of their products, *Enchufe.tv's* producers were able to flourish in a heavily controlled media environment. Nevertheless, in most of their videos there is a clear carnivalesque component, and, in some of them (such as the series *Mundo al revés*), one of social satire.

Russian critic Mikhail Bakhtin developed pioneering work on the notions of carnival in his analysis of the popular culture of sixteenth-century France, situating Rabelais's comic, satirical, and grotesque writing in the context of diversion, rituals, and spectacle. According to Bakhtin (1984), carnival captures and rearticulates the sharp wit and cruel humor of ordinary people expressed in the unofficial spaces of popular culture where they can mock authority and the status quo. Carnival, then, is marked by the suspension of certain norms and prohibitions of usual life (Bakhtin 1984, 15). Bakhtin emphasized the dialogic nature of carnival, which constitutes "the people's second life, organized on the basis of laughter" (Bakhtin 1984, 8). In this double-voiced discourse, our "first world" is suspended in the "second world" of carnival by setting aside the usual etiquette surrounding discussions of, for example, bodily functions (like copulation and defecation) and using irreverent and profane language. At the same time, carnival language practices regenerated and reproduced new ways of thinking by mocking the language conventions of the "first world." Carnival behavior is transgressive because it overturns conventional oppositions (high and low, mind and body, the spiritual and the profane, culture and nature, male and female). It is a space that breaks down barriers; it creates a world upside down, in which critique of the status quo is possible. As Achter (2008) highlights, carnival is a prevailing mood or spirit of fun mixed with social criticism, and its self-reflexive, playfully discursive practices mark the enduring value of humor and laughter in the public arena. Carnival's comic rhetorical posture submits that situations are up for grabs, which suggests that they can be remedied or fixed. In this sense, satire, a form that holds up human vices and follies to ridicule and scorn, is intrinsically linked with carnival. As with the carnivalesque, satire makes its point by use of parody, irony, travesty, and grotesquery, and is characterized by reduction or exaggeration and use of wit. It is "an attack on or criticism of any stupidity or vice in the form of scathing humor," and it is also a critique of "dangerous religious, political, moral, or social standards" (Cuddon 1991, 202). These types of social vices and prejudices are attacked in *Enchufe*'s *Mundo al revés*.

Mundo al revés is *Enchufe.tv*'s series of videos that turn prevailing views about sociocultural stereotypes upside down. The idea of the world upside down is an ancient trope traceable to the Middle Ages (Donaldson 1970) and a central component of carnival culture. Connected to the tradition of Menippean satire, it seeks to offer an inverted (and perhaps clearer) perspective on reality in order to test the "solidity" of our conventional ideological beliefs (Chiang 2004). The observation of the normal world from this unconventional viewpoint forces us to rethink our most common assumptions. In this sense, *Mundo al revés* is a carnivalesque world in which inverted values ridicule the social and cultural prejudices embedded in stereotypes, a process with political implications. For example, in the sketch "Gringos y latinos,"[7] working- and middle-class Americans immigrate en masse to Latin America, searching for a better life. Many of them (the poorest ones) cross the border without documents in search of the Latin American dream. A border official shoots them while calling them "malditos ilegales" ("damned illegals") and spitting on the floor with the rifle smoking in his hand. When they arrive, the American immigrants face constant discrimination and challenges to find work because of their undocumented status and poor language skills. They are stereotyped as ignorant people, potential criminals, or terrorists, generating paranoia in local society. At the same time, immigrant women are exoticized as sensual and good dancers, because "they have the rhythm in their blood."

Like most of *Enchufe.tv*'s sketches, the video of four minutes and 14 seconds is organized in parallel storylines that are intertwined. The other stories of "Gringos y latinos" change their approach to and perspectives on xenophobia and immigration in relation to social class and cultural capital. In one of the stories, a middle-class US family applies for a visa at the Ecuadorian Embassy. They dream about earning in Latin American currencies (pesos, bolívares, guaraníes, reales, soles, or sucres) and practice how to adapt to foreign culture (for example, the son practices singing the popular theme to "El Chapulín Colorado," an iconic Mexican TV series). When they finally pass the stressful process and obtain the visa, they celebrate, and the father comments, "I am going to earn more by cleaning the floor of McChancho there than by being a state agent here." This segment of the sketch not only points to the issue of sub-employment of professional and educated immigrants, but also to their willingness to acculturate as a demand of accessing the opportunities of the receiving society.

The final storyline focuses on the receiving society and how its elites, who travel around the world as tourists, have an ignorant and prejudiced view about the "other." In this segment, a middle-aged, rich Ecuadorian couple tells stories to a friend about their trips around the world. After showing pictures taken at the Statue of Liberty in New York, they complain about how dangerous these foreign countries are. Exhibiting her ignorance, the friend asks if the United States is an island, because "she really doesn't know anything about whatever is north of Mexico." The conversation is interrupted by the arrival of the couple's son, who is accompanied by a blonde girl whom he introduces as his new girlfriend. The parents are shocked and astonished, looking with contempt at the American girl who speaks with a strong foreign accent. "He screwed up our race [Nos cagó la raza]," comments the father with disappointment. The last seconds of the sketch show photos of the young couple's wedding and the

American bride exhibiting proudly her new legal residence card. Ignorance, entitlement, racism, and utilitarianism are exposed as prevalent characteristics of the dynamics between local elites and working-class immigrants. While racial "whiteness" is challenged (the American girlfriend is white), class "whiteness" is still displayed as the center of prejudiced views. The fact that the wedding is framed in relation to the "residence card" also highlights the prejudice and suspicion that immigrant/local marriages have more to do with utilitarian arrangements than love.

The satiric strategy is similar in the sketch "Gays y heteros,"[8] which criticizes homophobia. In this sketch, heteronormative values are inverted and being heterosexual is presented as a marginal deviance. The first story line deals with a heterosexual girl's dilemma of coming out of the closet to her gay fathers. They are shocked and horrified, and ask themselves what they did wrong in raising her. The gay couple explores a variety of resources to "fix" their daughter (for example, they search for a "de-heterosexualization" clinic and try to hook her up with a lesbian woman). However, these techniques do not work, and their daughter becomes the secret lover of Gabriel, a media celebrity whose conflict is the second storyline in the sketch. A star of the entertainment world, Gabriel hides his heterosexuality from his gay colleagues, the media, and his audience and fans. In his performance, he reproduces stereotypes: for example, even though he enjoys watching soccer games, he changes the TV channel to *Glee* when he is about to be discovered by his friends. In the public sphere, he maintains a gay profile, but he has a double life, keeping his relationship with his girlfriend in the shadows. When the situation becomes unbearable, he holds a press conference announcing to the world that he proudly accepts his heterosexuality, which generates a media scandal and public debate about heterosexual rights. A priest appears on TV denouncing heterosexuality as killing the family, while public protests in the streets call for legalization of straight marriage. In the last scene, Gabriel has married his girlfriend and they are unhappy with their family life. He complains about her inconsiderate laziness and how he is in charge of all the housework. She ends the sketch by saying, "At what moment was this shit legalized? (¿En qué momento legalizaron esta huevada)?" By positioning homosexuality as hegemonic and heterosexuality as marginal, the reversed replica presented in the sketch emphasizes the absurdity of misconceptions and prejudices based on sexual orientation. At the same time, it not only satirizes the arguments against same-sex marriage (a controversial topic in the country), but also, with the final scene, suggests the decadence of marriage as an institution in a predominantly Catholic society where the president, a declared Christian leftist, opposes same-sex marriage.

Other videos of *Mundo al revés* are "Hombres y mujeres,"[9] "Sexismo,"[10] "Belleza,"[11] and "Hombres y mujeres de fiesta."[12] From a perspective opposite to that of the dominant ideology, these videos ridicule stereotypes and sociocultural prejudices (such as xenophobia, sexism, homophobia, and canonical notions of beauty, among others). It is a carnivalesque space in which the spectator identifies him- or herself as marginal to an absurd system of values that, nevertheless, replicates inversely hegemonic values, exposing their arbitrariness. In this sense, *Mundo al revés* questions static identities and promotes understanding of difference, of the other. In the line of satire that seeks to ridicule social vices in order to fix them, *Mundo al revés* includes an optimistic spirit that reveals a desire for a better world. This critical humor has transgressed certain norms of the country's television and media culture (such as the use of profanity and new framing and treatment of controversial topics in Ecuador); however, its critical and transgressive spirit seems restricted by the sociopolitical context of the country and its own commercial nature. In other words, *Enchufe.tv*'s satire criticizes homophobia, xenophobia, sexism, and other social vices without risking its commercial development, because these topics resonate positively with the show's young target audience and their treatment does not cross the limits set by the government's policing. This does not mean that *Enchufe.tv* is not controversial. Their parody of *El Chavo del Ocho*, analyzed in the following section, was polemic, but had no negative consequences. On the contrary, it was highly effective in reaching an international audience. These tensions between commercialism and satiric risk also reflect *Enchufe.tv*'s calculated hybrid nature, which partially explains its regional success.

Hybridity, Parody, and *El Chavo del Ocho*

The relationship between US culture and Latin America has long been characterized as a one-sided, unfettered flow of dominant cultural products, with the increasing penetration of the US media as a foreign corporate and cultural force into the region (Schiller 1991; Tomlinson 1991; Miller et al. 2005; Dorfman and Mattelart 1975). However, theories of "cultural imperialism" have been updated to reflect a more complex reality created by globalization and transnational culture.[13] Scholars have argued that globalization produces the emergence of a variety of "hybrid," "creolized," or "glocal" phenomena, in which local elements are incorporated within globalized forms and other combinations (Robertson 1995). While hybridity and *mestizaje* are intrinsic characteristics of postcolonial Latin America, the production and consumption of cultural products represent a struggle for meanings between classes within countries, between high and popular cultures, and among local, national, and imported cultural traditions (García Canclini 1995; Kraidy 2005). For Martín-Barbero (1993), this reveals the syncretic nature of popular culture that both adopts and resists the dominant culture, and also transforms it. In this sense, hybridization describes a process in which elements of different cultures are synthesized together into new forms that reflect elements of the original cultures, but constitute distinct new ones (García Canclini 1995).

In this scenario, global formats must tap into local culture to find audiences at new locations (Straubhaar 2007; Moran 2009). According to the notion of "cultural proximity," audiences tend "to prefer and select local or national cultural content that is more proximate and relevant to them" (Straubhaar 1991, 43). The consequential process of hybridization then becomes a negotiation between structure and culture, and its success partially depends on its ability to allow space for local specificities (Straubhaar 2007; Kraidy 2005; Pieterse 2009). While audience preference still largely depends on the cultural proximity of the local and the national (Straubhaar 1991), regional programming also holds significance, highlighting the relevance of Latin America as a geolinguistic market (Sinclair 2004). Nevertheless, the national and the regional are far from being natural and homogeneous categories, but rather are televisually manufactured and market-tailored products (Piñón 2014).

Enchufe.tv is an essentially hybrid or glocal product. In many interviews, the producers have defined their creative work as "Hollywood (or the American audiovisual tradition) at the service of Ecuadorian (or Latin American) idiosyncrasies" (pers. comm.). They adapt transnational formats, styles and genres, and combine them with local themes, stereotypes, and popular culture. The resulting intertextual dialogue is made evident by the producers: "Citamos estos referentes en nuestros videos: 'Día de la Madre' está cubierto por un tratamiento de Indiana Jones; 'Cuatro héroes en el espacio' está cubierto por un tratamiento de Armageddon"[14] (Jorge Ulloa, pers. comm.).

The ethnic diversity of their actors also highlights *Enchufe*'s hybrid aspect. In a Latin American television and advertising system where white actors and models are still predominant in the media, *Enchufe.tv*'s casting of multiethnic, *mestizo* Ecuadorian actors offers local verisimilitude to the narratives. At the same time, their physical or racial attributes rarely define their roles, which avoid the reinforcement of discriminatory stereotypes. From another angle, the use of local expressions and colloquialisms[15] is a recurrent mark of *Enchufe*'s process of glocalization by manufacturing national identity: "Hay una frase que dice que para ser universal tienes que pasar por la aldea. Cuando pensábamos hacer el proyecto mucha gente nos decía que lo hiciéramos en inglés o que si íbamos a usar español, que sea neutral para que todos lo entiendan. Pero nosotros hemos convivido con el 'órale' de México, el 'che' de Argentina, porque no tuvieron miedo de mostrarnos cuál era su idiosincrasia y su cultura verbal. Y es súper lindo saber que afuera ya hay gente que dice 'Chuta,' sólo por ver *Enchufe. tv*" (Jorge Ulloa, pers. comm.).[16]

One of *Enchufe*'s most controversial videos reveals more clearly its hybrid and multidimensional creation. On July 6, 2014, *Enchufe.tv* uploaded a parody trailer of a fake movie spinoff based on *El Chavo del Ocho*,[17] a Mexican television sitcom widely broadcast since 1971 in Latin America as well as in Spain, the United States, and other countries. Created by famous Mexican comedian Roberto Gómez Bolaños, also known as Chespirito (a diminutive Hispanization of "Shakespeare"), *El Chavo del Ocho* tells of the adventures and misfortunes of a poor orphan (nicknamed "el Chavo") and other inhabitants of "the vecindad" (the neighborhood), a fictional low-income housing complex in Mexico. At the peak of its popularity during the mid-1970s, *El Chavo del Ocho* was the most watched show on Mexican television and had a Latin American audience of 350 million viewers per episode. The show continues to be immensely popular as a comedy emblematic of "clean" humor for the whole family. Markedly different, *Enchufe.tv*'s parody (titled *El Chico del Barril*) has a similar plot to *The Da Vinci Code* and copies the style of Christopher Nolan's action movies. It features two agents, one American and the other Middle Eastern, who are searching for the real name of "el Chavo." The trailer presents a dark, violent, sexualized configuration of the beloved sitcom characters.

Parodies of the most famous characters from *El Chavo del Ocho* appear in *El Chico del Barril*, making references to their popular catchphrases and configurations from a twisted perspective. The trailer ends with the US agent discovering the classic squeaky hammer of the "Chapulín Colorado" (another character created by Chespirito) in the desert.

A few hours after uploading the YouTube video, the controversy began. Mexican radio and TV (and later diverse Latin American media) disseminated the news. Actors from the original Mexican series *El Chavo del Ocho*, such as Édgar Vivar (who personified the characters of Ñoño and *el señor Barriga*), Carlos Villagrán (Quico), and María Antonieta de las Nieves (*la Chilindrina*) publicly accused *Enchufe's* parody of distorting and twisting their creations (El Comercio 2014b). Roberto Gómez Fernández, the son of Chespirito, initially also accused *Enchufe's* producers of profiting from his father's work and criticized the trailer for its shocking images. Televisa, the Mexican TV network that owns the rights to *El Chavo del Ocho*, requested YouTube take the video down. While the video was taken down for a few hours, *Enchufe's* producers defended their product as an original tribute to the iconic show. The video became public again and the controversy ended when Roberto Gómez Bolaños's son praised *Enchufe's* work, accepting the tribute to his father (El Comercio 2014c). By then, the video had already had millions of visits in just a few days, and *Enchufe's* audience had grown 700 percent in Mexico (Varas 2014).

Enchufe's parody of *El Chavo del Ocho* is an interesting and representative textual object for understanding *Enchufe's* hybrid or glocal dimension. First, as a parody, it already implies a combination, dialogue, and juxtaposition of different texts in order to create a new one. As Achter noted, the term "parody" refers to "a composition in which the characteristics, style and themes of a particular author or genre are satirized by being applied to inappropriate or unlikely subjects, or are otherwise exaggerated for comic effect" (2008, 280). The preposition "beside" (para) is an indicator that a parodic text implies an original and an imitation juxtaposed in a carnivalesque dialogue. The case of "El Chico del Barril" is a double parody, of both the local/regional tradition and the global one. It is a tribute to one of the most important referents in Latin American popular humor, developed through the trailer format of a Hollywood action movie. The objects of parody are also revealing. On the one hand, *El Chavo del Ocho*, a symbol of uncontroversial and innocuous comedy, is not only a Mexican referent, but also belongs to most Latin American countries, where several generations watched daily repeats of the show on national TV for decades. On the other hand, the movie *The Da Vinci Code* and filmmaker Christopher Nolan's style are representative of the most effect-driven and commercial Hollywood action films. Both objects of parody are connected by their huge regional/global commercial successes.

The parody of both audiovisual products is based on transgression of the codes and themes of their respective genres. In the case of *El Chavo del Ocho*, *Enchufe*'s parody distorts the configuration of the original naive characters (children played by adults): they carry guns, have blood on their clothes, and have erotic encounters, while maintaining the traits and dress codes of their original models. In relation to *The Da Vinci Code* and Nolan's movies, the focus is on the formal aspect: the parody adopts the narrative visual strategies of Hollywood action movies' trailers, while evidencing the artificial and spectacular techniques employed to catch the audience's attention in the service of an absurd plot. In this sense, the parody works at the content and formal levels.

From another perspective, *The Da Vinci Code* is in itself an interpretation of a previous mass-culture product: the best-selling novel by Dan Brown, which has the same title and has motivated a variety of literary and audiovisual parodies itself. At the same time, Nolan's style also has an intertextual dimension: he is known for his reboot of the Batman film franchise, having made a successful trilogy. Chespirito's work also has a parodic aspect, especially in relation to his character "El Chapulín Colorado" (which is also referenced in *Enchufe*'s trailer). Embodying many aspects of Latin American and Mexican culture, "El Chapulín Colorado" is a critique of the unrealistic image of American superheroes. In contrast to Superman or Captain America, the "Chapulín" is imperfect, clumsy, and timid, but he is good-hearted and succeeds at the end of his adventures (most of the time, by sheer good luck). The final text involved in the parody is non-existent: it is the script for the movie that the trailer promotes. In this sense, *Enchufe*'s trailer parody becomes an intertextual and meta-textual object with several layers of parody that reflect its hybrid discursive universe. Combining diverse cultural traditions, audiovisual genres, and levels of reality, *Enchufe*'s discourse appeals to different audiences that could relate to any (or many) of the different layers at the local, regional, and/or global levels. Consequently, it also reveals the manufactured condition of its carnivalesque hybridity as a commercially successful strategy for independent digital media that seeks a transnational audience. While the parody of *El Chavo del Ocho* became popular in many Latin American countries, it was targeted at Mexico, where *Enchufe.tv* has its biggest audience. The producers' plans to shoot new episodes in different Latin American countries, with local talent, highlight a similar strategy for glocalizing their audiovisual production further.

Conclusion

In times when traditional media is seeking new formulas to make their online operations profitable, the case of *Enchufe.tv* reveals a successful and sustainable business model for independent digital media and online TV. Its formula is that of a production company that funds a risqué, high-quality, and innovative product as a showcase for its talents and potential in order to obtain advertising clients. This risqué product fills a gap in local media production, consolidates an audience, and expands to other platforms (such as national TV). The operation is developed by the constant and sustained production of innovative content and an active strategy on social media platforms. After the project becomes profitable through online advertising and "sponsors" (advertising clients), the content production combines commercial placements with comedy sketches on the same YouTube channel. The next phase includes consolidating an international audience by targeting specific countries with glocalizing strategies.

In a tense political climate between government and media in Ecuador, the development of *Enchufe.tv* exhibits a process of discursive negotiation about its own critical/satirical limits within the national mediascape. While Correa's government has restricted satirical critique and freedom of expression, *Enchufe.tv*'s producers seem ambivalent about defining their humor's critical intentions. However, due to its humor's carnivalesque nature and characteristics, *Enchufe.tv* also manifests its desire to question social prejudices and vices, such as homophobia, sexism, xenophobia, and racism, among others that inevitably have a political dimension. Its satirical spirit is especially shown in the series of videos *Mundo al revés,* which question the status quo and static identities, by satirizing stereotypes and suggesting the fluidity of identities in today's postmodern and global world.

Cultural globalization clearly permeates the hybrid and glocal dimension of *Enchufe.tv*, which "puts Hollywood at the service of Ecuadorian and Latin American idiosyncrasies." The hybrid components are present at *Enchufe.tv*'s diverse discursive levels, as shown in the analysis of the parody of *El Chavo del Ocho*. At the same time, the case of *Enchufe.tv* also illustrates how this process of hybridization or glocalization is deliberately manufactured, exposing its artificial character. In other words, it shows how identities are commercially manufactured in transnational media.

Finally, the massive success of *Enchufe.tv* reveals its potential as a critical voice on cultural, social, and political topics at the local, regional, and transnational levels. The existence of other successful independent instances of critical humor and digital satire confirms the importance of this genre in popular culture in the age of the internet. As shown with the case of *Enchufe.tv*, the national sociopolitical context remains relevant to understanding the role of satire in negotiating the limits of dissent in media culture. Further research in this area of digital humanities should focus on the contrast and comparison of independent satiric cases from different countries of the region, to better illustrate their role in public debate through entertainment.

Notes

1. The video can be accessed here: https://www.youtube.com/watch?v=TyiM15doLwU

2. "Yapa" is a slang word that means something extra given as a bonus.

3. According to the report *El silencio asfixiante* (*The Stifling Silence*), developed by Fundamedios (2014), the year 2013 was characterized in Ecuadorian media by the new legal limitations imposed by the country's controversial Communications Law, the increase in censorship, and public officials' hostilities against the press. Most aggressions came from public officials, followed by the government in the form of administrative or legal measures.

4. Supermaxi is a supermarket chain; Claro and Movistar are two corporations that provide telephone services.

5. "There is a document of the Presidency that attests to a contract for eleven thousand US dollars, for social communication services, with *Touché Films*. It's dated December 2012. This issue brought many problems at the time, and the accusations that they were sellouts to the government."

6. These institutions were the Ministerio de Salud and the Ministerio Coordinador de Desarrollo Social, de Estrategia Nacional Intersectorial de Planificación Familiar y Prevención del Embarazo en Adolescentes.

7. The video can be accessed at: https://www.youtube.com/watch?v=n2ISkJZC6DI

8. https://www.youtube.com/watch?v=3at_j5JtDik

9. https://www.youtube.com/watch?v=ZU8zS-145ZA

10. https://www.youtube.com/watch?v=kgQNGwJ-xlg

11. https://www.youtube.com/watch?v=h7aSEuxaRjo

12. https://www.youtube.com/watch?v=4HlN4FPdi2w

13. In contrast to the notion of "international," the transnational defies binary oppositions between the national and the foreign (the local and the global) by emphasizing the permeable character of national borders, and the multi-spatial, multilayered, hybrid identities and cultures that coexist at cross-border, regional, and global levels (Piñón 2014).

14. "We cite these references in our videos: 'Mother's Day' is treated as *Indiana Jones*; 'Four heroes in space' is treated as *Armageddon*."

15. Local expressions such as "¿Quién dice?" (Who says that?) or "¡Chuta!" (an exclamatory expression) are recurrent on the show.

16. "There is a saying about how in order to be universal you have to go through the village. When we thought about doing the project, a lot of people told us to do it in English, or, if we were going to use Spanish, that it would have to be neutral so everyone could understand it. But we have grown up with slang from Mexico and Argentina, because they weren't afraid of showing us their idiosyncrasies and verbal culture. And it's great that now there are people using Ecuadorian expressions just from watching Enchufe.tv."

17. See https://www.youtube.com/watch?v=pQFzVr2YUGM.

11

~~~~~~~

No Blogger, No Cry

ORLANDO LUIS PARDO LAZO

> In the beginning was the Blog. But blogs were formless and empty. Repression was all over the blogosphere. And Cuban citizens saw the blogs were good. So lacking other channels of expression, the e-merging civil society occupied the blogosphere as a tool for dissent. Won't you help to share these blogs of freedom? Redemption blogs, redemption blogs to emancipate ourselves from the State.

As early as the summer of 2005, I started a blog to publish a literary and opinion magazine that three freelance Cuban writers had decided to edit in Havana: *Cacharro(s)*—in English, Jalopy(ies). Lizabel Mónica, Jorge Alberto Aguiar, and I were just posting our texts in cyberspace, hoping for a reader abroad to save us from the silence within. We couldn't imagine that in a couple of years our initial experiment would be largely dismissed from the history of the Cuban blogosphere, when our efforts to escape not only censorship, but also the mass-media mediocrity of the revolution, were completely displaced by new voices with high public impact within both the cultural and political fields.

This happened when the digital magazine *Consenso* (Consensus) became *Contodos* (With All) and started the website Desdecuba.com, managed by Reinaldo Escobar, Manuel Cuesta Morúa, Miriam Celaya, and Dimas Castellanos, among others, including a webmaster who, in April 2007, started a very simple WordPress blog called *Generation Y*. The trademark of Yoani Sánchez was born, as well as the first virtual revolution in the era of Castro. This was the genesis of an independent movement of citizen journalism and blogger-activism, which would shortly challenge the lack of transparency in the public sphere in Cuba, a country still without private internet service today.

Top-level Cuban intelligence commanders like Ramiro Valdés have stated that the internet is a "wild horse" that "must be tamed" before it is offered to the people.[1] After many promises and postponements, including the installation of a submarine fiber-optic cable that has connected us with Venezuela since 2011, we Cubans are still waiting for a digital miracle, although then vice-president Miguel Díaz Canel warned our press not to be objective but "loyal to Fidel, Raúl, and the Revolution," while Fidel himself determined that the "internet is a revolutionary tool."[2]

Elaine Díaz, blogger of *La Polémica Digital* (The Digital Polemic),[3] is known as a critic of certain official measures, but is also a professor of journalism at the University of Havana and was the 2014–2015 Nieman Fellow at Harvard University. In her doctoral dissertation on the Cuban blogosphere, published as "Blogs y periodismo en Cuba: entre el deber ser y la realidad" (Díaz 2009), she "scientifically" established, in terms of topics and chronology, that none of the renowned Cuban dissident bloggers were pioneers at all, thus diluting this phenomenon in an ocean of other blogs practically discovered by her, up to nearly 3,000 today, which outnumber by far the dozens of local independent bloggers.

Díaz quotes only those blogs that can be quoted in Cuba without risking her research position, like *Patria y Humanidad* (Homeland and Humankind),[4] managed since 2006 by Luis Sexto, a winner of the National Journalism Prize, and *La Isla y la Espina* (The Island and the Thorn),[5] administered since 2007 by Reinaldo Cedeño—both defined as open to "foreign authors" and to "heated debates" but, of course, within the temperature limits of political discipline on the island. Díaz acknowledges that the Union of Cuban Journalists (UPEC), and no less than the Ideological Department of the Central Committee of the Cuban Communist Party, authorized more than 1,000 official journalists to start blogs from their workplaces or privileged home connections, in order to—as Milena Recio wrote in her article "Cuban Blogs: An Entrenched Identity"—reproduce in cyberspace the same battlefield logic of street propaganda, to "counteract the distorted and oppositional speeches from hegemonic mass media" against the revolution (Díaz 2009, 8).

The Code of Ethics of UPEC rejects "hyper-criticism" in its article 7, while in articles 8 and 9 it reminds UPEC members to "maintain social and moral behavior in accordance with the principles and norms of our society . . . to promote the best of our national values and the constant improvement of our socialist society."[6] And after said paternalism comes a list of punishments, which includes imprisonment, as happened to a journalist from the Communist Party newspaper *Granma*, José Antonio Torres, accused of espionage after issuing one of his official reports.

At the Latin American Studies Association Conference in 2013, Díaz also proposed the "emancipatory and anti-capitalist usefulness of the new media and technology" in Cuba, and the need for "virtual symbols" for a country where "horizontal dialogue" is "possible," beyond power hierarchies and all kinds of social exclusion—through race, gender, sexual preference, economic status, etc. (Díaz 2013). Nonetheless, she omits the cause of all discriminations in Cuba: the political intolerance and hate speech of the revolutionary government since 1959, summarized by Fidel Castro in his speech to Cuban intellectuals in 1961: "Within the Revolution, everything; outside the Revolution, nothing" (Castro 1961).

Recently, this approach to dialogue has been updated by the website *Cuba Posible*,[7] run by Lenier González and Roberto Veiga, former editors of a Catholic Church magazine that published some civil debates in which certain civil society activists managed to participate. *Cuba Posible* claims that it stands for the complicit concept of "loyal opposition" to the regime. González and Veiga also urge Cuban dissidents not to accept all the support they receive from foreign NGOs, despite the fact that these authors defended such support when they were invited to Washington, DC in January 2015 by a compendium of US pro-Castro NGOs, like Philip Peters's Cuba Research.

During the last decade, the Cuban alternative blogosphere has expanded and contracted like the cycles of a claustrophobic universe. Its main communication strategies and activists have been reborn, only to remain identical. Since mid-2015, Cuba has launched dozens of Wi-Fi hot spots in public areas, although users must pay in hard currency for the service (the equivalent of around two dollars per hour). Many Cubans, many of whom receive remittances from abroad, and in particular the younger generations—who are much more enthusiastic about communications with the outside world than some of their elders—are taking advantage of this service to establish personal and professional relations that eventually could help them travel outside of Cuba, whether in a temporary or definitive way. Cuban social activists are also using this opportunity to send not only reports of human rights violations but also bigger audio and video files with more elaborate independent coverage of what is going on in the streets of Cuba on a daily basis. Thus the visibility of a closed society is expected to increase dramatically, and hopefully the impunity of the authorities will be contained, or at least denounced, almost in real time to the international public, whose opinion in turn will bounce back to the Cuban people through TV stations broadcasting from the US that are illegally but widely seen in Cuba thanks to networks of parabolic antennae in many neighborhoods.

Through my blog of fictionalized chronicles *Lunes de Post-Revolución*[8]—Post-Revolution Mondays[9]—and my photoblog *Boring Home Utopics*, I have witnessed most of this Cuban e-volution, with its pro-human rights achievements, and, unfortunately, with its drawbacks in the face of a state involved in a transition to capitalism without capitalists.

Most freelance Cuban blogs were originally linked to the websites HavanaTimes.org[10] (and VocesCubanas.com, no longer online), where one may find the famous *Generation Y* by Yoani Sánchez;[11] blogs from visual artists like the graffiti performer Danilo "El Sexto" Maldonado[12] (who has been jailed several times) and the photographer Claudio Fuentes;[13] blogs dedicated to new media and technologies, like that of Walfrido López;[14] blogs from independent lawyers who gave legal advice, like the unregistered Cuban Juridical Association of Wilfredo Vallín;[15] blogs from religious leaders like the Baptist minister Mario Félix Lleonart;[16] blogs of digital publications like *Cuadernos de Pensamiento Plural* (Plural Thought Notebooks), *Cuadernos para la Transición* (Notebooks for Transition), and the magazine *Voces* (Voices), edited by me; community participation initiatives like the *País de Pixeles* (Country of Pixels)[17] photo contest; and blogs of filmed debate projects, which then are uploaded to the web to influence public opinion, like *Estado de Sats* (State of Sats) and *Razones Ciudadanas* (Citizen Quests). Thanks to the volunteer amateur projects TranslatingCuba.com and HemosOido.com, many of these blogs are distributed beyond geographical isolation and the barriers of language.

Mainly in Havana, which is much closer to the World Wide Web than the Cuban pre-technological countryside, events have been held to shift from cyberspace to citizen mobilization, like the Blogger Academy, where we teach the technical rudiments of digital self-publication, as well as the primitive option of tweeting through an international SMS sent from the island, as local mobiles have no internet service in Cuba. Other events held in private homes, like the 2012 and 2013 editions of the Click Festival, had the privilege involving international blogging experts, and were consequently stigmatized by the governmental blogosphere as being part of a subversive conspiracy to disrupt social stability.

Indeed, cyberbullying was actually among the less-brutal responses of Castro's political police to Cubans exercising their right to freedom of expression. It was just a first step before threats, coercion, harassment, beatings, detention, etc. Two inflection points in this abusive battle of the government against its own citizenry occurred in 2011. First, Cuban TV showed a weekly series on cyber-mercenaries in which all independent activists were severely threatened with prosecution (coincidentally, Elaine Díaz was used an example of blogging "correctly"). Then a suspicious video leak came from State Security, in which an officer later identified on social media as Eduardo "Tato" Fontes Suárez delivered a seminar to the Ministry of the Interior to teach them how to manipulate the internet in the era of a US president "much worse than Bush"—yes, Barack Obama!—by establishing a clone blogosphere in which to reproduce Cuban official press and saturate the web with appropriate content. This includes creating authorized versions of Wikipedia (as *EcuRed*[18]), Facebook (as *La Tendedera*; this cannot be accessed from abroad), Twitter (as *El Pitazo*; this cannot be accessed from abroad), and locally controlled blogging platforms like *CubaVa*[19] (all of them hosted by .cu servers). This is a reminder of the theories of Evgeny Morozov regarding how disappointing the excess of web optimism may be, because repressors also learn how to take advantage of the interconnected world to channel and control social discontent for their own ends.

Unfortunately, since the 2013 migratory reform that, for the first time in decades, allowed Cubans to travel abroad without an exit permit, international recognition of Cuban civil society leadership has also meant a national weakening of our networks, and the dispersion of our already limited impact on the island. All peaceful movements and prominent personalities in Cuban civil society, which between 2008 and 2011 seemed about to integrate into a unified opposition front with political implications, have now splintered into their respective personal initiatives. The more successful their international reach, the more isolated their national projects. We Cubans still lack a culture of open polemics and an understanding of differences. After more than half a century, Castroism has Castrified even its opponents.

Here are some sad examples, as they are all my dear colleagues, and have been fighting quite a long time for a better future for Cuba:

1) The Ladies in White[20] have split more than once, in a fractal procedure that keeps the movement's numbers stagnant, and with an exponential increase in members fleeing to the US. Once in exile, most Cubans dissidents quit social activism, or, in the best cases, end up as secretaries in pro-human rights Cuban American NGOs. The legacy of their founding leader, Laura Pollán, has been at risk, to the benefit of the Ministry of the Interior, ever since their new leader, Berta Soler, carried out a shameful repudiation of one of the group's former members, and then had to hold a referendum to ratify her lifetime leadership. But Soler was in turn expelled by the daughter of Laura Pollán from her home headquarters in central Havana, where Laura Pollán junior expects to direct a new foundation that will monopolize use of her mother's name.

2) The Christian Liberation Movement (MCL)[21] has been headless since the 2012 extrajudicial killing in Cuba of their leaders Oswaldo Payá and Harold Cepero. Internal rearrangements in a dispute over the redemptive legacy of the martyrs, as well as which strategies should be implemented, have turned the MCL into a virtually exiled movement.

3) The Cuban Patriotic Union (UNPACU)[22] always has nearly half of its activists in jail. On one hand, UNPACU fostered the creation of an independent branch that broke from the Ladies in White, the Lady Citizens for Democracy. On the other hand, it is obsessed with detecting and denouncing—and sometimes converting to the cause of freedom—Castro's secret agents, like the infamous case of Ernesto Vera, but they lack a citizen mobilization strategy beyond their self-extinguishable street protests.

4) The Somos Más (We Are More)[23] movement, launched by Eliécer Ávila, relies solely on the charisma of his face and voice. Ávila was once a digital government soldier who conducted Operation Truth in the University of Information Sciences (UCI), directing a platoon of trolls devoted to defaming activists worldwide, distorting online forums and surveys dealing with Cuba, and hacking websites that expose the violations and fallacies of international

Castroism. Currently, Ávila is exiled in the United States, and his movement advocates for democratic changes in Cuba.

5) A bitter debate of mutual distrust and discredit continues between those close to blogger Yoani Sánchez and her brand-new *14yMedio.com* digital outlet—which is prone to take advantage of the new US-Cuba engagement to push the limits of censorship in Cuba—and other early digital citizen journalists. These include the staff of *Primavera Digital* (Digital Spring), who in turn last year publicly repudiated their Swedish funding partners, as well as the well-known Antonio Rodiles, from the very active audiovisual discussion project *Estado de Sats*, who practically accused *14yMedio* and other colleagues of collaborating with the regime's agenda of allowing foreign investment in Cuba with no guarantee of human rights, in a Putin-like or Chinese post-totalitarian model.

On the official side, in the monolithic digital headquarters of *Cubadebate*, general Raúl Castro, in his speech at the ALBA Summit in Caracas (March 2015), and many other op-eds published in tandem, have warned that the "Internet can be for the best and be very useful, but, at the same time, it can also be for the worst."[24] As well, the international ultraconservative right is again deploying its mass media weapons to use the "concept" of "civil society of those in power and their mass media empires,"[25] with the purpose of "deceiving and manipulating the people" and "attacking progressive governments" from the hemispheric left.[26]

Cubadebate has even applauded the official repudiation that Cuban dissidents—so-called mercenaries—received at the Summit of the Americas in Panama (April 2015), because critics of Castro all are "conceived, paid, and directed as drones from the US and the EU, through NGOs, supposedly for the promotion of human rights, but in fact having met with confessed terrorists like Luis Posada Carriles in Miami, and in addition directly financed by secret institutions of American imperialism, including the Pentagon and the CIA" (Montesinos 2015).

Echoing the Castro regime's rhetoric, *Cubadebate* still proudly calls Cuban social activist leaders "Washington's puppets, in the line of dictators Fulgencio Batista in Cuba, Carlos Andrés Pérez in Venezuela, and Augusto Pinochet in Chile, whose mission, if they ever attain power, is to surrender the wealth of our nation to US monopolies." They depict dissidents as privileged white people who do not care about the "black, aboriginal, farmer and workers minorities" (Montesinos 2015). Paradoxically, it was, of course, Fidel Castro who dollarized the Cuban economy over 20 years ago, while his brother Raúl Castro is demanding financial credit from US banks and corporations. Furthermore, Afro-Cubans suffer much more than other dissidents in Cuba at the hands of (mostly white) State Security top officers, who assume that blacks owe more gratitude to them than do the rest of the Cuban people.

> Here are only some of the tragic examples in this respect: The death of the Afro-Cuban opposition activist Orlando Zapata Tamayo in jail, after a long hunger strike in 2009–2010 to stop torture against him; the 33 months that the Afro-Cuban member of the Ladies in White Sonia Garro and her husband spent in prison without charges and with no trial; the harassment and beatings against Afro-Cuban leader Jorge Luis García (Antúnez), usually prevented from stepping out of his own house in the town of Placetas; the arbitrary political arrests, plus the temporary or permanent invalidation of the passports of Cuban Afro-Cuban intellectuals and activists Manuel Cuesta Morúa and Iván Hernández Carrillo; the fascist-like mobs conducted by the government against the residences of Berta Soler and other Afro-Cuban peaceful women of the Ladies in White, including throwing tar—yes, tar—with impunity against their bodies, like recently happened to Digna Rodríguez Ibáñez; or staining them by force with red paint to emulate human blood, like they did to Mercedes La Guardia Hernández.

The White House's partial lifting of the US economic embargo should not negate the fact that a market economy is not a tropical liberation formula, since it has already been implemented by authoritarian systems as a tool of despotic control. The secret negotiators who expect to appease Castro's tyranny should remember that what has been good for free Americans since the eighteenth century is also good for Cuban citizens hoping to be free today.

The rationale that, after waiting for so long, Cuban democracy can wait a little longer is a discriminatory concept implicitly legitimized by the US press and academics in their search for a lost Latin American left. Maybe the hope of the White House is that the New Man will stop being a soldier and become the New Salesman, but bringing down the wall should mean

202 · Orlando Luis Pardo Lazo

more than opening up the wallet. For all the urgency of Google, Amazon, Delta, Netflix, Coca-Cola, and even Bacardi to re-conquer their "Pearl of the Antilles," they should not forget that we "Cubans have the right to have rights," as preached by Oswaldo Payá before the gerontocracy cruelly took his life. In any case, according to migratory statistics, Cubans are certainly making a lot of space for Yankees to come home to our island, as we keep escaping by legal or lethal means, in a kind of pedestrians' plebiscite, voting with our fleeing feet instead of our electoral ballots.

By the time of Fidel's funeral, the commander-in-chief had earned all the glories of history, which is the mother of all horrors, but also the frantic farewell of his own people—almost one-fourth of our population. This migratory crisis is what the US is really trying to stop by stabilizing the communist dynastic succession to the Castro 2.0 generation—which includes Alejandro and Mariela Castro Espín, among others, whether dandies or despots, many of them holding high-level positions in the Cuban establishment while receiving privileged visitor status in the US.

The hope would be to convoke a national plebiscite with international observers so that the Cuban people can freely and safely express their will for the first time since 1948. Otherwise, Cuba will become a Castro-centralized capitalist condominium, economically annexed to the US but with hyper-nationalist speech designed to justify impunity on the island, as well as alliances with despotic regimes elsewhere.

In the process of this plebiscite, which would involve the national and international campaign CubaDecide.org, led by Rosa María Payá, all Cuban citizens should be welcomed to mobilize, organize, and participate effectively and safely. This includes those nearly two million Cubans living abroad, as their Cuban nationality never expires. In many cases, including my own, the decision to establish themselves abroad has been provoked by Cubans' lack of fundamental freedoms, even (or especially) when the majority of new exiles may consider themselves more economic migrants than political refugees.

The Cuban government, which has never dared to conduct such a participative, inclusive, and competitive consultation—like the plebiscite carried out in Chile by Augusto Pinochet in 1988 with international surveillance—is now trying to limit the Cuban democratic struggle to those activists who permanently reside on the island, as they can be easily manipulated, harassed, beaten, incarcerated, and ultimately, again, forced to "commit exile." But a long-term and stable solution for a true

Cuban transition will necessarily have to depend on the know-how and the resources of a diaspora that does not deserve to be perpetual pariahs, as no Cuban from abroad can reside permanently in his or her own country again unless that person applies for a very restrictive process of repatriation.

The administration of Barack Obama could have chosen to extend a helping hand to the oldest Latin American dictatorship. Or it could have considered whether the Cuban people deserved to endure this apartheid until the last of the Castros left power. The free voices from the Cuban alternative blogosphere are still struggling not only to be heard, but also to be respected as protagonists of our own nation.

Fidelism 1959, the temperature at which fundamental freedoms burn. As time blogs by. As I lay blogging. The blogger in the revolution. From dictatorship to dictacracy. Blogged the Raven: Nevermore. Castrobamacare as the measure of all things. Won't you help to share these blogs of freedom? Redemption blogs, redemption blogs to emancipate ourselves from the States.

Notes

1. Ramiro Valdés's opinions are paraphrased in Peter Rugg, "Cuba's Black Market Internet is Booming," *Inverse*, Sept 18, 2015, available at https://www.inverse.com/article/6287-cuba-s-black-market-internet-is-booming.

2. See Omar Pérez Salomon, "Fidel Castro: 'Internet es un instrumento revolucionario,'" *La pupila insomne*, March 7, 2012, available at https://lapupilainsomne.wordpress.com/2012/03/07/fidel-castro-internet-es-un-instrumento-revolucionario/.

3. See https://espaciodeelaine.wordpress.com.

4. See http://luisexto.blogia.com/.

5. See http://laislaylaespina.blogspot.com/.

6. See "Codigo de Ética del Periodista," http://www.cubaperiodistas.cu/index.php/codigo-de-etica-del-periodista/.

7. See http://cubaposible.net/.

8. See http://www.orlandoluispardolazo.blogspot.com/.

9. See https://orlandolunes.wordpress.com/.

10. See http://www.havanatimes.org/.

11. See https://generacionyen.wordpress.com/.

12. See http://www.delsexto.blogspot.com/.

13. See http://www.claudioshooter.blogspot.com/.

14. See http://www.walfridolopez.com/.

15. See https://ajudicuba.wordpress.com/.

16. See http://cubanoconfesante.com/.

17. See www.paisdepixeles.blogspot.com/.

18. See http://www.ecured.cu/EcuRed:Enciclopedia_cubana.

19. See http://cubava.cu/.

20. See http://www.damasdeblanco.org/.

21. See http://www.oswaldopaya.org/es/.

22. See http://www.unpacu.org/.

23. See http://somosmascuba.com/.

24. See Raúl Castro, "Raúl Castro en la Cumbre de las Américas," *Cubadebate,* April 11, 2015, available at http://www.cubadebate.cu/opinion/2015/04/11/raul-castro-en-la-cumbre-de-las-americas-hasta-hoy-el-bloqueo-contra-cuba-se-aplica-en-toda-su-intensidad/#.XIly7ihKjIU.

25. See Patricio Montesinos, "A propósito de la Cumbre las Américas y la 'Sociedad Civil,'" *Cubadebate*, March 20, 2015, http://www.cubadebate.cu/opinion/2015/03/20/a-proposito-de-la-cumbre-de-las-americas-y-la-sociedad-civil/#.XI19rShKjIU.

26. See Ruben Abelenda, "El lenguaje de EEUU y la derecha internacional para confundir a los pueblos," *Cubadebate*, Nov. 16, 2015, available at http://www.cubadebate.cu/opinion/2015/11/16/el-lenguaje-de-eeuu-y-la-derecha-internacional-para-confundir-a-los-pueblos/#.XI16qyhKjIU.

12

Electronic Civil Disobedience

Before 9/11 and after 9/11

RICARDO DOMÍNGUEZ

Nine-eleven has been constructed as an ontological event that redefined the nature of all forms of political realism for both war and security, an event zone in which history was bifurcated between a bad end and a terrible restart; on that day, the neoconservative "End of History" narrative became the future-present "Operation Infinite War," all under the signs of speed and the instantaneous that radiated from the attack on the World Trade Towers. What is not always considered is the history of protest, of how activists, artists, and "artivists"[1] responded to this cultural shift long before the 9/11 event. Artivist formations, or "post-media"[2] swarms, never left the waves of histories as sites for critical interventions that sought to disturb the borders of the state and the border(less/ness) power of transnational flows—artivist groups like Electronic Disturbance Theater assembled "a new language of civil disobedience" (Critchley 2007, 123) that combined "social netwar" (Ronfeldt and Arquilla 1998, 1) and "tactical frivolity" (Critchley 2007, 124), first placing one under erasure and amplifying the other as a "meta-political disturbance." Artivist networks understand that the ontological core of 9/11 that is being sold under the "politics of fear" is one that cannot/could not completely seal away critical resistance, counter-publics, and the speed of dreams that had come before 9/11 or after.

This is not to say that artivists do not or did not understand that virtual artivism/digital disturbances, such as electronic civil disobedience (ECD), were not full of gaps, failures, and the

> persistent pitfalls in conceptions of "electronic activism:" on the one hand, the tendency on the part of some activists and scholars to romanticize electronic action, and on the other, the dismissal of contentious electronic tactics as ineffective, as distractions from "real" mobilization, or as a troubling "return of the mob." Either extreme represents a failure to carefully engage with and differentiate the wide range of tools and techniques that make up the electronic action repertoire, or to consider what "effective" might mean in this context. (Costanze-Chock 2003, 173)

Indeed, artivists diagrammed responses to these concerns by inventing gestures that went beyond "saying" or "showing" ECD—to "doing" ECD action after action, as a serious and necessary repetition before and after 9/11, and letting theory hit the ground-as-practice in order to shape the "ineffective/effective" dyad at the fault lines between computers and peace, bombs and bandwidth, networks and exploits.

While the age of insecurity began to stumble around with all the fury of a new manifest destiny that had been lost and re-found as early as 1999, the neoconservative dream of a new "Pearl Harbor" was set to play and record; the mission traced in *Rebuilding America's Defenses* (2000)[3] was to "fight and decisively win multiple, simultaneous major theater wars." It also made a nightmare-before-Christmas wish: "Further, the process of transformation, even if it brings revolutionary change, is likely to be a long one, absent some catastrophic and catalyzing event—like a new Pearl Harbor." Neoconservatives also hoped to deploy an expansion of internal controls of the multitude in the US, with "free speech zones"—holding pens far away from the power brokers—uncontrolled surveillance of US citizens, the indiscriminate gathering up of anyone who seemed "other" (those soon to be profiled as "enemy combatants"), and by making anyone who was not with the "Osama bin Bush" regime invisible to the dominant media.

Activists, artists, artivists, and international civil society would soon discover what the "new normal" would mean to the "movement of movements" (another name for the alter-globalization movement) during the World Economic Forum meeting on January 31, 2002, (held only four months after 9/11), which usually took place in Davos, Switzerland, and instead decided to teleport to New York City, to show that "Virtual Capitalism" was not shutting down, but only revving up for the next good war. Our choice was to march across the arcs of these realities without fear, to let loose the puppies of play, and that everyone would continue to share lateral tactics on the streets and online—we were all in a fractal agreement that the alter-globalization movements would not be shut down: "When the World Economic Forum website collapsed just as its meeting began, it seemed a major win for online anti-globalization activists. But the organizers of the 'virtual sit-in' are refusing to take credit for the takedown" (Shachtman 2002). Indeed, give credit where credit is due: it was the electronic multitude that downsized the World Economic Forum. "Although the streets of New York City remained relatively subdued while the World Economic Forum (WEF) met here, over 160,000 demonstrators went online to stage a 'virtual sit-in' at the WEF home page" (ibid.). Electronic Disturbance Theater did not proactively seek to take the honor for what had happened; we instead offered this response: "I think that something else happened to the WEF URL or, perhaps, the WEF infrastructure is as badly built as the WEF's economic vision during the last 31 years" (ibid.). For the artivists, being able disconnect the internet access of the most powerful individuals representing the richest nations on our planet was not important—what was important was to be able to state that the transnational flow of the WEF was faulty at all levels.

Back to the Future: Critical Art Ensemble (CAE) and ECD

Critical Art Ensemble staged the theory of ECD as a gamble against a specific form of the all-too-present future of "dead capital." Electronic disturbances would be the core gestures that initiated a "performative matrix" that was deeply linked to Hakim Bey's dream, which observed that

> These nomads chart their course by strange stars, which might be luminous clusters of data in cyberspace, or perhaps hallucinations. Lay down a map of the land; over that, set a map of political change; over that, a map of the Net, especially the counter-Net with its emphasis on clandestine information-flow and logistics—and finally,

over all, the 1:1 map of the creative imagination, aesthetics, values. The resultant grid comes to life, animated by unexpected eddies and surges of energy, coagulations of light, secret tunnels, and surprises. (1991, 107–108)

While this was true of trajectories of counter-flows, it was also true of "virtual class." *The Electronic Disturbance* remaps the flows of nomadic power in the chapter "Nomadic Power and Cultural Resistance" as new shifting zones in which "The location of power—and the site of resistance—rest in an ambiguous zone without borders. How could it be otherwise, when the traces of power flow in transition between nomadic dynamics and sedentary structures—between hyperspeed and hyperinteria?" (Critical Art Ensemble 1994, 11).

CAE argues that "dead capital," otherwise known as "late capital," was being constituted as an electronic commodity form in constant flow. Capital had been, was, and would continue reassembling itself; we were witnessing "the flight of capital into cyberspacial realms that it is even now more difficult to see . . . [a]s the contemporary elite moves from centralized urban areas to decentralized and deterritorialized cyberspace" (ibid., 13). The answer to this riddle was to teleport the system of blockage and trespass that was historically anchored to civil disobedience (CD) to this new phase of economic flows in the age of networks:

> The strategy and tactics of ECD should not be a mystery to any activist. They are the same as [those of] traditional CD. ECD is a nonviolent activity by its very nature, since the oppositional forces never physically confront one another. As in CD, primary tactics in ECD are trespass and blockage. Exits, entrances, conduits, and other key spaces must be occupied by the contestational force in order to bring pressure on legitimized institutions engaged in unethical or criminal actions. Blocking information conduits is analogous to blocking physical locations; however, electronic blockage can cause financial stress that physical blockage cannot, and it can be used beyond the local level. ECD is CD reinvigorated. What CD once was, ECD is now. (Critical Art Ensemble 1996, 18)

Indeed, it was the open and transparent connection between CD and ECD that would enable the performative power of mass nonviolent direct action online to actualize. This asymmetric formation was a tool for the disturbance of digital capitalism and a new counter-network that would move the ontology of the dominant circuit of communication and documentation, as the only possibility of action for the "networks of struggle," to a stage where the multitude would soon be able to march across the ephemeral lanes of this new superhighway. In 2004, in the book *Multitude: War and Democracy in the Age of Empire,* Michael Hardt and Antonio Negri write that "basic traditional models of political activism, class struggle and revolutionary organization have become outmoded and useless" (68); for CAE it was clear that cyberspace, as it was called then, was the next stage of struggle, and that it would mean that instead of the easy-to-see signs of command and control, it would be necessary to re-configure the command lines of code flows and shift their value registers and data patterns. "CAE has said it before, and we will say it again: as far as power is concerned, the streets are dead capital! Nothing of value to the power elite can be found in the streets, nor does this class need control of the streets to efficiently run and maintain state institutions" (Critical Art Ensemble 1996, 18).

In the strange days that were to come, it would become difficult to distinguish a technical failure in the system from a social gesture of mass cyber-presence. So it became extremely important to make sure that all ECD actions were disturbances transparent to a system that was all too willing to give itself over to its desire for the borderless "battlespace" of "cyberwar," "cyberterrorism," and the very tight dream of "homeland security."

Flip_Forward: Digital Zapatismo

> Anderson traced "hacktivism" to the 1994 Zapatista guerrilla uprising for greater democracy and Indian rights in the southern Mexican state of Chiapas.
>
> Wolf 2001

The conditions for a performative matrix in which to stage ECD as a practice came from a world beyond digital networks; it came from south-ernmost state of Mexico: Chiapas. It was here that "hacktivism" would arise on January 1, 1994, as the North American Free Trade Agreement (NAFTA) was rolled out, which just happened to be the moment when the web browser Mosaic (released in February 1993 for X-Windows on Unix computers) was starting its very first flights, which just happened to occur as the neoliberal vision for globalization was being rolled out and David Ronfeldt and John Arquilla had just published "Cyberwar is Coming!" in the Summer 1993 issue of *Comparative Strategy*. These events cascaded into one another to manifest as invisible rebellion by indigenous groups to become the first "postmodern" revolution. The new browser-based networks felt the first seismic information swarm, and they all started riding the waves—all of them moving at the speed of dreams. The Zapatista rebellion allowed the emerging artivist networks to traverse the gap between the impossible and possible, between fantasy and protocols, between critical theorization and direct action gestures—bombs and bandwidth could be disturbed and rerouted.

As the RAND Corporation tried to keep pace with the rise of the swarming "peace networks," bits and pieces of the new (lo)balization (an early type of peer-to-peer movement), designed to counter the neoliberal glocalization (top-down drop-in global economies, such as Starbucks Coffee) process, began to play out as multiple lateral moves. One of the most important lateral networks was that of the digital Zapatistas, who were changing the master frame of "cyberwar," "cyberterrorism," and the soon to come post-9/11 "war on terror"; they were "literally dispatches from the future" (McKenzie and Domínguez 2001, 118). At the same time, other (lo)balization movements were seeking to alter the form and function of globalization-as-glocalization (the dominant media used the phrase "anti-globalization movement," which is far more reflective of the desire of transnational business trajectories than of anything else) to shift the top-down and bottom-up style of glocalization toward the hyper-connective lateralization of (lo)balization that flowed among hi-fi, low-fi and no-fi cultures.

The (lo)balization movements are not anti-globalization, but are instead seeking to invent another type of globalization. (Lo)bal movements are not centered or decentered social formations; instead, they spread out across the arcs of realities as distributed networks that seek to link with all those who are left out of the neoliberal globe. They are peer-to-peer networks that were and are more about the humans on the ground than about those who had or have access to the network—the networks became networks for the network-less:

The temporal fractalization of dead capital has allowed a spasm of micro-invention to emerge and flicker in the liminal space of the

Lacandona jungle; occurring somewhere between the imaginary borders of the American hologram and the real Taco Bell power of neoliberalism's NAFTA: the Zapatistas. In the Lacandona, a jungle in delirium, floats a temporary construction of plant, flesh, and circuits that is attempting to play out a rhizomatic disturbance, an "ante-chamber" of a "revolution that will make revolution possible. . . ." The Zapatistas are not the first postmodern revolution, but the last; they are a vanishing mediation between the breaking mirror of production (dead capital) and the shattering of the crystal of (de) materialization (virtual capital). (Domínguez 1995)

The "tipping point" was now streaming and ready to shout out as a full-spectrum force of (lo)bal movement(s), which were flung into the twenty-first century by the avant-garde of the indigenous. The Zapatistas not only ripped into the electronic fabric of first-world networks as an information distribution node, but, more importantly, they created new types of political subject(s) and new condition(s) for agency on a global scale. They created a diagram for a new (lo)bal name, which offered a guiding anchor for the emerging (lo)balization movement(s) through their "strategic occupation of [the] universalistic terrain of international rights and international law that provides the leverage of a local political articulation that has had global effects" (Critchley 2007, 107). It was a local-to-local call that established deep connections between slow micro-politics and the speed flows of transnational articulations—(lo)balization is a feedback loop for those who were willing to invent other social formations beyond the flexible zones of precariousness being pushed forward by the "free market" ideology that was ready to take over Canada, Mexico, and the United States in 1994.

The "intergalactic" emergence of the Zapatistas, digital Zapatismo, and (lo)balization came to be framed as a movement of movements that "exemplifies a new approach to social conflict" (Ronfeldt and Arquilla 1998, 1), and that RAND promoted as an important type of "social netwar." This research was prepared for the US Army by the RAND Arroyo Center as a tracing of a new social formation that did not fit the "cyberwar" and "cyberterrorism" paradigm, but instead created a transversal activism that was not seeking to "crush the state" and "seize power"— (lo)bal movements, like the Zapatistas, "draw on the power of 'networks' and strengthen 'global civil society' in order to counterbalance state and market actors" (ibid., 5). This new formation of (lo)bal publics was also linked to reconfigured modes of protest that took the measure of glocal-ization around the world. "It is in protest that globalization's true contours begin to be perceived: it is only with the Zapatistas that the meaning of a North American Free Trade Association becomes clear; it is only with hacktivism that the politics of the internet is uncovered; it is only with culture jamming that the absurdities of postmodern advertising are laid bare" (Jordan and Taylor 2004, 64).

Flip_Out: When Theory Hits the Ground, or Digitally Incorrect Hacktivism

Since our first encounters with analytic machines, we have flickered from the machine-smashing Luddites of 1811 to Augusta Ada Byron King, Count-ess of Lovelace, writing code for the "difference engine" in the mid-1800s; between utopia and apocalypse; between labor saving and loss of jobs; be-tween the ordinary and the all-too-new; between bad machines and good machines. The artivist group the Electronic Disturbance Theater (EDT) was among the first to develop a relationship among bad technology, inef-ficient code, and rebellion with a good cause—EDT operated/operates in "contradiction to cyberspace" (Jordan and Taylor 2004, 74). EDT created a mass demonstration machine (FloodNet) that connects to mass actions on the streets that was and is intimately linked to the Zapatistas and the alter-(lo)balization movements—a performative matrix that shifts the core of the network from communication and documentation to one of mass direct action online, a gesture that attempts to suture individuals and browsers, the virtual mass, and mass demonstrations in public spaces that are local and (lo)bal at the same time.

"Virtual sit-ins," as EDT came to name these network-based actions, were a direct echo of the CAE vision for ECD, but rather than the CAE version of a cadre of secret and efficient hackers, EDT created a transpar-ent and artivistic reconfiguration of ECD—one that, by all the laws of well-made code, should never work. But since when does art need to be well-made to spill out into the world? It was a new social poesis that allowed EDT's version of ECD to negotiate with pre-9/11 state and transnational powers over the discursive mobilizations of "cybercrime," "cyberwar," and "cyberterrorism," and shift the frame to that of Civil Disobedience (CD) and its legal histories in relation to ECD—without giving up the "art" in artivism or the "activism" this hybrid term contains:

> Electronic Disturbance Theater illuminates a new set of possibilities for understanding the relation between performance, embodiment, and spatial practice in cyberspace. Unlike a number of other performance artists who have explored the relation of the body to technology through the literal encounter of individual physical bodies to machines—Orlan's livecast surgeries; Stelarc's cybernetic experiments—EDT, in turn, has placed the very notion of "embodiment" under rigorous question, and thought to understand the specific possibilities for constituting presence in digital space that is both collective and politicized. . . . Those actions suggest that performance in cyberspace can reproduce—rehearse or practice—cyberspace in ways that produce an alternate form of spatiality. For EDT, as for the Zapatistas, cyberspace can be practiced as a new public sphere, a runway for the staging of more productive "lines of flight" for those struggling for social change. (Lane 2003, 131)

The plane of EDT's group composition was predominantly artist-centric and extremely focused on its version of ECD being simple and highly distributable from its inception. But perhaps its most transgressive and aberrant decision was to be completely transparent, or as transparent as a "databody" can be via the signature to the "real" body. Since at that point in cyber-time the call to utopian anonymity was a core doctrine for hackers, phreakers, crackers, and every company selling the internet to the world from 1994 on—no one had to know your gender, your race, or your class—being "no-body" was the new freedom. EDT chose to disturb this social ontology of immateriality by making a clear connection between "names" and action: Carmin Karasic (artist, interface design, and graphic designer for FloodNet), Brett Stalbaum (Java programmer, artist, and author of the FloodNet Applet), Stefan Wray (theorist, writer, and agitator), and myself, Ricardo Dominguez (organizer, agitator, artist, and theorist). These were the designations that we gave ourselves on the Electronic Disturbance Theater website in 1998 and the roster that we added to every e-mailed call to action. In this manner, we were able to create a performative context that gave us a high degree of control over the question of signification (Is this "cyberwar" or "cyberterrorism" or a "cybercrime" or a new form of CD?), and made a gesture toward the transparent—as the networks of digital Zapatistas, artists, activist, online strangers, governments, military, and dominant media all knew what we were going to do, when we were going to do it, why we were doing it, and where they could find us—if one wanted even more information.

EDT's choice to translate the Gandhian "Satyagraha"[4] to connect our "databodies" to our real bodies created a form of "digitally incorrect" artivism, which routed around the future of post-9/11 "fear-based" networks developed by US and transnational policies. This choice to connect the out-side and in-side of the cybernetic continuum also allowed ECD, as an artivist gesture, to instantiate a gesture against the "hegemony of communication" (Genosko 2002, 227). The last footnote of the last chapter of *Felix Guattari: An Aberrant Introduction* by Gary Gonosko points out that

> Deleuze raised this idea: "the key thing may be to create vacuoles of noncommunication, circuit breakers, so we can elude control." A kind of creativity, then, that was not linked to communication but broke it at some point by establishing cavities through which its messages could not pass or, to put in positive terms, passed too well . . . an example of the former vacuole suggests more virulent forms of network attacks of the sort developed by hacktivists such as the creation of disturbances . . . using FloodNet software that swarms sites and saturates lines. (Genosko 2002, 227)

FloodNet created an extreme form of informatic transparency and a counter-communication system that not only saturates the network with a new form of mass embodiment but also creates a simple flight of gaps-as-meaning that parasitically attach themselves to the "disappeared" and the "missing" in the databases of dominant power and make them visible—with the Dadaist force of the "404_file not found."

Brett Stalbaum, a cofounder of EDT, frames this "404_file not found" gesture within the frame of conceptual network art (net.art) history: "FloodNet is an example of conceptual net.art that empowers people through activist/artistic expression. By the selection of phrases for use in building the "bad" URLs, for example using "human rights" to form the URL "http://www.xxx.gb.mx/human_rights," the FloodNet is able to upload messages to server error logs by intentionally asking for a non-existent URL. This causes the server to return messages like 'human rights not found on this server'" (Stalbaum 1998).

This aberrant function of browser-based technology allows the weightless dreams of cyberspace to reinforce what is absent from the infrastructure of governance and the neoliberal drive that was solidifying a relationship between the global market and information in Mexico under NAFTA at that time.

ECD never was, nor is it now, about cyber-bombs and bandwidth, but about a style of "sustainable pulsing" (Ronfeldt and Arquilla 1998, 10) that is now possible for the social formations that emerged in 1990s (the Zapatistas, digital Zapatismo, tactical media, hacktivism, cultural jammers, and the alter-globalization networks) and entangled the communities in Chiapas, Mexico, the streets, digital infrastructures, software, and semantic interventions on a (lo)bal level.

For the RANDs, the prospect of ECD in 1998 as practiced by EDT would create "divisive effects, possibly leading to a split between those proponents of netwar . . . who believe that new, real-world organizational designs should be the basis for activist doctrines and strategies, and the more anarchistic proponents who believe that theatrical technological strikes—'digital Zapatismo'—should lie at the heart of doctrine and strategy" (Ronfeldt and Arquilla 1998, 73). Within a couple of years (from 1998 to 2000), EDT's version of ECD was able to integrate itself into the typical menu of tactical gestures available to activists and artivists "across arcs of the realities," as Zapatistas enjoy singing.

Jon McKenzie's diagram of EDT's recombinant gestures and entanglements manifested a priori futurities as an intimate condition of its possibilities in its past, which allow the ECD gestures to route around the post-9/11 syndromes of "fear as politics," social "insecurities," and the constant information war alarms of digital electrons being "10 feet tall." McKenzie de-stratified the "noopolitiks"[5] of EDT's style of ECD as an ontological time machine:

It would be interesting to trace how physical, syntactical, and semantic interventions each unfold on the three levels of major performance I've identified: the level of discourses-practices (i.e., words and gestures, the level where most artists still work; formal and conceptual experimentation), the level of sociotechnical systems (i.e., social groups and organizations, such as cultural, educational, and corporate institutions), and the level of onto-historical strata (i.e., formations of power/knowledge that largely define "what is" for a giving society over long period of time). Minor performances operate across these three levels to destratify the forms and functions of major performativity. . . . Moving to the level of onto-historical strata not only requires situating today's knowledge-formations and power-mechanisms in order to anticipate and indeed rehearse future modes of destratification. For me, the most striking thing about EDT's FloodNet technology is not its messages but its potential as an unheard-of writing machine: it literally dispatches the future. (McKenzie and Domínguez 2001, 118)

This movement between stratifications and destratifications was also linked to the question of the law(s), both within the US and internationally, in relation to the history of CD, and what part of this history could be established with ECD and its relation to local/global law paradigms and electronic practices.

To Nomos and Back: Is Electronic Civil Disobedience Civil Disobedience?

The stratum of the law was an early encounter in the recombinant performance by EDT. Over and over this question was asked by activists, artists, and security forces: Is ECD legal? The question itself became part of the performance as a "politics of the question" that called for a response that had already been formulated by CAE: ECD is CD now. The establishment of an epistemological connection between ECD and CD as part of the aesthetic trajectory of CAE in theory and EDT in practice created the necessity of response to this meta-pattern by all involved—so that the question became not, "How is this not CD?" but, "In what ways does ECD fit the legal definition of CD?"

In 1998 the question was often framed as EDS being potentially illegal, a "cybercrime" known as DoS (Denial of Service) or DDoS (Distributed Denial of Service): A denial-of-service attack (DoS attack) or distributed denial-of-service attack (DDoS attack) is an attempt to make a computer resource unavailable to its intended users. Although the means to, motives for, and targets of a DoS attack may vary, it generally consists of the concerted, malevolent efforts of a person or persons to prevent an internet site or service from functioning efficiently or at all, temporarily or indefinitely. EDT was consistently clear that this was not the proper question, since ECD was a social ontology question and not a technological question—this was not about code qua code between machines, but about a new form of social contestation and the law(s).

John Rawls, in his essay "Civil Disobedience and the Social Contract," states that civil disobedience is "a public, nonviolent, and conscientious act contrary to law usually done with the intent to bring about a change in the policies or law of the government" (1996, 356). He also expands on a number of other legal phases of CD that function to create a counter-public space: "Civil disobedience is a political act in the sense that it is an act justified by moral principles which define a conception of civil society and the public good. . . . Civil disobedience is a public act which the dissenter believes to be justified by the conception of justice and for this reason it may be understood as addressing the sense of justice of the majority in order to urge reconsideration of the measures protested and to warn that in the sincere opinion of the dissenters, the conditions of social cooperation are not being honored" (ibid., 358).

For EDT, the performative matrix of teleporting CD into cyberspace was an important anchor for the future of ECD. Local, national, and international courts as construed by EDT, and any group that functions within the scripts that have been established by EDT, must judge ECD as a transparent civil act of disobedience and not as a "cybercrime." As Dorothy E. Denning of Georgetown University stated in her testimony before the Special Oversight Panel on Terrorism's Committee on Armed Services in the US House of Representatives on May 23, 2000, "EDT and the Electrohippies view their operations as acts of civil disobedience, analogous to street protests and physical sit-ins, not as acts of violence or terrorism. This is an important distinction. Most activists, whether participating in the Million Moms March or a web sit-in, are not terrorists." ECD is not about a secret group of anonymous individuals or networks "cracking" into and enslaving servers in order to set off Distributed Denial-of-Service attacks (DDoS). Such actions only represent "crackers" who break into systems and then use those systems secretly. ECD is the product of mass agency online in a civil and transparent protest—whose main goal is to question and spread information about what those involved feel is a social condition that must be corrected to create a better society for all. This act of digital transparency is important for civil society and the courts to understand—ECD is and should be treated as another digital condition intimately tied to the long and deep Western tradition of civil disobedience—nothing more and nothing less.

Lawyer and legal scholar William Karam, in his 2000 essay "Hacktivism: Is Hacktivism Civil Disobedience?," sees links to ECD that go beyond the "modern theoretical roots of the late 1800s[;] the jurisprudence of civil disobedience involves a global narrative stretching from Aeschylus and other Athenians, to a visionary prisoner in an Alabama jail, to nomadic protesters opposing globalization." For Karam, the ECD practice that Electronic Disturbance Theater uses in its campaigns fits two important conditions of CD: deliberate unlawfulness and accepting responsibility. The members of EDT "have commonly used their real names and openly accepted responsibility for their actions. . . . Although such practices are still far from the norm, there is . . . a recognition that Thoreau's ideas are equally applicable to hacktivism in the information age . . . in short, if hacktivism is to be treated as civil disobedience there will have to be a continued increase in the willingness of hacktivists to accept responsibility and punishment for their acts."

For EDT, the establishment of a plane of consistency between the legitimacy of CD and ECD was extremely important; not only at a state level but a transnational level, it was now a question of having legal theory connect with legal practice as the outcome of EDT's ability to tune into "futural patterns" of post-9/11 illegal/legal models.

In 2005, a legal case in Frankfurt, Germany, was developing over an ECD action against Lufthansa in response to the immigrant deportation business it was doing with the German state. EDT was invited by two important activist groups in Germany, No One is Illegal and ¡Libertad!, to speak in different cities in the country in June 2001 about the history of ECD and EDT's use of mass nonviolent direct action online since 1998. EDT helped to spread the word about the virtual sit-in on Lufthansa that would take place during the yearly shareholder meeting on June 20th, 2001. We spoke to small and large groups of activists, media, artists, and hacktivists, as well as all the major newspapers, and radio and television outlets. The "Deportation-Class Action," as it was called, followed all the protocols of transparency that had been established for ECD. All the activists, artists, and artivists announced the dates, times, and reasons for the action online, all the actions in the streets, and inside the shareholders meeting—nothing was hidden. Some 13,000 people joined online that day to protest, and the Lufthansa website went off-line. The outcome was quite positive for the communities protesting: Lufthansa ended its deportation-class business with the German government.

On June 14, 2005, Andreas-Thomas Vogel went on trial in the lower court of Frankfurt, Germany. Vogel was the activist who had registered the domain libertad.de, where in 2001 the call for the Lufthansa action had been published. Vogel was prosecuted in a high-security courtroom where, normally, terrorist trials are held. The outcome of the hearing at

> the first-instance court of Frankfurt found initiator Andreas-Thomas Vogel guilty and sentenced him to a fine of 90 days' pay. The court found the demonstration to be a use of force against Lufthansa as a website operator as well as against other Internet users; specifically, the airline had suffered economic losses from the campaign, while other Internet users had been prevented from using Lufthansa's website. The online demonstration was found to be a threat of an appreciable harm as defined by German Penal Code 11 Section 240; Vogel was therefore found to be inciting people to commit coercion.[6]

One could see that the lower court was reading the question of ECD between the frame of market drives and "cybercrime"—and not as a form of CD represented by the constitutional rights of German citizens. A year later, newspapers reported that "the First Penal Senate of the Higher Regional Court of Frankfurt" had "overruled the initial verdict. The Higher Court found that the online demonstration did not constitute a show of force but was intended to influence public opinion. This new interpretation left no space for charges of coercion, and the accused was found not guilty."[7]

This decision by the higher court was and is an important step in introducing the theory and practice of ECD that was established by the critical aesthetics of EDT into the emerging legal language of the (lo)bal, which counters the disappearance of constitutional presence and rights under the erasure of the rule-less rule of law by global markets and the "war on terror." This connection was foregrounded by the German activists; for them, ECD action was not about the law and technology, but about the law and inhuman conditions for the "migrants" who were being killed by the hyper-violence of the lawless law of deportation: "As Libertad spokesperson Hans-Peter Kartenberg put it, 'Although it is virtual in nature, the internet is still a real public space. Wherever dirty deals go down, protests also have to be possible.' He also called on everyone not to forget the actual goal of the online protest in light of all the legal turmoil. According to Libertad, some 20,000 people are forcefully deported each year. Kartenberg reminds everyone that this 'inhumane policy' causes hundreds of deaths each year."[8]

For the "Libertad" activist, and for EDT, ECD is technology as an amplification gesture for those who do not have access to the biopolitical rules of globalization or state laws, both within and without, both for citizens and immigrants. These days, no one is exempt from "the state of exception" post 9/11; it will also continue to be the case that to "the extent that hacktivist efforts remain committed to responsibly and conscientiously drawing attention to important social issues, justice and human right issues, they will continue to be successful in meeting . . . the model of civil disobedience."[9]

Notes

1. Artivist is a portmanteau word combining "art" and "activist." Artivism developed in recent years while alter-globalization and antiwar protests emerged and proliferated. A typical short-term goal of artivists is to reclaim public space, especially by subvertising or destroying ads in urban areas or city transportation systems. Artivists also engage in different media like the internet for reasons other than actions that could be described as hacktivism. Further information is available at http://en.wikipedia.org/wiki/Artivist.

2. The independent forms of communicative agency which have emerged over the past years in free radios, mediactivism, telestreet, subvertising, etc. can be seen as the expression and prefiguration of what Félix Guattari called a "post-media civilization." Their independence is a challenge to the powers that be. To understand its meaning, one needs to go back to the Guattarian notion of "collective assembling" and to reflect upon the difference between the concepts of technical automatism and that of technical arranging. Information available at http://multitudes.samizdat.net/spip.php?article2719.

3. See "Rebuilding America's Defense: Strategies, Forces and Resources for a New Century," report of The Project for the New American Century, 2000, available at https://wikispooks.com/wiki/File:RebuildingAmericasDefenses.pdf.

4. Gandhi called his overall method of nonviolent action Satyagraha. This translates roughly as "truth-force."

5. "Noopolitik is an approach to statecraft, to be undertaken by nonstate actors, that emphasized the role of soft power in expressing ideas, values, norms, and ethics through all manner of media. This makes it distinct from [R]ealpolitik, which stresses the hard,

material dimensions of power and treats states as the determinants of world order" (Arquilla and Ronfeldt 1999, 27).

6. "Higher Regional Court says online demonstration is not force," *Heise Online*, June 2, 2006. Archived at https://post.thing.net/node/1370.

7. Ibid.

8. Ibid.

9. William Karam, "Hacktivism: Is Hacktivism Civil Disobedience?," University of Ottawa, Faculty of Law, Department of Graduate Studies, 2000, on Karam's home page, 27. (This home page and essay is no longer available online as of April 2007. A hard copy of the essay is in the author's hands).

IV

Interviews

13

On DH in Argentina

An Interview with Gimena del Río Riande

HÉCTOR FERNÁNDEZ L'HOESTE AND JUAN CARLOS RODRÍGUEZ

1. Could you please tell us a bit about how you came to the field of digital humanities (DH)?

I came to the field of DH (at that time, new technologies/*nuevas tecnologías*) when I started my PhD, by 2004, in Spain. I had moved from Argentina to Spain that year, as I had been awarded a grant from the Consejo Superior de Investigaciones Científicas (CSIC, Madrid) to start my PhD. I was working on an annotated critical edition of King Dinis of Portugal's Songbook, and my director, Dr. José Manuel Lucía Megías, was also working at the University Complutense of Madrid on the concepts of hypertext, hypertext editions, etc. In those days, some European projects were also offering online resources for medievalists, such as Base de Datos da Lírica Profana Galego-Portuguesa (https://www.cirp.gal/), Bibliografia Eletronica dei Trovattori (www.bedt.it/), and Rialto (www.rialto.unina.it/), among many others.

I started thinking about how to work on a "hypertext edition" for my dissertation, and some years later, I got the chance to work on Dr. Mercedes Brea's project, Base de Datos da Lírica Profana Galego-Portuguesa, and I became interested in working with databases. One interesting thing is that we never called these projects or works digital humanities/*humanidades digitales*, not even humanities computing/*informática humanística*. With the exception of new technologies/*nuevas tecnologías*, there wasn't a name for what we were doing. Many years later, by 2011, I had started working on the Bibliografía de Escritoras Españolas Database (http://www.bieses.net/) with Dr. Nieves Baranda at UNED-Madrid, and that year I also started my first DH project with Drs. Elena González-Blanco and Clara Martínez Cantón, Repertorio Métrico de la Poesía Castellana, ReMetCa (www.remetca.uned.es/). We called it a DH project by 2012!

I moved back to Argentina in 2013 as a CONICET researcher and I started here [both] the Asociación Argentina de Humanidades Digitales (AAHD) (http://aahd.net.ar/) and the first projects in digital humanities developed in the country (that is, not just collaborations with other northern projects), like Diálogo Medieval (http://dialogo.linhd.es/), Obras Completas de José Luis Romero (http://jlromero.com.ar/), and Pelagios South (https://recogito.pelagios.org/document/wzqxhk0h3vpikm).

2. Could you please describe your current work as a DH professional at CONICET?

I am a full-time researcher at the National Scientific and Technical Research Council (CONICET) in Argentina: I work at the Instituto de Investigaciones Bibliográficas y Crítica Textual (IIBICRIT), and I direct the Digital Humanities Laboratory at Centro Argentino de Información en Ciencia y Tecnología (CAICYT) (https://hdcaicyt.github.io). I also teach postgraduate courses at the University of Buenos Aires related to Medieval Studies (especially medieval Hispanic songbooks, https://reistrobadores.wordpress.com/, but also philological edition courses), and I co-coordinate the online DH master's certificate at UNED (Spain, http://linhd.es/).

My research work is nowadays mostly devoted to study and putting into practice open methods and tools for digital scholarly editions and for developing *humanidades digitales* (HD) projects. I research on medieval texts, from a philological perspective, but I am also dedicating most of my research time to analyzing how digital humanities can become a scientific field in Argentina, as *humanidades digitales* (HD). I publish scientific literature on DH, I coordinate and direct projects, I teach special courses, I am part of the board of directors of many DH journals such as

Digital Studies/Le Champ Numérique, Revista de Humanidades Digitales, Bibliographica, Relaciones, ArtyHum. I also organize many workshops and events related to DH with the Argentine Association of Digital Humanities (AAHD), the DH association I founded with other colleagues in 2013. DH has many faces; researching is not enough. You also need different types of hands-on work, and you also need to build a community of practice to see it in action. I also try to take part in the global aspects of DH, being part of associations and consortia outside Argentina, such as *Humanidades Digitales Hispánicas* (HDH, Spain), Pelagios Commons, FORCE11.

3. Explain the emergence of DH in Argentina.

The emergence of DH is related mostly to individuals, researchers, professors, librarians, and educators who believe that the impact of technology in their area of expertise is creating a new knowledge and that new knowledge is also shared in very different spaces, inside and outside academia. It is a movement based in communities of practice. Also, DH is related not only to "pure" humanities, but also to the social sciences (history, anthropology, sociology) and to educators. It is also a topic in the Open Access, Open Education, and Open Science movements inside and outside academia. In a country that is one of the so-called developing countries, a country in which most digital and non-digital infrastructures for research are obsolete, in which institutional funding for projects is almost nonexistent, and in which the "digital divide" is still a problem to solve, the emergence of DH is related to how a discipline that uses technology to explain itself and for its practices can develop, and how it may help improve digital and computational literacy. It is also a tool for democratizing knowledge for everyone on the web.

4. Who are some key figures or pioneers in the field in Argentina?

I can name Mela Bosch, a computational linguist who took part in one very interesting project on a big corpus developed in the 1980s: *El Derecho en Disco Láser* (Law on LaserDisc). The project aimed at digitizing a large part of Argentine jurisprudence (23 volumes of legal code). One very interesting thing about it is that Father Busa (the renowned forerunner of DH) was the project's counsellor, and he was invited to a meeting held at the Catholic University of Argentina in 1988 to talk about his experience with concordances and text technologies in his *Index Thomisticus* project. Mela Bosch also directed the Centro Argentino de Información en Ciencia y Tecnología (CAICYT, CONICET) between 2014 and 2017.

Alejandro Piscitelli, in his Cátedra de Datos (university data seminar), and through his very prolific work, has also been working on digital culture and some approaches to DH and outreach, not only in Argentina but also in many countries in Latin America.

I would also like to mention some figures who, without having worked in DH, helped start the field. This is the case with Germán Orduna, renowned Argentinean philologist who directed the IIBICRIT (former *Seminario de Edición y Crítica Textual*, SECRIT) and its academic journal, *Incipit* (http://www.iibicrit-conicet.gov.ar/ojs/index.php/incipit/index). *Incipit* published many of the most important articles on humanities computing in Spanish (*informática humanística*), thanks to Orduna's open mind and vision for future research.

I can also consider, very humbly, myself a pioneer. When I moved back to my country in 2013, I founded the Argentine Association of Digital Humanities (AAHD), after a series of meetings at the National University of La Plata and the Doctor Amado Alonso Institute of Philology and Hispanic Literatures that came after the first call to start a DH association at the Argentine National Library, on September 27, 2013. In fact, everything had started a few months earlier at the THATCamp Buenos Aires, on July 22nd of that same year. Since that first THATCamp Buenos Aires, I have been working with the AAHD in building a community of practice interested in addressing the complexities of the impact of the digital on research and teaching in the humanities and the social sciences. We have also worked to understand the multiple common areas of interest with computer science, libraries, information and communication technologies, studies on science, technology and society, or open and citizen science, among many other disciplines and fields of knowledge.

5. What is the current state of DH in Argentina? Comment on the challenges and the opportunities of DH in Argentina.

In Argentina, the *humanidades digitales* have led to the development of different lines of research and to the creation of a diverse community that circulates their theories, practices, and new objects of study, not only within the academy but also in peripheral areas, through collaborative spaces and methodologies. Thus, global guidelines intersect with local conditions, giving rise to new experiences that progressively define the field.

One of our challenges is to keep our community of practice working firmly in a scientific field of its own, but also to design a curriculum in digital humanities that could be real and possible in a region that suffers social inequality, the obsolescence of infrastructures and the lack of adaptation to technologies. As I mentioned, in Argentina, the digital humanities have led to the development of different lines of research and to the creation of an interdisciplinary community. Thus, global guidelines intersect with local conditions, giving rise to new experiences that progressively define the field. Our challenges deal with working at these intersections of center-periphery, theory-practice, global-local, digital humanities-*humanidades digitales*.

6. What kind of projects and work are being developed in DH in Argentina? Which is the most representative work of DH in Argentina?

Most of the projects developed in the country are either small activities carried out over shorter periods and always of a more experimental nature, or they are part of international collaborations with projects from countries of the Global North. This has a clear explanation, and it is access and the possibility of using software and infrastructures that have an impact on the possibilities of production, exhibition, and preservation of projects. In Europe we have large projects funded by research agencies, but also by European consortia that invest millions of euros in personal or group projects (think about the calls for Horizon 2020, ERC, DARIAH). In the United States, the NEH supports a large number of DH projects. Then, those same infrastructures preserve the developed materials. There is a whole scientific context that supports and endorses DH research. In Argentina and in most Latin American countries, we do not have this type of infrastructure at a national or regional level, which makes our projects smaller, shorter, or more experimental. We sometimes develop our projects with the help of other international projects, or in collaboration with them.

I can mention my DH projects. At the IIBICRIT and the Humanidades Digitales Lab (CAICYT) I am working on:

Digitization and digital tools for journal editing: Digitization has been a relegated work inside institutions in the country. At IIBICRIT we started a project on digitization of our historical *Incipit* journals (1981–2010) with a DIY open hardware scanner. We also started working with and adapting Open Journal Systems (OJS) for editing and preparing online issues of these old journals (http://www.iibicrit-conicet.gov.ar/ojs/index.php/incipit/issue/archive?issuesPage=2#issues), and also for ones we have created (together with UNAM México and UNED Spain), like the *Revista de Humanidades Digitales* (http://revistas.uned.es/index.php/RHD/index).

DH Taxonomies: Projects on DH taxonomies aim to collaborate with the content on DH at CAICYT's semantic server (http://vocabularios.caicyt.gov.ar), structuring the information relevant to digital humanities and making it more easily recognizable, while opening a space for institutionalization and authority in Spanish, and linking us with different international research groups such as DARIAH, the POSTDATA-UNED project, etc.

With the members of the DH lab at CAICYT we worked on the translation to Spanish and adaptation of the Taxonomy of Digital Research Activities in the Humanities, TaDiRAH, developed by DARIAH: http://www.vocabularyserver.com/tadirah/es/.

Our taxonomy (in Spanish) of digital research activities applied to the humanities was used on many sites and projects promoted by the digital humanist community, like the DayofDH 2017 website.

We have been modelling other taxonomies, such as the one developed for the POSTDATA project (UNED) that seeks to communicate the terminology developed over the years in the different poetic traditions. (See http://www.vocabularyserver.com/lab/postdata/portalthes/home.php).

Digital Scholarly Editions: At IIBICRIT, we started the first Digital Scholarly Edition project, Diálogo Medieval, in which we studied the encoding on TEI of a corpus on medieval Hispanic dialogue poems. We also developed our own tools and resources: http://dialogo.linhd.es/.

I also coordinated the digital edition of José Luis Romero's complete works (http://jlromero.com.ar/). José Luis Romero was an Argentinean historian, and we used the TEI to encode the articles he published during the twentieth century.

GIS and semantic annotation: At the DH Lab at CAICYT, and thanks to different Pelagios Resource Development Grants, we developed in 2017 a project called Pelagios al Sur (Pelagios South, http://commons.pelagios.org/2017/12/pelagios-south-researching-teaching-and-learning-final-report/). This project aims to explore the relationships between Spain and Latin America through their historical, literary, and cartographic sources using Pelagios Commons tools and resources. Pelagios al Sur aimed to identify the names assigned to places in Spanish and indigenous languages, such as Guaraní and Charrúa, from the sixteenth to the nineteenth centuries in the Río de la Plata territory. We mostly studied, mapped, and annotated collectively Ruy Díaz de Guzmán's *La Argentina manuscrita*. A second moment of this initial project is the one I am carrying out with my team at HD CAICYT lab together with Karl Grossner from the World-Historical Gazetteer (USA), Werner Stangl from HGIS-Indias (Austria), Albert Palacios from LLILAS Benson Latin American Studies and Collections (USA), and Ben and Sara Brumfield from Brumfield Labs (USA). Our project, LatAm, funded by a second Resource Development Grant from Pelagios, will develop a linked dataset for colonial Latin America based on two primary sources: Antonio de Alcedo's *Diccionario geográfico-histórico de las Indias Occidentales ó América* (1786), a gazetteer describing places within the New World from a Spanish colonial perspective; and George Alexander Thompson's *Geographical and Historical Dictionary of America and the West Indies* (1812), an expanded, English-language version of Alcedo's *Diccionario*. The primary goal of the LatAm project is to use Alcedo's *Diccionario* to create a generally useful dataset that can contribute to the emerging linked data network of historical places, including resources such as Pelagios's Recogito and Peripleo applications and the World-Historical Gazetteer. The secondary goal is to develop tools and protocols that will enable scholars working with historical gazetteers to prepare digital editions and GIS datasets from those documents.

Actually, I think that the most representative DH work here is the one related to building a community, so I would say that my work with the Argentine Association of Digital Humanities (AAHD) in the organization of events and conferences is the most representative DH work. Since the first THATCamp Buenos Aires, the AAHD has been working as a community of practice interested in addressing the complexities of the impact of the digital on research and teaching in the humanities and the social sciences. Over these five years, the AAHD has organized a large number of talks, workshops, meetings, and symposia in Argentina and in collaboration with other research groups in Latin America and Spain, such as The Day of the Digital Humanities/DayofDH. The most outstanding activities were the AAHD's two major events: the First National Conference of Digital Humanities: Culture, Technology and Knowledge (2014), and the Digital Humanities Congress: Local Constructions in Global Contexts (2016). These two events were held at the Centro Cultural San Martín and the Centro Cultural de la Cooperación, in the city of Buenos Aires. These spaces do not belong to any university and are public cultural centers. The events did not have a previous budget. The AAHD has published the proceedings of the two events. All the information about them and the proceedings can be found at https://www.aacademica.org/jornadasaahd and https://www.aacademica.org/aahd.congreso. In 2018, we will celebrate our third conference in the city of Rosario, province of Santa Fe, with the aim of federalizing our proposal. More information about the event can be found at: https://www.aacademica.org/congreso.aahd2018.

7. Discuss the level of institutional support given to DH in Argentina.

The level of institutional support is difficult to define. On the one hand, in many cases, universities seem to be interested in knowing what DH is about, they support events in DH (like conferences and workshops), but they still do not foster a master's degree or certificate in DH. We could define it as an informal institutional support. However, I think it is just a question of time. Sooner or later, and maybe through different labels (digital culture, digital social sciences, digital humanities), the research paradigm in humanities and social sciences will start including these approaches. I only wish this could be done in a coherent way, proposing a more real and democratic digital curriculum that takes into account our digital literacies, our disciplines, our traditions, and the strengths and weaknesses in the region inside academia.

8. How could conditions improve to spur further development of DH in Argentina?

Conditions could improve if institutions started supporting our work and financing projects that can call themselves DH projects. Conditions could improve if libraries started working with researchers, professors, students. We need better infrastructures that can support and preserve our work. In the case of a scientific field such as digital humanities, where the use of digital tools and resources is a key element for the construction of projects' epistemology, infrastructures become an essential support that also regulate their value. Sadly, we don't have the same technological infrastructures around the world and, consequently, research is affected by the (non)existence of infrastructures.

9. With the coming elections, do you foresee any impact on the field in Argentina?

No, and it's really difficult to foresee a positive impact on what is related to funding science and technology projects, as the government has announced that universities and CONICET won't receive most of the funding for next year and almost no researchers will be incorporated in tenured positions. This context is especially negative for humanities and social sciences, areas that do not receive much funding.

10. In terms of DH, how does Argentina compare to other countries in the Spanish-speaking world?

DH in Argentina is very much dominated by approaches that come from the social sciences or literary criticism. There is a lot of work reflecting on the impact of the digital on research in humanities and social sciences, a lot of interest in e-literature, e-poetry, and many people from those groups also take part in our conferences, but there are still very few practical approaches. Moreover, those practical approaches are more experiments than projects. I can also say that DH is also very much understood as public humanities, as a field that can also relate to open science and citizen science. I think that that relationship is supported by our work as a community of practice, something that other countries, through more formal associations or master's degrees that have suddenly appeared, haven't taken into account.

11. Name some appealing work in DH in other Latin American nations.

I think that the most appealing thing in Latin America since 2012 has been the emergence of DH associations that have been organizing events and publishing materials in Spanish: the Red de Humanidades Digitales (RedHD) in Mexico, the Associação das Humanidades Digitais (AHDig) in Brazil, the Asociación Argentina de Humanidades Digitales (AAHD) in Argentina, and the Red Colombiana de Humanidades Digitales (RCHD) have done great work in this sense. Also, all the approaches on openness in DH, making materials more accessible on the web, are very relevant. DH has proved that a more global openness model is possible, not only in terms of access but also in terms of methods, best practices, and opportunities for collaboration.

I like the work of the people of the Programming Historian in Spanish, though I think it is a project that still needs more openness in fostering collaboration in terms of cocreation with Spanish speakers. One great work is that of the Biblioteca Digital de Autores Uruguayos, https://autores.uy/colecciones/190, which includes an Open Data approach to the project, very much in consonance with the Open movement in Latin America (Open Access, Open Data, Open Science, Open Research, Open Education, Open Government).

12. What is your view of DH in the anglophone world?

Northern DH is very much based on funded and collective projects, where you can find students and programmers and researchers paid by that project. It is also very much based on the use of software (proprietary or open) and infrastructure. As I have stated before, this is a very institutionalized DH, where we can find a context that supports the field through funding (Mellon foundation, NEH, etc.), infrastructures (DARIAH, CLARIN, DH labs and centers), through a curriculum (master's, PhD, certificates), and through publications (*DHQ*, *Digital Studies/Le Champ Numérique*, etc., and collective anthologies such as the *Companions*). I can't say this is a model I do not like, though I still seek some more reflection on how to foster open collaboration in terms of cocreation among researchers from different parts of the world. DH practitioners need to read about what other researchers are doing in other nations. In that sense, we could think of an open infrastructure development in DH from the perspective of globalized participation, not only for Europe or for North America. If we consider that DH as a discipline is in the midst of a significant "global turn" that has come to question many aspects of our personal, linguistic, technical, and administrative practice, we should be focusing in the same way on access, diversity, and interrogating privilege in tools, resources, and infrastructures. Here, our field has been characterized by national and/or regional efforts that have not made global interoperability and participation a primary concern. Also, the use of languages for science should be a primary concern, but not during conferences. DH journals and anthologies should support the use of the most representative languages in academia, or translations.

13. How could the relationship between Argentinean DH and US DH evolve and improve?

The relationship between Argentinean DH and US DH could evolve and improve through cocreation of DH projects, through partnering. From my point of view, the idea of collaboration as "please, join my project, collaborate with us," and once the project is finished, our collaboration too is over, does not work. What we need to find is a common interest and projects in which we find partners from north and south in equal conditions. In that way you can foster collaborative creation and sharing of knowledge and information, and cocreation. The open-source software movement or other digital environments like Wikipedia can give us good examples for improving a dialogue between DH and HD, for instance. Also, creating global DH journals, anthologies that make use of different languages for science, or organizing events with different partners (ACH and AAHD, for instance).

14. How is the renegotiation of trade treaties and/or the evolution of the economy likely to affect the development of the field in Argentina?

Funding science and technology is vital for research. This is a big problem in my country. Research work, mostly in the humanities and social sciences, is poorly funded. We can't fund our work and we can't afford to buy expensive technology. As I have explained in other places, this context is a problem for the development of *humanidades digitales*, as their epistemology is very much based in technology. I envision a future related to very short projects based on open minimal computing approaches.

15. How do you envision the future of digital humanities in Argentina?

I envision the future of digital humanities in Argentina very much related to the movements of Open Access, Open Software, Open Science, and Open Education, because they are paying a lot of attention to the ways the digital can help democratize knowledge and make it available inside and outside academia. I envision DH as communities of practice that foster cocreation and also find ways to fight the digital divide. I envision DH as a movement with very strong theories that will work on critical approaches to technology and redefine the humanities for the twenty-first century.

14

On DH in Brazil

An Interview with Ana Lígia Silva Medeiros

HÉCTOR FERNÁNDEZ L'HOESTE AND JUAN CARLOS RODRÍGUEZ

TRANSLATED BY HÉCTOR FERNÁNDEZ L'HOESTE

1. Could you please tell us a bit about how you came to the field of digital humanities (DH)?

In today's society, it is impossible not to align oneself with the study of the impact of the digital on the production and diffusion of knowledge. New questions arise in terms of research methodology, availability of tools, and even about the way scholars think. We are possibly experiencing a moment of transition in which the ways of thinking and acting in society no longer respond to the demands that arise.

In this sense, when I undertook the direction of the Center for Memory and Information (CMI) at the Fundação Casa de Rui Barbosa (FCRB), I had as one of the main goals to align the institution with the current issues that affect institutional assets. I understood that the patrimony was not only the collection accumulated by the memory sectors under the custody of the FCRB, but also the intellectual production of researchers in several areas, which represents the fundamental social capital of the institution.

It should be noted that the FCRB, as of November 30, 2018, is a federal body subordinated to the Ministry of Culture (MinC), whose purposes are the development of culture, research, and teaching, highlighting intellectual work, democratization and access to collections, and preservation of national memory, literary, intellectual, and humanistic production.

The structure of the FCRB is composed of two centers: the Memory and Information Center (CMI), responsible for the management of the collection of the institution, and the Research Center (CP), in which research is conducted in the areas of law, philology, history, cultural politics, and *Ruiana* (archives having to do with Rui Barbosa). In addition to these, the FCRB also has the General Coordination of Planning and Administration (CGPA) and the Postgraduate Program in Memory and Information (PPGMA).

The CMI is responsible for the management, in particular, of the preservation, treatment, and restoration of patrimonial collections—museological, archival, bibliographic, architectural, and environmental—in order to secure the technical and technological references from its initiatives. It also develops research in the areas of performance.

In order to achieve this ideal, a diagnosis was made to understand how the technologies were being incorporated into the daily life of the institution, not under the instrumental aspects, but with the objective of perceiving the capacity of the institution to assimilate the possibilities of exploiting digitization in the research and services offered.

Thus, the situation encountered was below the threshhold that digitization made possible. In this way, a team consisting of one employee and four fellows was created with the intention of updating and expanding the possibilities of access to information. Therefore, we began research of an applied nature, updating the bibliography on the subject, and developing benchmarking to discover the best practices of similar institutions and to initiate the implantation of new tools. Consequently, our understanding is that digitization transcends the cold establishment of new means of searching, making it necessary to add a critical reflection, without which there is a waste of financial resources and personnel.

It is important to note that the application of the concept, in a broad sense, of digital humanities (*HDs*, in Portuguese) made it possible to build the foundation for the actions to be taken from that moment. However, it was fundamental that actions be coordinated, reflected, and mainly taken in conjunction with researchers, not only in the work of the CMI but also of the CP. Subsequently, a practical community was created informally where it is possible to discuss the implementation of innovative tools and to plan the [necessary] methodologies.

2. Could you please describe your current work as a DH professional at FCRB?

We are developing initiatives that contribute to the access, preservation, dissemination, information retrieval, innovation, and creation of new knowledge through the use of digital research methods linked to DH. These include: the Rui Barbosa Repository of Cultural Information (Rubi),[1] the Memory and Information Periodical,[2] the FCRB Memory and Information Center blog,[3] and other digital products.

An example of research and use of DH with an application of the concept of community of practice was the "Mostra Leandro Gomes de Barros: Poet of the *Sertão*," exhibited from March 5 to April 10, 2018, which it was only possible to develop . . . by gathering research efforts and [through] organization of the CMI staff (library officers, scholarship librarians, historians and systems analysts, museum staff, publishing staff, library staff who provided leaflets for exhibit at the show, etc.).

The study and future application of the Transcribe Bentham initiative in the archival collections of the Archive of Brazilian Literature Museum (AMLB) of the FCRB are quite noteworthy. This project is made possible through community participation with the institution, since this will contribute to the transcription of manuscripts belonging to the collections. This adoption will ratify the consolidation of DH at FCRB.

We can also list some coding of access to the websites produced by researchers from the institution, the result of interaction between technology and research, which can be considered DH. The following are some of these initiatives:

Machado de Assis (http://machadodeassis.fflch.usp.br/): This is a search site for the universe of quotes and allusions that Machado de Assis makes in his fiction to other works, authors, characters, anonymous sources, etc. It is the result of Marta de Senna's research.

Slavery, Abolition, and Post-Abolition (http://rubi.casaruibarbosa. gov.br/handle/20.500.11997/1186): The purpose of the site is to contribute to research on these topics and also to encourage the formation of new researchers. Recommended for internet users of all ages, it offers the following areas: scanned documents, controlled vocabulary, links, and games.

Rui Barbosa Online (http://rubi.casaruibarbosa.gov.br/handle/20. 500.11997/1190): This site brings together the different databases and research tools organized for the dissemination of the collections of books, documents, and objects that belonged to Rui Barbosa as well as his work and what was written about him.

Cordel: Popular Literature in Verse (http://rubi.casaruibarbosa.gov. br/handle/fcrb/520): The project is aimed at the preservation, conservation, and availability of this collection, unique in the world. Given its characteristics of rarity, originality, and antiquity, it is necessary to guarantee its preservation against the wear and tear of time and handling, subjecting the collection to specific technical and technological treatments, ensuring the restoration of leaflets, the making of envelopes adequate for the custody and the digitization and availability of the *cordel* collection through the FCRB portal, as well as the insertion of its catalogues in the Foundation's database, making it possible to carry out studies and research on this manifestation of Brazilian popular culture.

Memory Project: Rui Barbosa—Justice and Freedom (http://rubi. casaruibarbosa.gov.br/handle/20.500.11997/1183): This is a site commemorating the 150th anniversary of Rui Barbosa's birth. Besides presenting aspects of his life and work, illustrations, and photographs, "Rui Barbosa—Justice and Freedom" established discussion groups with researchers, jurists, and people interested in the author. In addition, the Memory Project pays homage to 12 other personalities.

Developed in partnership with the Instituto Moreira Salles (IMS) at the beginning of the second half of 2018, the Portal of Brazilian Chronicles is also particularly significant. The chronicle is an important Brazilian literary genre. The Portal will enable the digital integration of the collections of main Brazilian chroniclers such as Rubem Braga and Otto Lara Resende. Soon, the Portal will promote the dissemination, research, memory, and preservation of said collections.

It is also worth mentioning that we are focused on DH training for the institution's employees, through the promotion of training, courses, and lectures. Every year, we hold the Technology and Culture Seminar, with a specific desk for DH, which counts on the presence of institutions from several states of the federation.

Digital Humanities Laboratory

The FCRB Memory and Information Center (CMI) organized the FCRB's Digital Humanities Laboratory, established by Portaria nº 73, June 2018.

The Digital Humanities Laboratory aims to meet the growing demand of the body of internal and external researchers of FCRB in the application of information and communication technologies as a new research method. It contributes to the access, preservation, dissemination, information retrieval, innovation, and creation of new knowledge through the use of digital research methods linked to the digital humanities.

The Digital Humanities Laboratory is supported by the Research Group on Technologies and Communication in Memory Institutions (GPTICIM) and has three pillars: research, product development, and academic production.

Research was organized according to the understanding of the information access needs of researchers and the community through meetings and requests. Subsequently, we devised strategies so that the use of the techniques met the demands of researchers through the creation of products. We highlight below some of the products developed:

- Rui Barbosa Repository of Cultural Information (RUBI);
- Periodical memory and Information;
- Blog of the Center of Memory and Information of FCRB;
- Open Conference Systems (OCS).

Finally, the results of the research and implementation of the generated resources will be archived as a dossier at FCRB's institutional archive and will have generated a scientific production on the research carried out.

3. Explain the emergence of DH in Brazil.

The expansion of DH is fundamental for a wider awareness on the part of researchers of the possibility for the use of technology in their work. Although the research process depends more and more on technology, it is essential to take advantage of all the possibilities offered.

In addition, digitization of collections needs to be intensified so that researchers and the wider community can access documents.

However, this need is affected by three factors:

- The need for diffusion of DH in Brazilian academic and scientific spaces;
- Budget reduction in the Ministry of Culture (MinC), of which the FCRB is a part, which delayed the project by custodial institutions to accelerate the process of digitization. In addition, there is no funding application for equipment and personnel for the development of projects linked to HDs;
- Ministries' budget cuts, affecting public universities and research centers. The cut announced to the budget of the Ministry of Science, Technology, Innovations, and Communications (MCTIC) for 2017 was of approximately 40 percent in relation to 2016—and of almost 56 percent compared to 2014. Although the national scientific community has objected, overall, this cut was maintained.

4. Who are some key figures or pioneers in the field in Brazil?

I quote some names that I consider active in the area, at the risk of omitting some other names. The information on these personalities was obtained using the platform Lattes.

Aquiles Ratti Alencar Brayner: He graduated [with undergraduate degrees] in Psychology from the Federal University of Ceará (1994) and in Languages and Cultures of Latin America from Leiden University (1996). He holds a Master's in Languages and Cultures of Latin America from Leiden University (1998), a Master's in Librarianship and Information Science from the City University of London (2011), and a PhD in Brazilian Literature from King's College London (2006). He held the position of Digital Curator of the British Library (BL), where he was responsible for developing new products and management models for BL's electronic resources. He acted as university professor at several British universities. In 2017, he was awarded a research grant to hold the position of Researcher in Residence at the National Library Foundation. He currently works with several research institutions and memorials for the development of activities in the area of digital curatorship. In addition to having publications in the areas of literature and history, he carries out research in information science, digital humanities, bibliographic historiography, and music.[4]

Claudio José Ribeiro: He holds a PhD in Information Science from the Universidade Federal Fluminense/MCT-IBICT agreement, a Master's in Information Science from UFRJ/MCT-IBICT (2001), and an MBA in Knowledge Management from COPPE/UFRJ-Dataprev (2005). He also holds a degree in Civil Engineering from the State University of Rio de Janeiro (1984) and a certification in Systems Analysis from PUC-RJ (1986). On the subject of content management, he has ECM Practitioner and ECM Specialist certifications issued by the US-based Association for Information and Image Management (AIIM). He has experience in the areas of Computer Science and Information Science, both in technical work and in activities as a university professor, working mainly on the following topics: domain analysis, information systems, information architecture, social security, content management, and knowledge management. He is adjunct professor of UNIRIO (Federal University of the State of Rio de Janeiro).

Jair Martins de Miranda: He graduated in Archivology from the Federal University of the State of Rio de Janeiro (UNIRIO, 1983). He has a specialization in Systems Analysis (1984) and Planning and Archives Management (1985), a Master's in Social Memory from the Federal University of Rio de Janeiro (1995—when it was still called Administration of Cultural Centers), and a doctoral degree in Information Science from the UFRJ / IBICT Agreement. He is currently an associate professor in the Department of Archives Studies and Processes at the Center for Human and Social Sciences at UNIRIO, Coordinator of the Laboratory for the Preservation and Management of Digital Collections (LABOGAD), and president of the Center for Reference and Information on Arts, Entertainment, and Brazilian Culture (CRIAR). He works in research, teaching, and extension in the areas of social archivology, digital collections, creative economics, social networks, and organization and representation of knowledge, especially in the field of Afro-Brazilian culture and the history and social memory of samba. He coordinates the "Samba Global" projects; "Memorable Samba"; "Portal do Carnaval," the annual "International Meeting of Samba and Carnival," and the biannual "Samba National Congress," in addition to the "Edison Carneiro Prize," which encourages academic, literary, journalistic, entrepreneurial, and cultural promotion initiatives in the areas of samba and carnival.

José Eduardo Santarem Segundo: He holds a PhD and Master's in Information Science from São Paulo's Júlio de Mesquita Filho State University (UNESP-Marília /SP); is professor in the Department of Education,

Information, and Communication, Faculty of Philosophy, Sciences, and Letters of Ribeirão Preto, University of São Paulo (USP); and is professor in the Graduate Program in Information Science of UNESP/Marília in the Information and Technology track. He is coordinator of GT8-Information and Technology, part of the National Association of Research and Graduate Studies in Information Science (ANCIB). His research focuses on digital environments and technologies applied to information and communication—with emphasis on Semantic Web, Linked Data, Open Data, and Digital Collections. He is the leader of the Semantic Web and Open Data Study Center (NEWSDA). He received the Best Thesis Award from the National Association for Research and Graduate Studies in Information Science (ANCIB) in 2011. He also received an Honorable Mention for the Capes de Teses Award in 2011 (Applied Social Sciences).

Ricardo Medeiros Pimenta. He is a type-2 researcher with CNPq (productivity grant) and Young Scientist at our State FAPERJ (2018?–2020). He is a research associate of the Brazilian Institute of Science and Technology Information (IBICT) of the Ministry of Science, Technology, and Innovation (MCTI). He is permanent professor in the Graduate Program in Information Science (PPGCI / IBICT-UFRJ), and a historian (2003) of Gama Filho University (UGF), with a graduate degree in the history of Brazil (2005) from Cândido Mendes University (UCAM). He has a master's degree in Social Memory and Documentation (2006) from the Federal University of Rio de Janeiro (UNIRIO), and a PhD in Social Memory (2010) from the same institution, having held a postdoc (2007–2008) from the École des Hautes Études en Sciences Sociales (EHESS) in Paris.[5] He is the leader of the Information, Memory, and Society Research Group (http://www.memoriaesociedade.ibict.br), registered in the CNPq directory, and coordinates the Digital Humanities Network Laboratory of IBICT (Larhud/COEPE/IBICT). He is a Research Associate of the Interdisciplinary Laboratory on Information and Knowledge (LIINC/UFRJ) and a member of the Latin American Network of Surveillance, Technology, and Society Studies (LAVITS). During the two years from 2012–2014, he was a member of the Higher Studies Commission of the Center for Reference to Political Struggles in Brazil (1964–1985)—Revealed Memories in the National Archive. He is interested in the field of dialogues and analyzes information, memory, and their places/devices; political and economic aspects of information control; their surveillance mechanisms;

and cyberspace in sociological and historical perspective. He is also interested in reflections concerning the role of the document and technology in studies of memory, forgetfulness, and the digital humanities.

Luis Antonio Coelho Ferla. A professor of undergraduate and graduate programs in the History Department of the Federal University of São Paulo, Guarulhos Campus, he has been an alumnus of the Graduate Program in Applied Computation of the National Institute of Space Research since May 2017. He holds a degree in History from the University of São Paulo (1998) and a PhD in Economic History from the University of São Paulo (2005). He holds an honors degree from UNEP/UNESCO/University of Dresden (1995). He has experience in teaching and research in history, with emphasis on contemporary history, working mainly on the following themes: phenomena of modernity, history of science, history of the body, and history of the city. Currently, he develops research aimed at the use of new digital technologies in the historian's work, especially those related to geoprocessing (historical GIS). He was a visiting researcher in the Department of History of Science of the Consejo Superior de Investigaciones Científicas in Madrid in 2007 and 2010, and at the Spatial History Laboratory of Stanford University in the United States in 2012.

5. What kind of projects and work are being developed in DH in Brazil? Which is the most representative work of DH in Brazil?

It is a model of what happens in many countries. The trend in Brazil is the creation of laboratories, groups, or research centers directed at DH. Some examples are:

- USP Digital Humanities Research Group;
- Laboratory for Preservation and Management of Digital Collections LABOGAD (UNIRIO);
- FGV Digital Humanities Laboratory;
- Laboratory in the Network of Digital Humanities (IBICT and UFRJ);
- Research Group History, Maps and Computers—Himama (Federal University of São Paulo / Archive of the State of São Paulo);
- Research Group TEMA DIDÁTICO—Technology, Education, and Didactic Materials (Federal University of Santa Catarina);
- LabDH, FCRB Digital Humanities Laboratory, Fundação Casa de Rui Barbosa [Casa de Rui Barbosa Foundation])

According to the published research by Oliveira and Martins (2017), the areas studied by research groups are divided into five topics of study: linguistics, literature, history, information science, and communication.

It would be difficult to nominate exemplary work, as each initiative turns to a particular area. Here are a few examples, bearing in mind the following criteria:

Pioneerism: Brasiliana USP (University of São Paulo, https://digital. bbm.usp.br/handle/bbm-ext/1). The Brasiliana Guita and José Mindlin Library,[6] at USP, pioneered the digital humanities. Since 2005, when it was created, the library has gathered experts, hosted projects, and supported study initiatives, developing activities around four fields of knowledge: 1) Brazilian studies; 2) history of the book and reading; 3) knowledge technology and digital humanities; and 4) preservation, conservation, and restoration of books and paper. According to their website:

> This Library, according to the bylaws, seeks to preserve, disseminate, and facilitate the access of students, researchers, and the general public to the collection, and to promote the dissemination of studies of Brazilian subjects through specific programs and projects. In this sense, it has acted as an interdisciplinary center for documentation, research, and scientific diffusion of Brazilian studies, book culture, information technology, and digital humanities, becoming an organ of integration of several academic initiatives of inter-sectorial and transdisciplinary interest.

Training: Events related to DH are important to consolidate the field and stimulate discussions. Recently there have been two events, one with national coverage and another one of an international nature, that can be mentioned as examples.

The Second Technology and Culture Seminar, held by FCRB, took place in November 2017 and addressed two topics that may become complementary: DH and information competence. The importance of an event like this is that it provides a local forum for discussion of the topic. Thus, we were able to verify how the field is perceived by Brazilian researchers and professionals, besides generating a scientific production important for the area.

The first International Congress on Digital Humanities/HDRio,[7] held in Rio de Janeiro from April 9 to 13, 2018, brought together academics, scientists, and technologists from the arts, the cultural sector, and social, human, hard, and computational sciences. It was organized by the Getúlio Vargas Foundation (FGV), through the Laboratory of Digital Humanities (LHuD) of the School of Social Sciences/CPDOC, and UNIRIO, through the Laboratory for Preservation and Management of Digital Collections (LABOGAD), with the support of FCRB's CMI. This international event was able to offer the visions of foreign researchers, which helps in the discussion between our researchers and professionals in the field.

The event was divided into eight research tracks: Contemporary Thought and the Digital World; Technology, Culture, Politics, and Society; Representation of Knowledge, Semantics, and Open Data; Large Collections of Textual Data in the Digital Humanities; Digital Arts and Expressions; Visualization, Sonification, and Analysis of Networks; Digital Humanities and Brazilian Reality; and Digital Collections and Social Memory. Ana Lígia Medeiros (CMI/ Fundação Casa de Rui Barbosa [Casa de Rui Barbosa Foundation]), Aquiles Alencar Brayner (British Library), and Jair Martins de Miranda (LABOGAD/CCH/UNIRIO) coordinated the last track.

As an example of the diversity of projects, I mention the experience of the Research Group for Digital Humanities at USP, created in 2009. Its webpage brings together some works that can illustrate very well the types of projects and works developed by Brazilian institutions and researchers related to DH. They are:

- They Are Now Swearing at My Skin (M.A.P., https://humanidadesdigitais.org/projetos-atuais/recursos/): This includes writings of and on women in Portuguese America. The digital catalogue of the M.A.P. is still a work in progress, started in October 2017. The base document was built in XML, and the first forms of visualization are already available: a geo-referenced catalogue, complete records, and simple lists (table access). The object was to construct a digital catalogue of written documents by and about women in Portuguese America in the sixteenth, seventeenth, and eighteenth centuries, with the aim of coding and making visible for future research a set of scarce and immensely important sources for philological studies and studies on the history of language, social history, the history of writing and reading, and the history of women in Brazil.

- Caminhos do Romance (Universidade Estadual de Campinas, http://www.caminhosdoromance.iel.unicamp.br/): This is an interdisciplinary thematic project financed by FAPESP, developed through the collaboration of two professors in the area of literature (Márcia Abreu [IEL/UNICAMP] and Sandra Guardini T. Vasconcelos [FFLCH/USP]), two professors in the area of history (Nelson Schapochnik [FE/USP] and Luiz Carlos Villalta [FAFICH/UFMG]), and their supervisors. Taking as chronological starting points the middle of the eighteenth century and the end of the nineteenth century, the project investigates the process of implantation and consolidation of the Romanesque genre in Brazil by examining the novels in circulation, the reading practices they raise, and the spaces in which these practices took place.

In addition to USP's experience, it is worth mentioning other studies developed at the State University of Campinas (UNICAMP) and Federal University of Bahia (UFBA):

- Transatlantic Movement of the Press (http://www.circulacaodosimpressos.iel.unicamp.br/): The Globalization of Culture in the Nineteenth Century (State University of Campinas): The project promotes familiarization with the press and the ideas circulating among England, France, Portugal, and Brazil in the "long nineteenth century" (1789–1914). Its main objectives are to identify and analyze the cultural, political, and economic processes set in motion by the circulation of printed matter and ideas on a transnational scale, analyzing the appropriations of these ideas in the four countries.
- Portuguese Corpus of Tycho Brahe (UNICAMP, http://www.tycho.iel.unicamp.br/corpus/index.html): This is an annotated electronic corpus, composed of texts in Portuguese written by authors born between 1380 and 1881. Currently 76 texts (3,302,696 words) are available for free research, with a system of linguistic annotation in two stages: morphological annotation (applied to 45 texts, totaling 2,012,798 words) and syntactic annotation (applied to 27 texts, totaling 1,234,323 words).
- Digital Edition of the Pamphlets of Eulálio Motta (UFBA, http://www.eulaliomotta.uefs.br/): The digital edition of Eulálio Motta's

pamphlets is based on the concept of the hyper-edition, which, according to the American philologist Jerome McGann (1997), consists of hypermedia capable of including in the same environment conventional editions (critical, diplomatic, facsimile, etc.) integrated into various types of iconographic, filmographic, sound, and textual documents, with zoom, hypertext, and animation features.

- eDictor (https://humanidadesdigitais.org/edictor/): This is a tool for electronic philological editing (USP and UNICAMP), the fruit of years of research by linguists, philologists, and computer scientists. It is free software for philological editing and linguistic annotation.

These are examples of works and projects developed in DH in Brazil, and almost all are available through the Association of Digital Humanities (AHDig).[8]

It turns out that the projects approach different aspects of DH, since they include digital libraries, catalogues, editing software, memory, and culture. There are other projects, but these exemplify well the diversity of application of *HDs* in the country.

6. What is the current state of DH in Brazil? Comment on the challenges and the opportunities for DH in Brazil.

Brazil is in the development stage of several initiatives, manifesting in both theoretical and applied projects and work. This is noticeable in that the creation of laboratories, centers, or research groups is growing, which will stimulate discussion and the emergence of other projects.

The challenges are to obtain resources for the development of projects and the promotion of exchange of experiences.

7. Discuss the level of institutional support given to DH in Brazil.

Support is still institutional, not targeted by specific public policies. Initiatives are the fruit of the commitment of researchers who identified in DH an important area of research for promoting new knowledge.

8. How could conditions improve to spur further development of DH in Brazil?

Brazil is going through a difficult time, with cuts to resources in several areas of activity. Universities and research institutions are unable to implement new activities. The situation of laboratories is still very precarious in general, depending on the initiatives of researchers. This situation is reflected in the scarce resources applied to DH in terms of personnel, technology, and financial resources, preventing the full development of activities.

9. With the coming elections, do you foresee any impact on the field in Brazil?

Brazil faces one of the biggest financial and institutional crises of recent times, aggravated over the last three years. Conservative tendencies gain space in the House of Representatives and the Federal Senate. Education and educational institutions, especially public ones, suffer from precariousness.

In 2017 Law n.13.415 was passed, which establishes the reform of secondary education, stipulating that Portuguese, mathematics, physical education, arts, philosophy, sociology, and English become mandatory. In contrast, natural sciences and humanities and social sciences become optional.

In the field of higher education, the web page of the Federal Senate has a legislative proposal aimed at terminating humanities courses at public universities. It argues these "are cheap courses that can easily be covered by private universities; the measure is to focus on professional courses (medicine, law, engineering, and others). Humanities courses may be conducted face-to-face and at a distance at any other paid institution" (https://www12.senado.leg.br/ecidadania/visualizacaoideia?id=100201).

The proposal already has 7,241 signatures; upon reaching 20,000, it will be debated by senators.

While Brazil is engaged in dialogue on the subject of DH, at the same time, it must defend the humanities in all spheres. This is a battle that started before the elections and [it] is believed [it] will extend due to this institutional and financial crisis.

10. In terms of DH, how does Brazil compare to other countries in the Portuguese-speaking world?

There are no safe statistics that provide the number of laboratories, research centers, university programs, or even the number of researchers dedicated to the subject, both nationally and internationally.

In the case of Brazil, in particular, this situation is exacerbated, since the area is under development and the term DH has not yet been assimilated by many researchers. Research conducted through sources such as Google Scholar, the research directories of CNPq, the CAPES portal of periodicals, and SciELO (the Brazilian Scientific Electronic Library Online) results in quite divergent data.

In relation to Portuguese-speaking countries, Brazil leads, together with Portugal, in the creation of centers, laboratories, research groups, or initiatives, a statement confirmed in the work presented at HDRio 2018, entitled "Panorama of Digital Humanities: Use and Trends," prepared by FCRB/CMI. This article illustrates the distribution of initiatives in DH around the world, considering only those registered by some associations or aggregators specializing in the area.

According to the article, it is clear that, among Portuguese-speaking countries, Brazil appears in eight of these registered initiatives, while Portugal appears in four, although the geographical size of Brazil is greater than that of Portugal. In addition, we find a great deal of Portuguese production on DH, in contrast with Brazil, which is still growing in terms of bibliographic production. In many Portuguese universities it is already possible, on their websites, to find the expression DH.

It should be noted that the intellectual production of researchers through articles, papers, and theses, among other [things], faces a series of language barriers, which reduces the wide dissemination of the international dimension.

The AHDig (2018), which stands out, is defined as a "network of researchers united by the Portuguese language and by the inclusion of the digital perspective in their research horizons" (https://ahdig.wordpress.com/associacao-das-humanidades-digitais/).

Despite work on several initiatives, such as the use of digital repositories, for example, it is evident that Brazilian institutions (universities) still do not address the use of these technologies or platforms as DH.

11. Name some appealing work in DH in other Latin American nations.

- Red de Humanidades Digitales de México: It promotes and strengthens the relationship in the digital humanities field, with emphasis on research and education in Latin America;
- Red Colombiana de Humanidades Digitales: The network does not belong to a specific institution, yet it aims to disseminate a thematic catalogue of tools, platforms, and software in digital humanities. All work is supported by members and proposed by them.

I would also like to mention the work of Gimena Del Río Riande, in Argentina.

12. What is your view of DH in the anglophone world?

Work presented at the event HDRio 2018, quoted in the [answer to the] previous question, can answer this question well. Based on a study by the Digital Humanities Research Group at USP, it is evident that in 2011 there were 114 initiatives (centers) in DH in the world, in 24 countries, of which the US and Canada have more initiatives among the English-speaking countries: 44 and 11, respectively. The article updated these figures based on aggregators of initiatives in DH; it was soon clear that, by 2017, the total number had increased to 176 initiatives in 34 countries. It then became evident that the US and Canada continue with more initiatives among English-speaking countries, with 63 and 18, respectively.

This may represent a major advance in DH discussions over the rest of the world, with more consistency and diversity of DH applications, and a greater view of integration between different areas of knowledge and the use of technologies.

13. How could the relationship between Brazilian DH and US DH evolve and improve?

At the moment, FCRB still does not have a formal relationship with US institutions, although it is essential for the growth and strengthening of the DH area to know and follow the experience of the United States.

14. How is the renegotiation of trade treaties and/or the evolution of the economy likely to affect the development of the field in Brazil?

We are in a moment of political and economic uncertainty that, hopefully, will be defined after the inauguration of a [new] presidency in January 2019. The candidates' proposals are not clear; in fact, we do not yet have a definitive list of candidates. We know that we will have candidates from the left, center, and right, but none is in a position [that guarantees victory]. The situation is still unpredictable.

15. How do you envision the future of digital humanities in Brazil?

There is a visible effort [on the part] of researchers to strengthen DH in Brazil, demonstrated by the creation of laboratories and research groups. However, due to the political situation and lack of resources, it is difficult to consolidate these efforts.

On the other hand, we hope there will be no global setbacks in the processes of strengthening an open access policy and in maintaining the democratization of the internet, focused on the communication of culture and science, not only for researchers but also for society as a whole.

Last but not least, it is essential to strengthen the field of DH through publications, seminars, and other activities that enable the wide exchange of experiences developed at national and international levels.

Notes

1. For more information, please see: http://rubi.casaruibarbosa.gov.br/.

2. For more information, please see: http://memoriaeinformacao.casaruibarbosa.gov.br/index.php/fcrb.

3. For more information, please see: http://centromemoriainformacao.blogspot.com/.

4. For more information, please see: https://www.escavador.com/sobre/1507422/aquiles-ratti-alencar-brayner.

5. For more information, see: http://www.memoriaesociedade.ibict.br/pesquisadores/ricardo-medeiros-pimenta/

6. For more information, please see: www.brasiliana.usp.br.

7. For more information, please see: http://eventos.fgv.br/hdri02018.

8. The main objective is to strengthen initiatives in digital humanities already active in the universe of Portuguese speakers and to promote new initiatives in this field among them (AHDig 2018).

15

On DH in Mexico

An Interview with Isabel Galina Russell

HÉCTOR FERNÁNDEZ L'HOESTE AND JUAN CARLOS RODRÍGUEZ

1. Tell me how you made it to digital humanities.

Well . . . I had been working with digital resources. Here at UNAM (the National Autonomous University of Mexico)—and, in particular, I was always attracted to the type of material, the publications, which had little in common with what one could find in printed form. That is, databases and things of the kind. And coming from humanities, because my field is literature, well, when I traveled for the doctorate, I wanted to work with digital resources, particularly with less-formal publications in the humanities. I studied library and information studies, for the doctorate, and I attended University College London; about two years after I graduated, the UCL Centre for Digital Humanities was opened. Claire Warwick was my supervisor and I also had the pleasure of meeting Melissa Terras. And they are the ones who introduced me to the term "digital humanities."

2. And as a digital humanities professional, since I imagine you started there, how do you manage at UNAM? How do you see yourself, and what is your role within the institution?

When I returned, I started as a researcher at the Institute for Bibliographic Research (Instituto de Investigaciones Bibliográficas), and one of my first research projects was on digital resources for the humanities. We had four workshops and we gathered people who were in the humanities and who had been working on some digital projects in a very wide sense. And there, I was already working with someone called Ernesto Priani, who also already had contact with digital humanities because he had been on sabbatical at Brown University, and the idea of digital humanities came from this contact with a lot of other people. And these four workshops were the seed for the formation of the digital humanities network (Red de Humanidades Digitales).

3. And within UNAM's structure, what is it you do here?

I do research, my position is as researcher in the Institute of Bibliographic Research. Then, my first research project was on digital resources for humanities and I'm now working on digital bibliographic heritage and digital preservation, because the Institute of Bibliographic Research is in charge of the National Library of Mexico (Biblioteca Nacional de México). My research subject is related to identifying which are the publications that must belong to our bibliographic patrimony and [that] are currently missing. I have focused the most on digital resources that are being produced in the digital humanities. They are materials in which there is a production of knowledge that does not go through formal channels or traditional means of publication, whether that may be called [an] editorial department, etc., and that, regardless, are valuable, they've received funding, they involve a knowledge that must be preserved.

4. So you must be identifying what must be digitized.

We do not digitize, we work with the digital projects that are being created. And thinking what the National Library can do to collect publications of this kind that are beyond the traditional scope of what is collected.

5. And is there some digitization of elements that are not digital? Digitization of material that has been published in a more traditional manner.

Yes, yes, many. I identify the projects that are available; some involve digitization. Some others create the material and it is born digitally. Then it's a matter of identifying both kinds of origins and how they can be included in the collection.

6. If you had to suggest a very brief version of the birth of digital humanities in Mexico and of its pioneers in the field, how would it be?

I think we're still identifying and building that history. It's very clear that people have been working on digital humanities for a long time, but it wasn't necessarily called digital humanities. The parallel that I find is with open access, where it turns out open access in Latin America has existed for a very long time, it's just that we didn't call it open access. There is probably much more work in DH in Mexico than what we have identified so far, but under other names. Some of the pioneering studies that we've encountered are the corpus of the dictionary of Mexican Spanish and the work done by the Colegio de México with computational linguistics. Those have been some of the projects we've managed to identify, but that is still a pending task. In itself, as digital humanities, with that name and conceived as such, in 2011, with the formation of the Red de Humanidades Digitales and those workshops that I told you about . . . but that is already with the label "digital humanities," but that does not mean there hasn't been earlier work.

7. Are you working on open access in general? I mean, are you related most of all to open access efforts? I am simply asking because of the following: first, the other day I met Luis Gantus. Do you know him? He's someone who moves really well within Mexican comics circles and organizes a conference called Conque in Querétaro. He mentioned he has a good collection; that, in fact, Sixto Valencia, the cartoonist for *Memín Pinguín*, had somehow asked him, before passing away, about what could be done with his collection. So Gantus has a collection. It's a story that hasn't been told. It has been published, written, but there isn't a place. Right? And, in that sense, there is a gap within what is the collection of certain [kinds of] Mexican cultural production. There's a second example: there's a magazine, you must know it, *Chamuco*, which does political satire with comics. And they publish, but in printed form, but it's obvious they're very advanced in the transition to doing things digitally. What they sell is all digital, so, in that sense, within the frame of more private efforts, my question is whether someone in the Mexican academic scene is documenting or collecting that part of cultural production.

There have been efforts to work with private collections, collections from companies, absolutely. I'm thinking that, for example, we worked with *El*

Universal, the newspaper. They've been wanting to rescue their historic collection for a long time—projects, for example with ICA (a civil engineering company) and its photographic collection. Those are some of the digitalization projects that I know of. And, talking about comics, now that I think about it, the National Library (of Mexico) has one called http:// pepines.unam.mx that is very difficult to find but which exists, which perhaps may interest you.

8. Thanks for the info. Well, we went onto a side topic, but then again, in terms of origins, what would you say about what you mentioned, or are there concrete names?

Luis Fernando Lara, of the Colegio de México, who worked on computational linguistics. He was the keynote speaker during the second congress of digital humanists we celebrated in 2016. These were the people from Colegio de México: Luis Fernando Lara, María Isabel García Hidalgo, and Roberto Ham Chande. I believe they were the pioneering linguists in the use of computational methods. There must be others.

9. How would you define the current moment of digital humanities in Mexico and its challenges and opportunities?

I think that, right now, we're in a very effervescent moment for digital humanities in Mexico. I think it is important that the digital humanities conference will be in Mexico. For the first time, it won't be celebrated in a European country, Canada, the US, or the Australian setting. Then, I think there is a lot of interest for what is being done. That is, we're on the map, which I think is very important. Um, challenges . . . I think one of the biggest challenges is to make sure that we define our own agenda and not have it defined by others.

And above all, [it is important] that we manage our relationship with the digital humanities of other parts of the world as a matter of collaboration and not of dependence or imitation. Another challenge is that digital humanities suffer a bit of a problem in terms of self-identification, here and elsewhere.

10. You mean a problem with the definition of the field.

For us in Mexico, it's not just about how we situate ourselves, but also our context. Another thing that I think is very important is the work that we may be doing looking toward the Global South. I believe that we're making a lot of progress in everything else.

11. I'm going to propose an idea and you do whatever you wish with it, right?

Sure.

12. In the US, whenever there's a new field, criticism and concern has to do with inclusion in terms of ethnicity and race. In Latin America, we go for class, because we have a society that is more founded on social prejudice, right? So if I were to ask you about racial prejudice, it would be an imposition. Nonetheless, that is what matters to lots of people in the Anglo world. How would you contextualize what can be done in terms of development of digital humanities in Latin America dealing with the issue of racial prejudice, in a way such that there could be a dialogue with the criticism of exclusion in terms of identity in the Anglo world? In other words, to make it plain, the big worry of Latin Americans and Latinxs in the US is that it is developing as an eminently Anglo discipline and with an exclusive discourse. That's why ethnicity. But in Latin America, that may not apply, although there is racism, right? But the primary source of exclusion is class. What do you suggest?

OK. It's not an easy question.

It is clear to me that the digital humanities—as we are dealing with them—have been developing principally in academic institutions where, well, there's already a certain privileged situation. What we have tried to do—and I think there is an important connection that identifies us, which I believe is what makes digital humanities in Latin America special—are two things. First, many interesting digital projects that are being developed, and really change things and have an impact, are digital projects in, for instance, Mexican indigenous communities. Unfortunately, what we haven't yet managed is to identify and establish those collaborations that I believe could be very good. We have worked a bit with the people from the Wikipedia Foundation, as they're very involved with those types of things. We have also worked with anthropological studies. One of the keynote speakers for DH 2018 is someone who has worked on an application for the learning of the Zapotec language, for example, right? Then, it's a matter of trying to connect with this work. This is a field in which there is still much to explore. Another important topic is the connection between digital humanities and hacktivism, citizens' laboratories, etc., which has to do with the critical use of technologies, people who are questioning not only what are people using Facebook for or what are people using Twitter for or these types of studies, right? But also, let's see, what does it mean to us, culturally, that our relationships are going through Facebook or Twitter or through—right?—some other technologies that are not developed in our culture.

This is a topic that is among those that could be included in the digital humanities. I know colleagues who are working on it. For example, Paola Ricaurte from the TEC of Monterrey is one of the people working on it along the lines of media studies, right? It would also be interesting [to contemplate] what is being done in Latin American studies. But much of this work that is being developed is not under the umbrella of digital humanities, neither should it be—right?—if they do not wish, but what is interesting is that we could establish a dialogue.

13. The intersection. . . .

In one of the meetings that we had as digital humanists there was a presentation by a person whose name I haven't been able to find that I thought was extremely interesting because she was talking exactly about the fact that we're using platforms that were developed in other contexts, so it's very cool to say she/he uses Omeka or uses the timeline this or that, it's only that we have to include in our results a reflection about what this mediation means. That seems to me like a very interesting topic that I hope, right, is still being developed.

14. How would you define the degree of institutional support?

Varied, yes . . . I wrote an article about that, about the evaluation of digital resources for the humanities, where we did some research on the topic (http://revistas.uned.es/index.php/signa/article/view/16909).

What we found out was that basically, on one hand, there was a lack of recognition for the value when you work on or produce digital scholarship, when your academic products are not a book or a printed journal. If it's not something traditional, then the problem is the value given to this kind of products.

15. Lettered prejudice, that is, not in the most traditional way.

Yes, and also, we identify it as a problem, yes, on one hand as prejudice, but also in other cases in which the evaluation committees do have the tools. That is, even if they did not share prejudice, even if they were quite open, they still lack the tools to be able to evaluate. So that made us develop a guide for the evaluation of digital resources in the humanities, that's how we've tried to promote some change.

16. Do you have it online?

Yes, it's online. On the page of HumanidadesDigitales.net (http://humanidadesdigitales.net/evaluacion/). We've been trying to promote it so that it is in some way useful. It is available in both Spanish and English.

17. In some way standardize [it] so everyone is. . . . The field levels off a bit, at the very least, I imagine, in terms of evaluation.

Or that the committee may say we were given this, how can we evaluate it? Well, here you have a first tool that may help. This, on one hand, and on the other, the lack of recognition. In the digital humanities, however, we do not have many problems in terms of funding, especially compared with whether you study classic Mayan or some of those other disciplines. . . .

18. So, there's funding everywhere?

Yes, not like in the US, the amount of funding is still more modest, but it's relatively easy to find any type of support even if it's little. Um . . . [laughs].

19. How do you think the conditions sponsoring the development of digital humanities in Mexico could be improved?

Then, well, I was saying. . . . Funding, there's funding available. They're not the amounts common in other countries. Here at UNAM, for example, the PAPIIT projects, which are forms of funding that have been very common for a very long time, appreciate digital products. There is also something called PAPROTUL, which is exactly for digitization. They are funds to digitize, and then CONACyT (National Council of Science and Technology), lately, for example, has been issuing a call for three years for the development of repositories. This funding is pretty good, like a million pesos; at most, a million pesos. It's big funding.

20. So CONACyT on one hand, but the other two are from UNAM.

From UNAM.

21. So, UNAM has one called . . . PAPIIT?

PAPIIT, which is the Program for the Support of Research Projects and Technological Innovation. So they're—generally, what I've seen—well, I don't know, but intuitively—that they've been, they've funded digitization projects, websites, databases, online catalogues, um, e-books. PAPIIT belongs to DGAPA, which is the Dirección General de Apoyo (General Directorate of Support). . . . They award funding. . . . Ah, there are PAPIITs and PAPINes. Here, as well as in other countries, the digital humanities are very attractive to administrators, right? Because they're modern, because they have money. . . .

22. Because they have money.

And because there's something concrete.

23. There's a visible result, right? Administrators love that.

But the problem is a bit that then you have all this funding, but then the degree of recognition for your career, the evaluation formats, etc., etc.

24. So in terms of professional development in your career, will you find obstacles in terms of recognition of your efforts? That is, I mention [it] simply because UNAM is a global school, so, in this sense I imagine that, when you go through tenure, if you develop something, it's less tangible for people with a traditional perspective. So I ask myself, have there been cases of this nature?

Yes. In my case, I haven't had any problems, because I've also made sure to publish articles and chapters because I know that. . . . In other words, it's a bit. . . . Those are the rules. . . . It's a lot of work. That is, you end up working more, right?

25. So you're compensating for the system's deficiencies.

Yes, yes. Another obstacle that I see, at least at UNAM, is that we have different job positions, the creation of "figures"—for example, we have research positions, we have academic technician positions, and we have professor positions. I'm a researcher. I have a research position. Ernesto

Priani, the other person with whom I work a lot, has a professor's position. But then the type of people that we need to work on projects of this type. . . . For example, we need to work with programmers. The role of academic technician is much more associated with people who provide some kind of service, right? So, service . . . to work in the Computer Science Department. Then, to try to develop these networks for, like, collaboration has not been easy. It's already hard when, institutionally, the idea is that academic technicians serve in research teams as support for research.

26. Do you code?

No. I know enough about coding to ask someone to please do it for me [laughs].

27. It's just curiosity. I don't agree with such a definition; it seems very narrow. Well, my bachelor's is in electrical engineering.

I see. . . .

28. And I ended being a cultural studies scholar, so. . . .

Then, this, this, actually . . . I believe that these figures that allow us, like, to form more flexible groups for collaboration, very characteristic of digital humanities projects. . . . Everything is an obstacle.

29. Do the coming elections in Mexico have any impact on your field?

Well, perhaps in matters of digital strategy at the Department of Culture of . . . here in Mexico (Secretaría de Cultura). There is an office that I think is called Digital Agenda, and the head is a person who is a fellow digital humanist. He's one of the few people with a master's in digital humanities in Mexico. Well, I'd like to think that, independently from who will be the next president, nothing will change for this kind of initiatives.

30. So the field is a little shielded from political instability, right?

I hope. . . .

31. Because there are positions that do change, right?

Yes, yes, but I think it's very important. My connection with digital humanities is focused on patrimony, right? Cultural patrimony, bibliographic patrimony, etc. Then, that the Department of Culture is thinking and has a digital office and that a digital humanist is handling it seems like, like a very important topic. We talked about companies, universities, but we haven't talked about government. And I think government is important in this, like, setup.

32. Yes, that's precisely why I ask you this question. I know that, in [the] Mexican context, the state is everywhere. Uh, how do you compare the current status of the field in Mexico with that of other Latin American nations? Do you think you're ahead, leading, or about the same?

Well, Mexico has managed, through these international contacts that we have, to enjoy a very important visibility within the international community, which is basically [the ADHO] (Alliance of Digital Humanities Organizations), but I don't know whether that means that we have done more, that we're more advanced than others, right? I believe that the others are like a bit along the same process as we are, which is to see who are—let's not say digital humanities started in 2011, we're going to try to see what has been done, right, that is not called digital humanities and that will also help us to try to see how is it that we will understand digital humanities.

33. So for you, it's mostly a matter of visibility?

Right now, yes. Ah, I forgot to tell you, one of the terms that we're sure that there must be many of, where we can find digital humanities, is in ICTs, which are very common in Mexico—information and communication technologies, right? So, ICT has been the term and it's very related to teaching, pedagogy, and distance learning. . . . None of these fields are currently represented in our DH network. . . . These are the kinds of people that we've have to continue identifying, but they are not necessarily [in the] digital humanities. I don't know whether they see themselves as part of DH.

34. Governments have given ICTs money, sure, because, for a politician, what we said before, it looks good, right?

Yes, at UNAM, there has been much talk about ICTs. And we—I then did want to go a lot more over the term "digital humanities" to avoid confusion with ICTs.

35. Tell me about your connections with DH networks in Latin America.

In Colombia, there is the Red Colombiana de Humanidades Digitales. Stefania Gallini from the National University (Universidad Nacional de Colombia) and Omar Rincón from the Universidad de los Andes. The latter offers a digital humanities MA program. And the excellent work being done at the National Library of Colombia. They are a very solid group.

Gimena del Río is the contact at the Asociación Argentina de Humanidades Digitales. They just published the call for their congress, which will be in November of this year [2018], in Rosario. And us in June, when DH2018 takes place in Mexico City, we will have a meeting of the Latin American associations of digital humanities.

Our first contact with Brazil was with somebody called Maria Clara Paixão de Sousa, with whom we even have an article: "Las humanidades digitales en español y portugués en el Anuario Americanista Europeo" [see http://e-spacio.uned.es/fez/eserv/bibliuned:352-Egonzalez20/Gonzalez_Blanco_Elena_humanidades_digit.pdf]. It is about the emergence of digital humanities in Ibero-America. In April, there was a congress on digital humanities in Brazil.

36. Was the language difference a challenge?

Aside from collaboration with Maria Clara, we worked with Daniel Alves from Portugal on that very article. I think it's possible to overcome language barriers with a little extra effort.

37. What's your vision of digital humanities in the anglophone word? That is, as a Latin American, as Mexican.

Well, I like it a lot when I go to conferences and things of that kind; I think it's a very interesting community. It is an open community, I think. That is, the kind of discussions about inclusiveness that are being held I haven't seen in other communities.

38. The controversy?

Aha, the controversy, and it's very good that people talk about these things. What I do sometimes feel is that there are some really big projects, very visible, but also that there are many smaller projects that are not so big. I think there are four, five, ten very big projects, but all the remaining projects also share not such huge aspirations like some of the ones we develop here in Mexico. What there really is in the US or Europe is an institutionalization of digital humanities that we do not have. That is, there are many centers of digital humanities. Only recently the first master's program in digital humanities started here in Mexico.

39. With UNAM?

No, at the Universidad del Claustro de Sor Juana, very close with communication, the School of Communication.

40. How could the relationship in digital humanities evolve and improve between Mexican DH and US DH? And, with the NAFTA renegotiation, how could it affect digital humanities?

Well, there's a language factor that is very important. Then, it is very clear to me that there is very strong research in Latin American studies or Hispanic studies, where I believe there is a connection point that may be interesting. We, for example, have the National Digital Newspaper Library of Mexico, and there have been some contacts with the research on newspapers from over there, with the newspapers from over here, projects that I think are very valuable, like the one of First Books (Primeros Libros), where it's also about re-creating collections that are dispersed because many of the materials remain in libraries at universities in the US. Then the process of digitalization and work on digital editions of this type of material seems to me a natural and feasible point to start collaboration of this nature.

41. Don't you think that. . . . Well, sometimes linguistic prejudice affects a lot the relationship between the US and Latin America, and particularly at this moment with what is happening in Mexico. There is acute ignorance about Mexico, right? Doesn't it ever affect you?

In my case, for example—I could only answer for me—not particularly. But it does have important consequences for many. Now, in general, the type of relationship that we have is with people who are in universities so then, maybe also. . . . Then, I'm also bilingual, so I believe that also helps. That is something that sometimes does limit a lot the field of digital humanities here in Mexico—the ones who do not speak English, well, they may not participate or [may] feel excluded from some networks. Because the discourse is in English, right?

Not long ago I was interviewed on digital humanities and language when this topic came up. We, for example, who are now organizing the [upcoming] Digital Humanities conference, have decided to make it bilingual. It's twice the work; it's . . . it's a lot of work. And, for example, right now we're in an international project; there's Finland, Germany, England, the Netherlands, [and] the US, among other countries that are participating. It's a great project. But for example, we decided to write blog posts; each country has to put out a description of the data they'll be using for this newspaper collection. They're digitized newspapers from the nineteenth century, and then everyone said, well, then it's published in English, right? And also in the language of the country—but then suddenly we've thought, well, we have to do it in English and Spanish, and those who only speak English only have to do it in English, right? Then, no, there isn't even a consciousness that, that we, if we want things to be in Spanish, it's our obligation that that happens, right, and to get the resources and other things to attain this bilingualism. So, the. . . .

42. [It's] part of the risk of translation, right? Which proposes an interpretation of whatever is being digitized. So it's much more preferable that you do it instead of someone from elsewhere, but there's always a mediation.

Yes, but the onerous part of translation, of multilingualism, is on those of us who speak two languages, it isn't on those who speak only one, especially when that one is English.

Now, I know that applies to all around the world, etc., etc., and especially, when you're thinking about digital humanities projects where many times you'll have sources from different languages, it's a topic that is very important unlike, for example, in physics or mathematics, where most likely the original material—you don't have the creative part of the material that will be in two languages. They also have their problems, but I think in digital humanities it's a topic that is key.

43. That deals a bit with ethnocentrism in [the] sciences and that affects digital humanities as well as any other field. But the part of NAFTA, no. . . .

The NAFTA thing, um, in truth it doesn't. . . . That is, it will have an impact in our lives in general, yes; on digital humanities in particular, I don't know. It struck me that the other day we held a meeting on projects funded by CONACyT and related to the European Union and, basically, all the projects had to do with the sciences except the two Digging into Data projects. . . . Anyway, several people mentioned that one of the great problems they had with completing the research projects was importing material and equipment. Issues related to customs—they went on saying, it's that we have, let's say, 24 months for the research project, and even though we receive the funds quickly, then the importing of tools takes eight months because they're stuck in customs, because they won't allow us, because etc., etc. So then I started thinking that, for instance, in digital humanities, once we start needing supplies for our equipment, we're going to start facing problems of this nature, because right now the only thing that we export and import are data, digital data. So, since we just send that, nothing happens. . . .

44. Nothing happens, but when things turn demanding in terms of equipment, then you will be affected.

Then I think it will affect us. That could happen. . . .

Afternote

From the 26th to the 29th of June of 2018, the annual Digital Humanities conference was held in Mexico City. I (Isabel Galina Russell) was the local organizing committee cochair. We had over 600 participants. Among the most notable issues for us was the fact that there were many more presentations in Spanish and from Mexicans than at other conferences, which makes sense, as the conference was held in Mexico. We think that this was a great opportunity for Mexican DHers to network, but also to showcase the work being done here. Many attendees got into the spirit of embracing bilingualism, trying to translate their slides, or say a few words in Spanish or even attend talks held in Spanish. The opening keynote speaker was Janet Chávez, an indigenous language activist from Oaxaca, Mexico, and her talk was extremely well received and, I think, opened up new worlds for many in the audience. Finally, we had a meeting of Latin American DH, and I am hoping this will turn out to be a landmark meeting as we move forward to find new ways to work and collaborate.

Coda

HÉCTOR FERNÁNDEZ L'HOESTE AND JUAN CARLOS RODRÍGUEZ

This book has involved revaluing several elements of the relationship between the digital humanities, a field that has emerged in English-speaking academe under an occasionally provincial scope promoted by monolingualism and androcentrism (in that order), and the Latinx American world, a transcontinental swath of land and people that admittedly comprises many contradictions and injustices when it comes to interweaving technology and social well-being. The fact that, since November 2016, the US has suffered from an extreme case of political dysfunction as well as mounting geopolitical isolationism does not bode well for an academy that, preferentially in cases of high visibility, tends to sustain a more enhanced international perspective within learned circles and transnationally interested contexts, drawing a sharp contrast with the widespread belief in the dogma of exceptionalism. Here, we speak as cognizant bearers of our privileged status as Latin/o American academics in the US, which is what brought us in the first place to conceive of a volume that would try to build bridges between US academe and a Latinx American reckoning of the practice of digital studies. But this is our caveat: We must acknowledge that, just as we were trying to strengthen these ties and watch carefully that we did not end up replicating the habitual power discrepancy implicit in US/Latinx American interaction, the ground beneath our feet shifted wildly. Since the last presidential election, many things have happened that we thought would never fly as normal north of the border, much to our chagrin as US citizens and immigrants. To claim things have gone topsy-turvy is an understatement. Social media has a lot to do with this development. Thus, we have focused more on laying a theoretical conduit for Latinxs and Latin Americans, while the English-speaking part of the academy makes peace and figures out how to deal with the new political and cultural order, which impacts the understanding and application of technology both within and beyond higher education.

Given the worrisome level of social disparity, access to technology ranks as one of the most defiant challenges of an uneven Latinx American modernity. People across the Americas are incredibly resourceful in their adoption of technology, yet this does not negate the fact that this part of the hemisphere lags behind considerably in terms of its use of technology as a tool for social egalitarianism. As long as technology is managed the way it has been thus far, controlled by a few brand names that have brought the US to a new age of robber barons amid the early twenty-first century—and countries across the globe, in Europe and Asia, emulate this model—its use as a tool for the lessening of differences between the metropolis and the periphery will remain beneath its sizeable potential. The current controversy surrounding emerging 5G technology and Chinese brands ZTE and Huawei only hints at the geopolitical implications of this challenge. Russia's use of social media during the last US presidential election is another indication. Whether Latinx America will heed warnings of this nature remains to be seen. For the time being, the outlook is not promising, given the fierce economic incentive to embrace less-expensive brands of telephony, computer equipment, and internet service, with very short-term interests in mind and scant consideration for the long term. Nonetheless, the texts included in this collection also suggest the speed with which technology is playing a preeminent role in cultural, political, and social relations, be it north or south of the border. And this is precisely where unpredictability cuts both ways. Just as technology serves to fortify dependence, it also may contribute to its rebuke.

Academics like Valdivia and Venegas may not define themselves exclusively—or even tangentially—as digital humanists, but it is undeniable that their work has a strong bearing on the field. Along the same lines, work by scholars like Ames, Arriaga, Chan, and Lozano, more committed to the field, alludes to complexities implicit in the role of technology at the inter and intra-national level. Case studies like Valecce's or Alonso's, more convergent and incidental but nevertheless highly relevant, offer greater introspection within the confines of national constructs and technologi-cal appropriation. In contrast, when it comes to assessing the potential of technology for the promotion of political equity, Pardo Lazo and Domín-guez come across as more jaded practitioners, hardened by experience. Also, the fact that all three interviewees describing the circumstances of digital humanities in Latin American enclaves are women is not coinci-dental. In Latin America and the Caribbean, just as in the US and Eu-rope, women are attending academic institutions at a higher rate than men (Ferreyra et al. 2017, 53). In this sense, contact with science at the higher education level tends to reinforce exposure to technology. It may be what comes afterward—the top-down, verticalized structures of ac-cess to power, the overwhelmingly patriarchal structure of the corporate and public sector worlds—that prevents both the enshrinement of this long yearned-for achievement and its corresponding structural corollar-ies. Still, we hope these texts, as well as ours, contribute to an enhanced portrayal of the ways in which the relationship with technology is being assessed by academics in the humanities and social sciences.

We harbor no quarrel with prevailing agendas or voices in the digital humanities, not even with its enduring penchant for definition—which we hope continues to evolve along the customary principles of flexibility, respect, and tolerance of others. We have certainly benefitted from much of the research and enjoyed the controversies, especially when they have bordered on disciplinary soul-searching. Yet, as Latinx American scholars interested in the promotion of cultural criticism and diversity within the field, we claim the right to nourish and intervene in its practices (and to serve as a vessel for others to communicate their accomplishments and concerns), to establish a space where those of us who relate well to a cul-tural tradition based on the practice of another language can approach and engage digital studies on more equitable terms. Along the very same lines, we do not profess ruling knowledge of the field or pontificate in terms of research. Our interest is merely to advance the consideration of Latinx American digital studies as a viable, discerning academic field and to promote its practice among scholars on both sides of the border. As well, we wish to contribute to a greater dialogue between scholarly worlds in Portuguese and Spanish and academic spheres in the Anglo do-main, which, like it or not, exhibit a remarkable propensity to reproduce hegemonic inclinations (both in the US and the UK), having excelled at conjugating technology and humanities thanks to a greater availability of resources. In addition, we would rather simultaneously advance our own, alternate research agendas, which at times cross the boundaries of Latinx American digital studies. In our view, given their transformational, pragmatic nature, digital humanities perform better as a critical means, rather than as ultimate research destination or exclusive academic object to be studied, produced, or reproduced. One can only fathom what could emerge from a sustained study of the impact of technology on the quality of education in Latin America and the Caribbean; or, for that matter, from detailed research on the way(s) technology has been employed to improve the standard of living and the level of human development of Spanish- and Portuguese-speaking communities both north and south of the border. What does it mean to work in digital humanities and/or digital Latinx American studies in an age of election hacking and digital whistleblowers? In this way, we surmise, it would be possible to focus more on technology in the service of disenfranchised populations rather than just as a tool for the enrichment of privileged sectors within the academy, in which utilitarian application regularly surpasses human interests by way of neoliberal prerogatives, sometimes leading to eccentricity and the mere corroboration of normative capitalism. In other words, as suggested by the volume's introduction—paraphrasing lightly García Canclini's master *oeuvre*—and following a very Latinx American temperament toward the function of technology in the enactment and understanding of modernity, we pursue the right to come in and out of digital humanities, lest we end up, as stated previously, becoming more digital than human. In and out of digital humanities could serve as a motto for the constant reexamination of the multiple intersectionalities of the digital and the humanities as materialized by the strategic and contingent endeavors of the different communities emerging from its call. We hope this volume will do justice to our efforts.

Works Cited

14ymedio.com (blog). n.d. http://www.14ymedio.com/blogs/generacion_y/

AAP staff. 2015. "AAP Health Initiatives: Media and Children Communication Toolkit." American Academy of Pediatrics. https://www.aap.org/en-us/advocacy-and-policy/aap-health-initiatives/pages/media-and-children.aspx.

ABC Color staff. 2008. "El proyecto 'Una Laptop Por Niño' comenzará a Funcionar En Paraguay." ABC Digital, September 25, 2008, 25–27.

Abelenda, Ruben. 2015. "El lenguaje de EEUU y la derecha internacional para confundir a los pueblos." *Cubadebate*. Available at http://www.cubadebate.cu/opinion/2015/11/16/el-lenguaje-de-eeuu-y-la-derecha-internacional-para-confundir-a-los-pueblos/#.XI16qyhKjIU.

Achter, Paul. 2008. "Comedy in Unfunny Times: News Parody and Carnival After 9/11." *Critical Studies in Media Communication* 25, no. 3: 274–303. doi: 10.1080/15295030802192038.

AfroCROWD. Accessed May 12, 2015. http://www.afrocrowd.org/

Ahmed, Sara. 2004. *The Cultural Politics of Emotion*. New York: Routledge.

Alsema, Adriaan. 2015. "Colombia received 12% more foreign Visitors in 2014: Govt." *Colombia Reports*. Feb. 18. Available at http://colombiareports.co/colombia-received-12-foreign-visitors-2014-govt/.

Alvarado Godoy, Percy Francisco. 2014. "La desvergüenza de un mercenario," June 19, 2014. Accessed on March 2, 2019. Available at http://percy-francisco.blogspot.com/2014/06/la-desverguenza-de-un-mercenario.html.

Ames, Morgan G. 2010. "Unpublished fieldwork notes." June–December 2010.

———. 2014. "Translating Magic: The Charisma of One Laptop per Child's XO Laptop in Paraguay." In *Beyond Imported Magic: Essays on Science, Technology, and Society in Latin America*, edited by Eden Medina, Ivan da Costa Marques, and Christina Holmes, 207–224. Cambridge, MA: MIT Press.

———. 2015. "Charismatic Technology." Proceedings of the 5th Decennial AARHUS Conference, 109–20. https://doi.org/10.1080/19447014508661941.

Ames, Morgan G., Janet Go, Joseph "Jofish" Kaye, and Mirjana Spasojevic. 2011. "Understanding Technology Choices and Values through Social Class." Proceedings of CSCW 2011, ACM Conference on Computer-Supported Cooperative Work and Social Computing. ACM Press, 55–64.

Ames, Morgan G., and Daniela K. Rosner. 2014. "From Drills to Laptops: Designing Modern Childhood Imaginaries." *Information, Communication & Society* 17, no. 3: 357–70. https://doi.org/10.1080/1369118X.2013.873067.

Ames, Morgan G, Daniela K. Rosner, and Ingrid Erickson. 2015. "Worship, Faith, and Evangelism: Religion as an Ideological Lens for Engineering Worlds." Proceedings of CSCW 2015, ACM Conference on Computer-Supported Cooperative Work and Social Computing. ACM Press, 69–81. https://doi.org/10.1145/2675133.2675282.

Ananny, Mike, and Niall Winters. 2007. "Designing for Development: Understanding One Laptop per Child in Its Historical Context." In *2007 International Conference on Information and Communication Technologies and Development: IEEE.* https://doi.org/10.1109/ICTD.2007.4937397.

Anderson, J. N. 2004. *A Can of Worms: Public Intransigence on the Public Airwaves.* Unpublished master's thesis, University of Wisconsin-Madison.

———. 2013. *Radio's Digital Dilemma: Broadcasting in the Twenty-First Century.* New York: Routledge.

———. 2016. "Illicit Transmissions: Engaging with the Study and Preservation of Pirate Radio." *Journal of Radio & Audio Media* 23, no. 2: 233–249.

———. 2017. "Right-Wing Pirates: Hateful but Rare." *DIYmedia.net*, August 28, available at https://www.diymedia.net/right-wing-pirates-hateful-but-rare/.

Anzaldúa, Gloria. 2007. *Borderlands/La Frontera: The New Mestiza.* 3rd ed. San Francisco: Aunt Lute Books.

Arquilla, John, and David Ronfeldt. 1999. *The Emergence of Noopolitik: Toward an American Information Strategy.* Santa Monica, CA: RAND.

Arthur, J., ed. 1996. *Morality and Moral Controversies.* 4th ed. New Jersey: Prentice Hall.

Asociación Jurídica Cubana (blog). n.d. https://ajudicuba.wordpress.com/

Avelar, Idelber. 2000. "Toward a Genealogy of Latin Americanism." *Dispositio/n* 22, no. 49: 121–133.

Bajak, Frank. 2012. "Peru's Ambitious Laptop Program Gets Mixed Grades." Associated Press. http://www.nbcnews.com/id/48057348/ns/technology_and_science-back_to_school/t/perus-ambitious-laptop-program-gets-mixed-grades/#.XWbvOuhKiM9.

Baker, Geoffrey. 2011. *Buena Vista in the Club: Rap, Reggaetón, and Revolution in Havana.* Durham/London: Duke University Press. Kindle Edition.

Bakhtin, Mikhail. 1984. *Rabelais and His World.* Bloomington: Indiana University Press.

Baldwin, Carliss Y., and Kim Clark. 2000. *Design Rules, Vol. 1: The Power of Modularity.* Cambridge, MA: MIT Press.

———. 2002. "The Option Value of Modularity in Design." Harvard NOM Working Paper No. 02-13; Harvard Business School Working Paper No. 02-078. Available at SSRN: http://ssrn.com/abstract=312404 or http://dx.doi.org/10.2139/ssrn.312404.

———. 2005. *Design Rules: Volume 1, The Power of Modularity.* Preface to the Chinese Edition. Cambridge, MA: MIT Press.

Barlow, Aaron. 2008. *Blogging America: The New Public Sphere.* Westport, CT: Praeger Publishers.

Barnouw, Eric. 1966–70. *A history of broadcasting in the United States.* 3 vols: *A Tower of Babel; The Golden Web; The Image Empire.* New York: Oxford University Press.

Barquero S., Marvin. 2017. "Ingreso de turistas de EE.UU. bajó este año en Costa Rica." *La Nación*. July 9. http://www.nacion.com/economia/indicadores/Ingreso-EE-UU-Costa-Rica_0_1645035492.html.

Barriendos, Joaquín. 2006. "MARCA PAIS/MéXICO. Único, diverso y más allá de la hospitalidad." https://studylib.es/doc/7930611/marca-pa%C3%ADs---m%C3%A9xico.-%C3%BAnico—diverso-y-m%C3%A1s-all%C3%A1-de-la-hosp.

Barron, B., K. Gomez, N. Pinkard, and C. K. Martin. 2014. *The Digital Youth Network: Cultivating Digital Media Citizenship in Urban Communities*. Cambridge, MA: MIT Press.

BBC. 2013. "Profile: Ecuador's Rafael Correa." *BBC News*, February 27, 2013. https://www.bbc.com/news/world-latin-america-11449110.

Beattie, Keith. 2008. *Documentary Display: Reviewing Nonfiction Film and Video*. London/New York: Wallflower Press.

Beltran, Cristina. 2014. "No Papers, No Fear: DREAM activism, New Social Media, and the Queering of Immigrant Rights." In *Contemporary Latina/o Media: Production, Circulation, Politics*, edited by Arlene Dávila and Yeidy Rivero, 245–266. New York: NYU Press, 2014.

Bender, Walter. 2007. "One Laptop Per Child: Revolutionizing How the World's Children Engage in Learning." https://techtv.mit.edu/videos/16206-one-laptop-per-child-revolutionizing-how-the-world-s-children-engage-in-learning.

Berry, David M. 2011. "The Computational Turn: Thinking about the Digital Humanities." *Culture Machine* 12: 1–22.

Bey, Hakim. 1991. *T.A.Z. The Temporary Autonomous Zone, Ontological Anarchy, Poetic Terrorism*. Brooklyn, NY: Autonomedia.

Biddle, Ellery Roberts. 2013. "Rationing the Digital: The Policy and Politics of Internet Use in Cuba Today." *Internet Monitor*, July 10, 2013. Berkman Center for Internet & Society, Harvard University. *Internet Monitor* Special Report Series No. 1; Berkman Center Research Publication No. 2013-15. http://dx.doi.org/10.2139/ssrn.2291721.

Blackwell, Maylei. 2011. *¡Chicana Power!: Contested Histories of Feminism in the Chicano Movement*. Austin: University of Texas Press.

Blizzard, Chris. 2006. "DOOM on the OLPC XO!" *OLPC News*, Nov. 28, 2006. http://www.olpcnews.com/software/third_party/doom_on_the_olpc_xo.html.

Blogazo por Cuba (blog). n.d. https://blogazoxcuba.wordpress.com/tag/blogazo-por-cuba/.

Blog Bang Cuba. 2014. Directed by Claudio Peláez Sordo. Cuba: Facultad de Comunicación de la Universidad de La Habana. https://www.youtube.com/watch?v=5HCebmSCJ9M&app=desktop.

Boas, Taylor C. 2012. "Mass Media and Politics in Latin America." In *Constructing Democratic Governance in Latin America*, edited by Jorge I. Dominguez and Michael Shifter, 48-77. Baltimore: John Hopkins University Press.

Bonilla, Marcelo, and Gilles Cliche. 2004. *Internet and Society in Latin America and the Caribbean*. Penang, Malaysia: Southbound.

Brand Finance. 2013. *Nation Brands 2013*. http://issuu.com/brandfinance/docs/brand_finance_nation_brands_2013.

Brouwer, Daniel C., and Robert Asen. 2010. *Public Modalities: Rhetoric, Culture, Media, and the Shape of Public Life*. Tuscaloosa: University of Alabama Press.

Brown, John Seely, Allan Collins, and Paul Duguid. 1989. "Situated Cognition and the Culture of Learning." *Educational Researcher* 18 (1):32–42. https://doi.org/10.2307/1176008.

Brunwasser, Mathew. 2015. "A 21st Century Migrant's Essentials: Food, Shelter and Smartphone." *New York Times*, August 25, 2015. http://www.nytimes.com/2015/08/26/world/europe/a-21st-century-migrants-checklist-water-shelter-smartphone.html?_r=1 (accessed 8/25/15).

Bulut, E. 2016. "Social Media and the Nation State: Of Revolution and Collaboration." *Media, Culture and Society* 38, no 4: 606–618.

Burkhalter, Byron. 1999. "Reading Race Online: Discovering Racial Identity in Usenet Discussion." In *Communities in Cyberspace*, edited by Marc A. Smith and Peter Kollock, 60–75. New York: Routledge Press.

Bush, Matthew, and Tania Gentic. 2015. *Technology, Literature, and Digital Culture in Latin America*. New York: Routledge.

Byrne, Dara. 2008. "The Future of (the) 'Race': Identity, Discourse, and the Rise of Computer-Mediated Public Spheres." In *Learning Race and Ethnicity: Youth and DigitalMedia*, edited by Anna Everett, 15–38. Cambridge, MA: MIT Press.

Carey, J. W. 1989. *Communication as Culture: Essays on Media and Society*. Boston: Unwin Hyman.

Casillas, I. D. 2014. *Sounds of Belonging: U.S. Spanish-Language Radio and Public Advocacy*. New York: NYU Press.

Castañeda, M. 2008. "The Importance of Spanish-Language and Latino Media." In *Latina/o Communication Studies Today*, edited by A. N. Valdivia, 51–68. New York: Peter Lang Publishers.

———. 2014. "The Role of Media Policy in Shaping the US Latino 186 Radio Industry." In *Contemporary Latina/o Media: Production, Circulation, Politics*, edited by Arlene Davila and Yeidy Rivero, 186–205. New York: NYU Press.

Castillo, Debra, and Edmundo Paz Soldán. 2000. *Latin American Literature and the Mass Media*. New York: Routledge.

Castro-Gómez, Santiago. 2006. "La hybris del punto cero: ciencia, raza e ilustración en la Nueva Granada (1750–1816)." *Universitas Humanistica* 62 (July–March): 447–453.

Castro Ruz, Fidel. 1961. "Palabras a los intelectuales." http://www.cuba.cu/gobierno/discursos/1961/esp/f300661e.html.

Castro Ruz, Raúl. 2015. "Raúl Castro en la Cumbre de las Américas" *Cubadebate*. April 11, 2015. http://www.cubadebate.cu/opinion/2015/04/11/raul-castro-en-la-cumbre-de-las-americas-hasta-hoy-el-bloqueo-contra-cuba-se-aplica-en-toda-su-intensidad/#.XIly7ihKjIU.

Ceisel, C. M. 2011. "El Rock Star Perfecto? Theorizing Juanes and New Directions in Cross-Over Celebrity." *Communication Theory* 21: 413–435.

Cepeda, M. E. 2001. "Columbus Effect(s): Chronology and Crossover in the Latin(o) Music Boom." *Discourse* 23, no 1: 63–81.

———. 2010. *Musical ImagiNation: U.S.-Colombian Identity and the Latin Music Boom.* New York: NYU Press.

Chacón, Hilda. 2018. *Online Activism in Latin America.* New York: Routledge.

Chan, Anita. 2014. *Networking Peripheries: Technological Futures and the Myth of Digital Universalism.* Cambridge, MA: MIT Press.

Chiang, H. C. 2004. "The Trope of an Upside-Down World: Carnival and Menippean Satire in Richard Brome's *The Antipodes.*" *Concentric: Literary and Cultural Studies* 30, no 2: 55–72.

Christen, Kim. 2012. "Does Information Really Want to Be Free? Indigenous Knowledge Systems and the Question of Openness." *International Journal of Communication* 6: 2870–2893. (http://ijoc.org/ojs/index.php/ijoc/article/view/1618).

Claudio (blog). n.d. http://www.claudioshooter.blogspot.com/.

Cleger, Osvaldo. 2010. *Narrar en la era de las blogoficciones.* Lewiston, NY: Mellen Press, 2010.

"CNN Latino Shuts Down Operations." 2014. *HuffPost Latino Voices.* http://www.huffingtonpost.com/2014/02/05cnn-latino-shuts-down_n_4733473.html.

Coleman, Gabriella. 2010. "Hacking In-Person: The Ritual Character of Conferences and the Distillation of a Life-World." *Anthropological Quarterly* 83, no. 1: 47–72.

———. 2013. *Coding Freedom: Hacker Pleasure and the Ethics of Free and Open Source Software.* Princeton, NJ: Princeton University Press.

"Colombia presenta su nueva marca país." 2012. *Revista Summa.* September 10. http://www.revistasumma.com/29716/.

Commonwealth Club. 2015. Chief Technology Officer of the US Megan Smith. September 30, 2015. https://www.commonwealthclub.org/events/archive/podcast/chief-technology-officer-us-megan-smith.

Constante, Soraya. 2015. "Correa recibe de su propia medicina en las redes sociales." *El Pais,* February 4, 2015.

Correa Díaz, Luis, and Scott Weintraub. 2016. *Poesía y poéticas digitales.* Bogota, Colombia: Editorial Universidad Central.

Coscarelli, Joe. 2011. "Brisenia Flores is Still Not Quite National News: Why?" *Runnin' Scared: A Voice News Blog.* January 28, 2011. http://blogs.villagevoice.com/runninscared/2011/01/brisenia_flores_1.php.

Costanza-Chock, Sasha. 2003. "Mapping the Repertoire of Electronic Contention." In *Representing Resistance: Media, Civil Disobedience, and the Global Justice Movement,* edited by Andrew Oppel and Donnalyn Pompper, 173–191. Westport: Praeger Publishers.

Cristia, J. 2012. "One Laptop per Child in Peru: Findings and the Road Forward." *IDB Blogs.* February 28, 2012. http://blogs.iadb.org/education/2013/02/28/one-laptop-per-child-in-peru-findings-and-the-road-forward/.

Cristia, J., P. Ibarrarán, S. Cueto, A. Santiago, and E. Severin. 2017. "Technology and Child Development: Evidence from the One Laptop per Child Program." *American Economic Journal: Applied Economics* 9, no. 3 (July): 295-320. https://www.aeaweb.org/articles?id=10.1257/app.20150385.

Critchley, Simon. 2007. *Infinitely Demanding.* New York: Verso.

Critical Art Ensemble. 1994. *The Electronic Disturbance*. Brooklyn, NY: Autonomedia.

———. 1996. *The Electronic Civil Disobedience and Other Unpopular Ideas*. Brooklyn, NY: Autonomedia.

Cubadebate (blog). n.d. http://www.cubadebate.cu/.

Cubaencuentro. n.d. "Eliecer Ávila estrena en Youtube el espacio de opinión 'Un cubano más.'" http://www.cubaencuentro.com/multimedia/videos/eliecer-avila-estrena-en-youtube-el-espacio-de-opinion-un-cubano-mas.

"Cuba, falso paraíso (Tres documentales en uno)." 2014. YouTube video. 25:37. Antonio O. Segade E. May 30, 2014. https://www.youtube.com/watch?v=13t1WpIJjDE.

Cuba Material (blog). n.d. http://cubamaterial.com/.

Cubano Confesante (blog). n.d. http://cubanoconfesante.com/.

Cuba posible (blog). n.d. http://cubaposible.net/

Cuddon, J. A. 1991. *The Penguin Dictionary of Literary Terms and Literary Theory*. London: Penguin Books.

Cuen, David. 2010. "Latinoamérica es el segundo mercado de celulares más grande del mundo." *BBC Mundo*, October 7, 2010. http://www.bbc.com/mundo/noticias/2010/10/101006_1046_telefonos_celulares_america_latina_dc.shtml?print=1.

Damas de blanco (blog). n.d. http://www.damasdeblanco.org/.

Daniels, Jessie. 2012. "Race and Racism in Internet Studies: A Review and Critique." *New Media and Society* 15, no 5: 1–25.

Dávila, A., and Y. Rivero, eds. 2014. *Contemporary Latina/o Media: Production, Circulation, Politics*. New York: NYU Press.

Dávila, Arlene. 2012. *Culture Works: Space, Value, and Mobility Across the Neoliberal Americas*. New York: NYU Press.

Dean, Jodi. 2010 "Affective Networks." *Media Tropes* 2, no. 2: 19–44.

De Greiff, Alexis, and Oscar Javier Maldonado. 2011. "Apropiacion fuerte del conocimiento: una propuesta para construir políticas inclusivas de ciencia, tecnología, e innovación en América Latina." In *Estudio social de la ciencia y la tecnología desde America Latina*, edited by A. Arellano Hernandez and P. Kreimer, 209–262. Bogota: Siglo de Hombre Editores.

Díaz, Elaine. 2015. "Los derechos humanos en Cuba, punto de confrontación con Estados Unidos." *Global Voices*, January 31, 2015. http://es.globalvoicesonline.org/2015/01/31/los-derechos-humanos-en-cuba-punto-confrontacion-con-estados-unidos/.

Diaz, Tony. n.d. *Tony Diaz—The Cultural Accelerator*. https://www.tonydiaz.net.

Díaz Rodríguez, Elaine. 2009. "Blogs y periodismo en Cuba: entre el "deber ser" y la realidad." *Revista Latina de Comunicación Social* 12, no. 64: 951–967.

———. 2013. "Deliberar en red: consenso y disenso en la blogosfera cubana." Paper delivered at LASA Conference 2013.

DiFilippo, Anthony. 1990. *From Industry to Arms: The Political Economy of High Technology*. Westport, CT: Greenwood Press.

Dixon, Kwame, and John Burdick, eds. 2012. *Comparative Perspectives on Afro-Latin America*. Gainesville: University Press of Florida.

Domínguez, Ricardo. 1995. "Run for the Border: The Taco Bell War." *CTHEORY*, December 13. Available at www.ctheory.net/articles.aspx?id=155.

Dominguez García, Maria Isabel, Idania Rego Espinosa, and Claudia Castilla García. 2014. *Socialización de adolescentes y jovenes: Retos y oportunidades para la sociedad cubana actual*. La Habana: Editorial de Ciencias Sociales.

Donaldson, I. 1970. *The World Upside Down: Comedy from Jonson to Fielding*. Oxford: Clarendon Press.

Dorfman, Ariel, and Armand Mattelart. 1975. *How to Read Donald Duck: Imperialist Ideology in the Disney Comic*. New York: International General Editions.

Dourish, Paul, and Genevieve Bell. 2011. *Divining a Digital Future: Mess and Mythology in Ubiquitous Computing*. Cambridge: MIT Press.

Drucker, Johanna. 2012. "Humanistic Theory and Digital Scholarship." In *Debates in the Digital Humanities*, edited by Matthew K. Gold. St. Paul, MN: University of Minnesota. http://dhdebates.gc.cuny.edu/debates/text/34.

Dzidzienyo, Anani, and Suzanne Oboler. 2005. *Neither Enemies nor Friends: Latinos, Blacks, Afro-Latinos*. New York: Palgrave Macmillan.

Earhart, Amy E. 2012. "Can Information Be Unfettered? Race and the New Digital Humanities." In *Debates in the Digital Humanities*, edited by Matthew K. Gold, 309–318. Minneapolis: University of Minnesota Press.

Echeverría García, Olga. 2011. "Flores for Brisenia." *LaBloga*, March 20, 2011. http://labloga.blogspot.com/2011/03/flores-for-brisena.html.

EcuRed (blog). n.d. http://www.ecured.cu/EcuRed:Enciclopedia_cubana.

El Comercio. 2014a. "La parodia del Chavo de Enchufe TV bajo los ojos de la prensa internacional." https://www.elcomercio.com/tendencias/parodia-chavo-enchufe-tv-ojos.html.

———. 2014b. "'Los de EnchufeTV son talentosos,' afirma el hijo de 'Chespirito.'" July 11, 2014. https://www.elcomercio.com/tendencias/youtube-enchufetv-televisa-trailer-derechos.html.

"Eliécer Ávila ridiculiza a Ricardo Alarcón." 2011. YouTube video. 48:47. FaraonCuba. April 23. https://www.youtube.com/watch?v=42T0BNNHZA0.

El Sexto (blog). n.d. http://delsexto.blogspot.com/.

Ericsson AB. 2015. "Latin America and the Caribbean." *Ericsson Mobility Report*. https://www.ericsson.com/en/mobility-report.

Estado de Sats Facebook page. https://www.facebook.com/estadodesats.

Evelin, Guilherme. 2015. "Boris González Arenas: 'Fui preso e demitido por querer falar.'" *Epoca*, January 20, 2015. http://epoca.globo.com/vida/noticia/2015/01/bboris-gonzalez-arenasb-fui-preso-e-demitido-por-querer-falar.html.

Everett, Anna. 2004. "On Cyberfeminism and Cyberwomanism: High-Tech Mediations of Feminism's Discontent." *Signs* 30, no. 1: 1278–1286.

———. 2008a. "Introduction." In *Learning Race and Ethnicity: Youth and Digital Media*, edited by Anna Everett, 15–38. Cambridge, MA: MIT Press.

———. 2008b. *Race and Ethnicity*. Cambridge, MA: MIT Press.

Federal Research Division. 2005. "Country Profile: Paraguay."

Fejes, Fred. 1981. "Media Imperialism: An Assessment." *Media, Culture & Society* 3, no. 3: 281–289. https://doi.org/10.1177/016344378100300306.

Fernández Mora, Evelyn. 2017. "Estudio: Marca país Esencial Costa Rica es la de mayor crecimiento en América." *El Financiero*, July 6. http://www.elfinancierocr.com/nego-cios/Marca-Pais-Esencial-Costa-America_0_1207679226.html.

Ferreyra, Maria Marta, Ciro Avitabile, Javier Botero Álvarez, Francisco Haimovich Paz, and Sergio Urzúa. 2017. *At a Crossroads: Higher Education in Latin America and the Caribbean*. Washington, DC: The World Bank Group. https://openknowledge.world-bank.org/handle/10986/26489.

Fiormonte, Domenico. 2014. "Digital Humanities from a Global Perspective." Laboratorio dell'ISPF. Vol. XI. http://www.ispf-lab.cnr.it/2014_203.pdf.

Fitzgerald, Deborah. 2010. *Every Farm a Factory: The Industrial Ideal in American Agriculture*. New Haven, CT: Yale University Press.

Flores-Yeffal, Nadia, Guadalupe Vidales, and April Plemons. 2011. "The Latino Cyber-Moral Panic Process in the United States." *Communication and Society* 14, no 4: 568–589.

Fogonero Emergente (blog). n.d. http://jorgealbertoaguiar.blogspot.com/.

Fontana, Yohandry. 2013. "Las mentiras de Yoani Sánchez en 2012 que deberían conocer en Miami." *Yohandry's Weblog*, April 3. https://yohandry.wordpress.com/2013/04/03/las-mentiras-de-yoani-sanchez-en-2012-que-deberian-conocer-en-miami/.

Forbidden Voices. 2012. Directed by Barbara Miller. Switzerland: FILMCOOPI Zürich AG, DVD.

Foucault, Michel. 1995. *Discipline and Punish: The Birth of the Prison*. 2nd edition. New York: Vintage Books.

———. 2001. "The Political Technology of Individuals." In *The Essential Foucault*, vol. 3, edited by James Faubion, 403–417. New York: New Press.

Foxley, Alejandro. 1983. *Latin American Experiments in Neoconservative Economics*. Berkeley: University of California Press.

Frajman, Eduardo. 2014. "Broadcasting Populist Leadership: Hugo Chávez and Aló Presidente." *Journal of Latin American Studies* 46, no. 3: 501–526.

Freedom House. 2015. "Gobierno Ecuatoriano Continúa Persecución contra Caricaturista." https://freedomhouse.org/article/gobierno-ecuatoriano-contin-persecuci-n-contra-caricaturista#.VQhKJhY8r5l.

French-Davis, Ricardo. 1980. "Liberalización de importaciones: La experiencia chilena en 1973–1979." *Colección Estudios CIEPLAN* 4: 39–78.

Fukuyama, Francis. 1992. *The End of History and the Last Man*. New York: Free Press.

Fundamedios. 2013. "Gobierno ecuatoriano pide que se penalice la opinión en redes sociales." http://www.ifex.org/ecuador/2013/09/03/penalice_opinion/es/.

———. 2014. "El Silencio asfixiante: La libertad de expresión en el Ecuador durante el 2013." http://www.fundamedios.org.ec/articulos/el-silencio-asfixiante-la-libertad-de-expresion-en-el-ecuador-durante-el-2013.

Fusco, C. 1995. *English is Broken Here: Notes on Cultural Fusion in the Americas*. New York: The Free Press.

Future Brand. 2013. *Country Brand Index Latinoamérica 2013*. http://www.futurebrand.com/images/uploads/studies/cbi/CBI_Latinoamerica_2013.pdf.

———. 2015. *Country Brand Index 2014–2015*. http://www.futurebrand.com/cbi/2014.

Galina Russell, Isabel. 2013. "¿Hay alguien allá afuera? Construyendo una comunidad mundial de Humanidades Digitales." *Red de Humanidades Digitales*. http://humanidadesdigitales.net/blog/2013/09/02/hay-alguien-alla-afuera/.

———. 2014. "Geographical and Linguistic Diversity in the Digital Humanities." *Literary and Linguistic Computing* 29, no 3: 307–316. https://doi.org/10.1093/llc/fqu005.

Gallon, Kim. 2016. "Making a Case for the Black Digital Humanities." *Debates in the Digital Humanities*, edited by Matthew Gold and Lauren Klein. Minneapolis: University of Minnesota Press. http://dhdebates.gc.cuny.edu/debates/text/55.

Galloway, Alexander. 2004. *Protocol: How Control Exists After Decentralization*. Cambridge, MA: MIT Press.

———. 2012. *The Interface Effect*. Malden, MA: Polity Press.

Galloway, Alexander, and Eugene Thaker. 2007. *The Exploit: A Theory of Networks*. Minneapolis: University of Minnesota Press.

Garambel, José. 2010. *Las luchas por la escuela in-imaginada del Indio: escuelas, movimientos sociales, e indigenismo en el Altiplano*. Puno, Peru: Universidad Nacional del Altiplano.

García, Modesto. "Futurebrand rediseña la marca turística de Costa Rica." *Brandemia*, September 17, 2013. http://www.brandemia.org/futurebrand-redisena-la-marca-turistica-de-costa-rica/.

García Borrero, Juan Antonio. 2013. *El perfecto analfabeto y otras bloguerías*. Santiago de Cuba: Editorial Oriente.

Garcia Canclini, Nestor. 1995. *Hybrid Culture: Strategies for Entering and Leaving Modernity*. Minneapolis: University of Minnesota Press.

———. 1999. *La globalización imaginada*. Buenos Aires-Barcelona-Mexico City: Editorial Paidos.

———. 2004. *Diferentes, desiguales y desconectados*. Barcelona: Gedisa.

———. 2007. *Lectores, espectadores e internautas*. Barcelona: Gedisa.

Gascó Hernández, Mila. 2007. *Latin America Online: Cases, Successes, Pitfalls*. Hershey, PA.: IGI Global.

Gee, James Paul. 2004. *Situated Language and Learning: A Critique of Traditional Schooling*. New York: Routledge.

Generación Y (blog). n.d. https://generacionyen.wordpress.com/.

Genosko, Gary. 2002. *Felix Guattari: An Aberrant Introduction*. New York: Continuum.

Gerbaudo, Paolo. 2012. *Tweets and the Streets: Social Media and Contemporary Activism*. London: Pluto Press.

Giang, Vivian. 2013. "Ranking America's Biggest Companies by Turnover Rate." *Business Insider*, July 28, 2013. http://www.slate.com/blogs/business_insider/2013/07/28/turnover_rates_by_company_how_amazon_google_and_others_stack_up.html.

Gil, Alex, and Ernesto Priego. 2013. "Global Perspectives: Interview with Alex Gil." *4 Humanities*, January 11, 2013. http://4humanities.org/2013/01/interview-with-alex-gil/.

Glissant, Edouard. 1997. *Poetics of Relation*. Ann Arbor: University of Michigan Press.

Gold, Mathew K., ed. 2012. *Debates in the Digital Humanities*. Minneapolis: University of Minnesota Press.

Gómez Peña, Guillermo. 2001. *The New World Border*. San Francisco: City Lights.

González Fernandez, Guissela. 2005. *El dolor americano: Literatura y periodismo de Gamaliel Churata*. Lima: Editiones San Marcos.

González Sandoval, Gilda. 2013. "Expertos en marcas critican y alaban la marca país 'Esencial Costa Rica.'" *El Financiero*, September 15, 2013. http://www.elfinancierocr.com/economia-y-politica/Marca_pais-Esencial_Costa_Rica-Comex_0_372562764.html.

Grecco, Albert N., Clara E. Rodríguez, and Robert M. Wharton. 2007. *The Culture and Commerce of Publishing in the 21st Century*. Stanford, CA: Stanford University Press.

GSMA. 2016. "Mobile Internet Users in Latin America to Grow by 50 Per Cent by 2020, Finds New GSMA Study." *GSMA*, September 20, 2016. https://www.gsma.com/newsroom/press-release/mobile-internet-users-in-latin-america-to-grow-by-50-percent-by-2020-finds-new-gsma-study/.

Guback, T., and R. Bettig. 1987. "Translating the Manifesto into English: Nineteenth Century Communication, Twentieth Century Confusion." *Journal of Communication Inquiry* 11, no 2: 3–16.

Guernsey, Lisa. 2007. *Into the Minds of Babes: How Screen Time Affects Children from Birth to Age Five*. New York: Basic Books.

Gustafson, B. 2009. *New Languages of the State: Indigenous Resurgence and the Politics of Knowledge in Bolivia*. Durham, NC: Duke University Press.

Habermas, Jürgen. 1991. *The Structural Transformation of the Public Sphere: An Inquiry into a Category of Bourgeois Society*. Translated by Thomas Burger and Frederick Lawrence. Cambridge, MA: MIT Press.

———. 2006. "Towards a United States of Europe." *Signandsight.com,* March 27, 2006. Translated by John Lambert. http://www.signandsight.com/features/676.html.

Hacker, K. L., and R. Steiner. 2002. "The Digital Divide for Hispanic Americans." *The Howard Journal of Communications* 13: 267–283.

Harber, Jonathan. 2012. "Datapalooza: A Game Changer for Education?" *Pearson Research & Innovation Network*.

Hargittai, E. 2011. "Minding the Digital Gap: Why Understanding Inequality Matters." In *Media Perspectives for the 21st Century*, edited by S. Papathanassopoulos, 231–239. New York: Routledge.

Hargittai, E., and A. Hinnant. 2008. "Digital Inequality: Differences in Young Adults' Use of the Internet." *Communication Research* 35, no 5: 602–621.

Harris, Olivia. 1995. "The Sources and Meanings of Money: Beyond the Market Paradigm in an Ayllu of Northern Potosi," In *Ethnicity, Markets, and Migration in the Andes: At the Crossroads of History and Anthropology*, edited by Brook Larson and Olivia Harris, 297–328. Durham, NC: Duke University Press.

Hartley, J. 2012. *Digital Futures for Cultural and Media Studies*. New York: Wiley-Blackwell.

Havana Times (blog). n.d. www.havanatimes.org.

"HD Noticias: Jaime Bayly entrevista a Eliecer Avila (Completo) 2013." 2013. YouTube video. 32:55. 72pantalla2. May 14, 2013. https://www.youtube.com/watch?v=YglTusAr0Fw.

Hernandez-Reguant, Ariana, ed. 2009. *Cuba in the Special Period: Culture and Ideology in the 1990's*. New York: Palgrave Macmillan.

Herring, Susan C., Inna Kouper, Lois Ann Scheidt, and Elijah L. Wright. 2004. "Women and Children Last: The Discursive Construction of Weblogs." In *Into the Blogosphere: Rhetoric, Community, and Culture of Weblogs*, edited by Laura Gurak, Smiljana Antonijevic, Laurie Johnson, Clancy Ratliff, and Jessica Reyman. Minneapolis: University of Minnesota. https://conservancy.umn.edu/handle/11299/172825.

Hetherington, Kregg. 2009. "Privatizing the Private in Rural Paraguay: Precarious Lots and the Materiality of Rights." *American Ethnologist* 36, no 2:224–41. https://doi.org/10.1111/j.1548-1425.2009.01132.x.

"Higher Regional Court Says Online Demonstration is Not Force." 2006. *Heise Online*, June 2. https://post.thing.net/node/1370.

Higuera, Silvia. 2015. "Críticas del presidente de Ecuador y amenazas de muerte llevan al cierre de cuenta satírica de Facebook." *Knight Center for Journalism in the Americas*, February 27, 2015. https://knightcenter.utexas.edu/es/blog/00-15945-amenazas-de-muerte-y-criticas-del-presidente-de-ecuador-llevan-al-cierre-de-cuenta-sat.

Hill, Adriene. 2014. "A Day in the Life of a Datamined Kid." *Marketplace*, September 15, 2014. http://www.marketplace.org/topics/education/learningcurve/day-life-data-mined-kid.

Hookway, Branden. 2014. *Interface*. Cambridge: MIT Press. Kindle Edition.

IBOPE. 2013. Media Penetration in Latin America. Edited by Media Link. No longer available.

Innis, Harold A. 2004. *Changing Concepts of Time*. Lanham, MD: Rowman & Littlefield.

International Telecommunication Union. 2013. http://www.itu.int/en/Pages/default.aspx.

IPS Inter Press Service en Cuba. 2015. "Proyecto ciudadano organiza encuentro en Estados Unidos." Jan 26, 2015. https://www.ipscuba.net/sociedad/proyecto-ciudadano-organiza-encuentro-en-estados-unidos/

Irani, Lilly. 2015. "Hackathons and the Making of Entrepreneurial Citizenship." *Science, Technology & Human Values* 40, no 5: 799–824.

Iriarte, Igor. 2013. "Argentina renueva su marca país." *Brandemia*, October 3, 2013. http://www.brandemia.org/argentina-renueva-su-marca-pais.

Ito, Mizuko. 2009. *Engineering Play: A Cultural History of Children's Software*. Cambridge: MIT Press.

Ito, Mizuko, Sonja Baumer, Matteo Bittanti, Danah Boyd, Rachel Cody, Becky Herr-Stephenson, Heather A. Horst, et al. 2010. *Hanging Out, Messing Around, and Geeking Out: Kids Living and Learning with New Media*. Cambridge: MIT Press.

jcediciones. 2010. "El terrorismo de mediático de Raúl Castro: Ataque al bloguero Ernesto Morales." *Cubaout*, December 13. https://cubaout.wordpress.com/2010/12/13/el-terrorismo-mediatico-de-raul-castro-ataque-al-bloguero-ernesto-morales/.

Jeffries, F. 2015. "Cyborg Resistance on the Digital Assembly Line: Global Connectivity as a Terrain of Struggle for the Commons in Alex Rivera's *Sleep Dealer*." *Journal of Communication Inquiry* 39, no 1: 21–37. doi:10.1177/0196859914550689.

Jenkins, Henry. 2002. "Blog This: Online Diarists Rule an Internet Strewn with Failed Dotcoms." *MIT Technology Review*, March 1, 2002. http://www.technologyreview.com/article/401372/blog-this/.

———. 2006. *Convergence Culture: Where Old and New Media Collide.* New York: NYU Press.

———. 2008. "Race in Digital Space (Revisited): An Interview with Sarah N. Gatson (Part One)." *Confessions of an Aca-Fan: The Official Weblog of Henry Jenkins,* December 1, 2008. http://henryjenkins.org/2008/12/what_fan_studies_has_to_learn.html.

———. 2009. *Confronting the Challenges of Participatory Culture: Media Education for the 21st Century.* Cambridge: MIT Press.

Jenkins, Henry, Katie Clinton, Ravi Purushotma, Alice J. Robison, and Margaret Weigel. 2009. *Confronting the Challenges of Participatory Culture: Media Education for the 21st Century.* The John D. and Katherine T. MacArthur Foundation Reports on Digital Media and Learning. Cambridge, MA: MIT Press.

Jimenez, Carlos. 2011. "I Don't Get It: It's Always Sunny in Philadelphia and Online Viewing as a Guide to Ethnic Humor." Master's thesis, UCSB.

———. 2016. "From Telephones in Rural Oaxaca to Mobile Phones among Mixtec Farm Workers in Oxnard, California." *New Media & Society* 19, no 12: 2059–2074.

Jiménez Román, Myriam, and Juan Flores, eds. 2010. *Afro-Latin@ Reader.* Durham: Duke University Press.

Jordan, Tim, and Paul A. Taylor. 2004. *Hacktivism and Cyberwars: Rebels with a Cause?* New York: Routledge.

Kane, Charles, Walter Bender, Jody Cornish, and Neal Donahue. 2012. *Learning to Change the World: The Social Impact of One Laptop Per Child.* New York: Palgrave Macmillan.

Karam, William. 2000. "Hacktivism: Is Hacktivism Civil Disobedience?" University of Ottawa Faculty of Law, Department of Graduate Studies. Unpublished paper.

Kellam, Marisa, and Elizabeth Stein. 2016. "Silencing Critics: Why and How Presidents Restrict Media Freedom in Democracies." *Comparative Political Studies* 49, no 1: 36–77.

Kelty, Chris. 2008. *Two Bits: The Cultural Significance of Free Software.* Cambridge: MIT Press.

Khan, Salman. 2011. "Let's Use Video to Reinvent Education." TED Talks. 2011. https://www.ted.com/talks/salman_khan_let_s_use_video_to_reinvent_education?language=en.

Kirschenbaum, Matthew. 2009. "The Making of Reading: Data Mining and the Digital Humanities." http://citeseerx.ist.psu.edu/viewdoc/download?doi=10.1.1.111.959&rep=rep1&type=pdf.

Koh, Adeline. 2012. "More Hack, Less Yack?: Modularity, Theory and the Habitus in the Digital Humanities." *Adeline Koh.* Accessed March 20, 2015. http://www.adelinekoh.org/blog/2012/05/21/more-hack-less-yack-modularity-theory-and-habitus-in-the-digital-humanities/. Page no longer online.

Koh, Adeline, and Roopika Risam. 2014. *Postcolonial Digital Humanities.* http://dhpoco.org/.

Kraidy, Marwan. 2005. *Hybridity, or the Cultural Logic of Globalization.* Philadelphia: Temple University Press.

Kuhn, Thomas S. 1970. *The Structure of Scientific Revolutions.* 2nd edition. Chicago: University of Chicago Press. http://projektintegracija.pravo.hr/_download/repository/Kuhn_Structure_of_Scientific_Revolutions.pdf.

La chiringa de Cuba (blog). n.d. http://www.chiringadecuba.com/.

"La cíber policía en Cuba." 2011. Vimeo video. 53:08. Coral negro. January 31. https://vimeo.com/19402730.

Laínez, Reneé Colato. 2011. "*The Cazuela that the Farm Maiden Stirred*—Virtual Book Tour and Giveaway." *Labloga.com.* http://spanglishbaby.com/finds/virtual-book-tour-the-cazuela-that-the-farm-maiden-stirred-giveaway/.

La isla y . . . la espina (blog). n.d. http://laislaylaespina.blogspot.com.

Lane, Jill. 2003. "Digital Zapatistas." *The Drama Review: The Journal of Performance Studies* 47, no 2: 129–144.

La Polémica Digital (blog). n.d. www.Espaciodeelaine.wordpress.com.

Lara, Tania. 2013. "Ecuadorian Legislators Approve New Communications Law." *Knight Center for Journalism in the Americas*, June 13, 2013. https://knightcenter.utexas.edu/blog/00-14044-ecuadorian-legislators-close-approving-new-communications-law.

Lave, Jean, and Etienne Wenger. 1991. *Situated Learning: Legitimate Peripheral Participation*. Cambridge, UK: Cambridge University Press.

Lee, Francis L. F., Louis Leung, Jack L. Qiu, and Donna S. C. Chu, eds. 2013. *Frontiers in New Media Research*. New York: Routledge.

Lenhart, A. 2015. *Teens, Social Media, & Technology Overview 2015*. Pew Research Center. http://www.pewinternet.org/2015/04/09/introduction-teens-tech/DATE.

Lerner, D. 1958. *The Passing of Traditional Society: Modernizing the Middle East*. Glencoe, IL: Free Press.

Levitas, R. 2010. *The Concept of Utopia*. New York: Peter Lang.

———. 2013. *Utopia as Method: The Imaginary Reconstitution of Society*. New York: Palgrave Macmillan.

Lindsey, Ursula. 2015. "Scholars Re-Examine Arab World's 'Facebook Revolution,'" *Chronicle of Higher Education*, March 9, 2015. http://chronicle.com/article/Scholars-Re-Examine-Arab/228293/.

Liu, Alan. 2012. "Where is the Cultural Criticism in the Digital Humanities?" In *Debates in the Digital Humanities*, edited by Matthew K. Gold. Minneapolis: Minnesota University Press. http://dhdebates.gc.cuny.edu/debates/text/20.

Liverman, Diana M., and Silvina Vilas. 2006. "Neoliberalism and the Environment in Latin America." *Annual Review of Environment and Resources* 31: 327–363.

Lopez, Dennis. 2010. "Good-Bye Revolution—Hello Cultural Mystique: Quinto Sol Publications and Chicano Literary Nationalism." *MELUS* 35, no 3: 183–210.

Lugo, A. 2000. "Theorizing Border Inspections." *Cultural Dynamics* 12, no 3: 353–373.

———. 2012. "Border Inspections, Then and Now." In *Mapping Latina/o Studies*, edited by A. N. Valdivia and M. Garcia, 123-152. New York: Peter Lang.

Lugo, Jairo. 2008. *The Media in Latin America*. Maidenhead and New York: Open University Press.

Lunes de Post-Revolución (blog). n.d. http://orlandoluispardolazo.blogspot.com/.

Luyt, Brendan. 2008. "The One Laptop Per Child Project and the Negotiation of Technological Meaning." *First Monday* 13, no 6. https://firstmonday.org/ojs/index.php/fm/article/view/2144/1971.

Madory, Doug. 2013. "Mystery Cable Activated in Cuba." *Dyn Research Blog*, January 20, 2013. http://research.dyn.com/2013/01/cuban-mystery-cable-activated/.

———. 2014a. "Cuban Fiber: Completo?" *Dyn Research Blog*, January 23, 2014. http://research.dyn.com/2013/01/cuban-fiber-completo/.

———. 2014b. "What's Next for Cuba?" *Dyn Research Blog*, December 18, 2014. http://research.dyn.com/2014/12/whats-next-cuba/

Manovich, Lev. 2001. *The Language of New Media*. Cambridge, MA: MIT Press.

———. 2013. *Software Takes Command*. New York: Continuum Publishing Corporation.

Marca Colombia. "Colombia presenta su nuevo logo y su nueva imagen." http://www.colombia.co/videos/colombia-presenta-su-logo-y-su-nueva-imagen.html.

Marcopoto, Talia. 2014. "Brazil Claims 'Victory' in World Cup." *CNN*, July 6, 2014. http://www.cnn.com/2014/07/16/travel/brazil-world-cup-tourism/.

Martin-Barbero, J. 1993. *Communications, Culture and Hegemony: From the Media to the Mediations*. Newbury Park, CA: Sage.

———. 2002. *Oficio de cartógrafo*. Mexico City and Santiago: Fondo de Cultura Económica.

———. 2007. "Latin American Cyberliterature: From the Lettered City to the Creativity of its Citizens." *Latin American Cyberculture and Cyberliterature*, edited by Claire Taylor and Thea Pitman, xi–xv. Liverpool: Liverpool University Press.

Martinez, Alejandro. 2013. "Ecuador's Controversial Communications Law in 8 points." *Knight Center for Journalism in the Americas*. https://knightcenter.utexas.edu/blog/00-14071-8-highlights-understand-ecuador's-controversial-communications-law.

Matheson, Donald. 2009. "What the Blogger Knows." In *Journalism and Citizenship: New Agendas in Communication*, edited by Zizi Papacharissi, 151–165. New York: Routledge.

Mato, Daniel. 2003. "Latin American Intellectual Practices in Culture and Power: Experiences and Debates." *Cultural Studies* 17, no 6: 783–804.

McCarty, Willard. 2003. "Humanities Computing." In *Encyclopedia of Library and Information Science*. New York: Marcel Dekker Inc. http://www.mccarty.org.uk/essays/McCarty,%20Humanities%20computing.pdf.

———. 2012. "A Telescope for the Mind?" In *Debates in the Digital Humanities*, edited by Matthew K. Gold, 113–124. Minneapolis: University of Minnesota Press.

McKenzie, Jon, and Ricardo Domínguez. 2001. "Dispatches from the Future: A Conversation about Hacktivism." *Connect: Art, Politics, Theory, Practice* 2: 115–122.

McKinley, Jesse, and Malia Wollan. 2009. "New Border Fear: Violence by a Rogue Militia." *New York Times* online edition, June 26, 2009. https://www.nytimes.com/2009/06/27/us/27arizona.html?mtrref=www.google.com&assetType=REGIWALL.

McPherson, Tara. 2012a. "US Operating Systems at Mid-Century: The Intertwining of Race and UNIX." In *Race After the Internet*, edited by Lisa Nakamura and Peter A. Chow-White, 21–37. New York: Routledge.

———. 2012b. "Why Are the Digital Humanities So White?" In *Debates in the Digital*

Humanities, edited by Matthew K. Gold. Minneapolis: Minnesota University Press. http://dhdebates.gc.cuny.edu/debates/text/29.

Medina, Eden. 2011. *Cybernetic Revolutionaries: Technology and Politics in Allende's Chile.* Cambridge: MIT Press. Kindle edition.

Medina, Eden, Ivan da Costa Marques, and Christina Holmes, eds. 2014. *Beyond Imported Magic: Essays on Science, Technology, and Society in Latin America.* Cambridge: MIT Press.

Mercer, K. 1994. *Welcome to the Jungle: New Positions in Black Cultural Studies.* New York: Routledge.

Mignolo, Walter. 2000. *Local Histories/Global Designs: Coloniality, Subaltern Knowledges, and Border Thinking.* Princeton, NJ: Princeton University Press.

Miller, Toby, Nitin Govil, John McMurria, Richard Maxwell, and Ting Wang. 2005. *Global Hollywood 2.* London: British Film Institute.

Mills, K. 2004a. "Changing Channels: The Civil Rights Case that Transformed Television." *National Archives* 36, no 3. https://www.archives.gov/publications/prologue/2004/fall/channels-1.html.

———. 2004b. *Changing Channels: The Civil Rights Case that Transformed Television.* Jackson, MI: University Press of Mississippi.

"Mincetur invertirá más de US $10 millones en campañas de turismo receptivo." 2014. *Gestión*, September 8. http://gestion.pe/economia/mincetur-invertira-mas-us10-millones-campanas-turismo-receptivo-imagen-pais-2107940.

Miniwatts Marketing Group. 2018. "Internet Usage and Population in South America." *Internet World Stats*, Feb. 25, 2018. https://www.internetworldstats.com/stats15.htm.

Mirabal, N. R., and A. Laó-Montes, eds. 2007. *Technofuturos: Critical Interventions in Latina/o Studies.* Lanham, KT: Lexington Books.

Miroff, Nick. 2014. "Ecuador's Popular, Powerful President Rafael Correa Is a Study in Contradictions." *The Washington Post*, March 15, 2014. https://www.washingtonpost.com/world/ecuadors-popular-powerful-president-rafael-correa-is-a-study-in-contradictions/2014/03/15/452111fc-3eaa-401b-b2c8-cc4e85fccb40_story.html?noredirect=on.

Mitchell, Timothy. 2005. "The Work of Economics: How a Discipline Makes Its World." *European Journal of Sociology* 46: 297–320.

———. 2008. "Rethinking Economy." *Geoforum* 39: 1116–1121.

Molina-Guzmán, I. 2010. *Dangerous Curves: Latina Bodies in the Media.* New York: NYU Press.

Montes, Amelia M. 2012. "Libro Traficante: A Focus on the Banned Books List by Amelia M.L. Montes (ameliamontes.com)." *Migrare/Migrate/Change*, March 4, 2012. http://migrare.wordpress.com/2012/03/04/libro-traficante-a-focus-on-the-banned-books-list-by-amelia-m-l-montes-ameliamontes-com/.

Montesinos, Patricio. 2015. "A propósito de la Cumbre las Américas y la 'Sociedad Civil.'" *Cubadebate*, March 20, 2015. http://www.cubadebate.cu/opinion/2015/03/20/a-proposito-de-la-cumbre-de-las-americas-y-la-sociedad-civil/#.XIl9rShKjIU.

Moraga, Cherríe. 2000. *Loving in the War Years: Lo que nunca pasó por sus labios.* 2nd ed. Cambridge: South End Press.

Moran, Albert. 2009. "Global Franchising, Local Customizing: The Cultural Economy of TV Program Formats." *Continuum: Journal of Media & Cultural Studies* 23, no. 2:115–125.

Moreiras, Alberto. 2001. *The Exhaustion of Difference: The Politics of Latin American Cultural Studies*. Durham and London: Duke University Press.

Mosco, V. 2004. *The Digital Sublime: Myth, Power, and Cyberspace*. Boston: MIT Press.

Mukherjee, R. 2005. *The Racial Order of Things: Cultural Imaginaries in the Post-Soul Era*. Minneapolis: University of Minnesota Press.

Muniesa, Fabian, Yuval Millo, and Michel Callon. 2007. "An Introduction to Market Devices." Special issue: *Market Devices*. Edited by Michel Callon, Yuval Millo, and Fabian Muniesa. *The Sociological Review* 55, no. 2: 1–12.

Murph, Darren. 2006. "OLPC XO Caught Playing Super Mario Bros. 3." *Engadget*, December 25, 2006. https://www.engadget.com/2006/12/25/olpc-xo-caught-playing-super-mario-bros-3/.

Nakamura, Lisa. 2002. *Cybertypes: Race, Ethnicity, and Identity on the Internet*. New York: Routledge.

———. 2008. *Digitizing Race: Visual Cultures of the Internet*. Minneapolis: University of Minnesota Press.

Nakamura, Lisa, and Peter A. Chow-White, eds. 2012. *Race After the Internet*. New York: Routledge.

Nearshore Americas. 2015. "Cuba's Readiness for ICT Transformation: Executive Summary." July 2015. http://www.nearshoreamericas.com/product/assessing-cubas-appetite-for-ict-transformation/.

Negra Cubana tenía que ser (blog). n.d. http://negracubanateniaqueser.com/.

Negrón-Muntaner, F., C. Abbas, L. Figueroa, and S. Robson. 2014. *The Latino Media Gap: A Report on the State of Latinos in U.S. Media*. New York: NALIP/CSER. https://www.latinorebels.com/2014/06/17/the-latino-media-gap-a-report-on-the-state-of-latinos-in-u-s-media/.

Negroponte, Nicholas. 2006. "No Lap Un-Topped: The Bottom Up Revolution That Could Redefine Global IT Culture." OLPC Talks, Keynote Address, NetEvents Global Press Summit. Hong Kong, December 2, 2006. https://web.archive.org/web/20071012165720/http://olpctalks.com:80/nicholas_negroponte/negroponte_netevents.html.

Negroponte, Nicholas, and Walter Bender. 2007. "The New $100 Computer." World Bank Group, May 31, 2007. OLPC Talks. https://web.archive.org/web/20071014221537/http://www.olpctalks.com:80/nicholas_negroponte/negroponte_world_bank_group.html.

Nowviskie, Bethany. 2014. "On the Origin of 'Hack' and 'Yack.'" *Bethany Nowviskie* (blog), January 8, 2014. http://nowviskie.org/2014/on-the-origin-of-hack-and-yack/.

Nyhan, Julianna, Melissa Terras, and Edward Vanhoutte. 2013. "Introduction." In *Defining Digital Humanities*, edited by Melissa Terras, Julianna Nyhan, and Edward Vanhoutte, 1–7. New York: Routledge.

Octavo Cerco (blog). n.d. http://octavocerco.blogspot.com/.

Offline. 2013. Directed by Yaima Pardo. Cuba: Aminta D'Cardenas. https://www.youtube.com/watch?v=PlPiG-pDvGA.

Ojos que te miran: entre redes. 2012. Directed by Rigoberto Senarega. Cuba.

OLPC staff. 2011. "Hardware Uniqueness." OLPC Wiki. 2011.

———. 2012a. "OLPC's Vision." OLPC Website. 2012.

———. 2012b. "OLPC Mission: Frequently Asked Questions." OLPC Website. 2012.

———. 2012c. "OLPC Principles and Basic Information." OLPC Wiki. 2012.

Ontiveros, Randy. 2014. *In the Spirit of a New People: The Cultural Politics of the Chicano Movement.* New York: NYU Press.

Oppenheimer, Andres. 2012. "Region's One Laptop Per Child Plan Has a Future." *Miami Herald,* April 30. http://www.recordonline.com/apps/pbcs.dll/article?AID=/20120430/OPINION/204300311&cid=sitesearch.

Ossandon, José. 2009. "The Enactment of Private Health Insurance in Chile." PhD diss., Goldsmiths College, University of London.

Oswaldo Paya (blog). n.d. http://www.oswaldopaya.org/es/.

Pais de Pixeles (blog). n.d. http://paisdepixeles.blogspot.com/.

Papacharissi, Zizi. 2002. "The Virtual Sphere: The Internet as a Public Sphere." *New Media and Society* 4, no. 1: 9–27.

———. 2007. "Audiences as Media Producers: Content Analysis of 260 Blogs." In *Blogging, Citizenship, and the Future of Media,* edited by Mark Tremayne, 21–38. New York: Routledge.

Papacharissi, Zizi, and Maria de Fatima Oliveira. 2012. "Affective News and Networked Publics: The Rhythms of News Storytelling on #Egypt." *Journal of Communication* 62, no. 2: 266–282.

Papert, Seymour. 2006. "Digital Development: How the $100 Laptop Could Change Education." USINFO. Webchat, via OLPC Talks. US Department of State.

———. 1993. *The Children's Machine: Rethinking School in the Age of the Computer.* New York: Basic Books.

———. 1980. *Mindstorms: Children, Computers, and Powerful Ideas.* New York: Basic Books.

Papert, Seymour, and Idit Harel. 1991. "Situating Constructionism." In *Constructionism,* edited by Seymour Papert and Idit Harel, 1–12. Norwood, NJ.: Ablex Publishing Corporation.

Paquito el de Cuba (blog). n.d. http://paquitoeldecuba.com/.

Pardo, Yaima, Helman Avelle, and Juan Carlos Rodríguez. 2014. "Interview with Yaima Pardo and Helman Avelle." Unpublished manuscript.

Pardo Lazo, Orlando Luis. 2013. *Boring Home.* Caracas: Los libros de El Nacional.

———. *Boring Home Utopics* (blog). n.d. http://vocescubanas.com/boringhomeutopics/.

———. "Article 1: Censorship without censoring." Cubalog.eu. http://cubademocraciay-vida.org/web/print.asp?artID=26482.

Parks, Lisa, and Nicole Starosielski. 2015. *Signal Traffic: Critical Studies of Media Infrastructure.* Champaign: University of Illinois Press.

Patria y humanidad (blog). n.d. http://luisexto.blogia.com/.

Penix-Tadsen, Philip. 2016. *Cultural Code: Video Games and Latin America*. Cambridge and London: MIT Press.

Pérez, E. 1962. *Warisata: La Escuela-Ayllu*. La Paz, Bolivia: Hisbol/CERES.

Pew Research Center. 2012. "Median Age for Hispanics is Lower Than Median Age for Total U.S. Population." http://www.pewresearch.org/daily-number/median-age-for-hispanics-is-lower-than-median-age-for-total-u-s-population/DATE.

———. 2016. "American's Internet Access: 2000–2015." http://www.pewinternet.org/2015/06/26/americans-internet-access-2000-2015/.

Philip, Kavita, Lilly Irani, and Paul Dourish. 2010. "Postcolonial Computing: A Tactical Survey." *Science Technology Human Values* 37, no. 1 (Jan 2012): 3–29.

Pieterse, Jan Nederveen. 2009. *Globalization and Culture: Global Melange*. Lanham, MD: Rowman & Littlefield.

Piñón, Juan. 2014. "Corporate Transnationalism: The US Hispanic and Latin American Television Industries." In *Contemporary Latina/o Media*, edited by Arlene Dávida and Yeidy Rivero, 21–43. New York: NYU Press.

Pitman, Thea, and Claire Taylor. 2017. "Where Is the ML in DH? And Where Is the DH in ML? The Relationship between Modern Languages and Digital Humanities, and an Argument for a Critical DHML." *Digital Humanities Quarterly* 11, no. 1. http://www.digitalhumanities.org/dhq/vol/11/1/000287/000287.html

Ponte, Antonio José. 2010. *Villa Marista en Plata: Arte, políticas, nuevas tecnologías*. Madrid: Editorial Colibrí.

Portes, Alejandro, and Bryan Roberts. 2005. "The Free-Market City: Latin American Urbanization in the Years of the Neoliberal Experiment." *Studies in Comparative International Development* 40, no. 1: 43–82.

Press, Larry, Grey Burkhart, Will Foster, Seymour Goodman, Peter Wolcott, and Jon Woodard. 1998. "An Internet Diffusion Framework." *Communications of the ACM* 41, no. 10: 21–26.

Priego, Ernesto. 2012. "Globalisation of the Digital Humanities: An Uneven Promise." *Inside Higher Ed*, January 26, 2012. https://www.insidehighered.com/blogs/globalisation-digital-humanities-uneven-promise.

Probidad Cuba (blog). n.d. http://probidadcuba.blogspot.com/.

Project for the New American Century. 2000. *Rebuilding America's Defense: Strategies, Forces and Resources for a New Century*. https://wikispooks.com/w/images/3/37/RebuildingAmericasDefenses.pdf.

"Qué país cambia de marca? . . . La respuesta es Colombia." n.d. *Brandemia*. http://www.brandemia.org/que-pais-cambia-de-marca-la-respuesta-es-colombia.

Rama, Angel. 1984. *La ciudad letrada*. Hanover: Ediciones del Norte.

Ramírez, Catherine S. 2008. "Afrofuturism/Chicanafuturism: Fictive Kin." *Aztlan: A Journal of Chicano Studies* 33, no. 1: 185–194.

Ramos, Isabel. 2012. "La contienda política entre los medios privados y el gobierno de Rafael Correa." *Utopia y Praxis Latinoamericana* 17, no 58: 65–76.

———. 2013. "Trayectorias de democratización y desdemocratización de la comunicación en Ecuador." *Iconos. Revista de Ciencias Sociales* 45: 67–82.

Ramos, Manuel. 2011. E-mail message to author [Jennifer Lozano]. April 27, 2014.

————. 2014. E-mail message to author [Jennifer Lozano]. July 21, 2014.

Ramsay, Stephen. 2013. "Who's In and Who's Out." *Defining Digital Humanities*, edited by Julianna Nyhan, Melissa Terras, and Edward Vanhoutte, 239–242. New York: Routledge.

Rawls, John. 1996. "Civil Disobedience and the Social Contract." In *Morality and Moral Controversies*, 4th edition, edited by J. Arthur. New Jersey: Prentice Hall.

Raymond, Eric. 2003. *The Art of UNIX Programming*. Reading, MA: Addison-Wesley.

Readings, Bill. 1996. *The University in Ruins*. Cambridge: Harvard University Press.

Recio Silva, Milena. 2013. "La hora de los desconectados. Evaluación del diseño de la política de 'acceso social' a Internet en Cuba en un contexto de cambios." *Consejo Latinoamericano de Ciencias Sociales (CLACSO)-Asdi 2013*, November 1, 2013. https://jcguanche.files.wordpress.com/2014/06/recio_trabajo_final.pdf.

Red Observatorio Critico (blog). n.d. http://observatoriocriticocuba.org/.

Reflejos (blog). n.d. http://cubava.cu/.

Rettberg, Jill Walker. 2008. *Blogging*. Malden, MA: Polity Press.

Risam, Roopika. 2015. "Across Two (Imperial) Cultures: Ballad of Digital Humanities & the Global South." HASTAC. https://www.youtube.com/watch?v=ttjEGiuR9ec.

Rivas-Rodriguez, Maggie. 2003. *Brown Eyes on the Web: Unique Perspectives of an Alternative U.S. Latino Online Newspaper*. New York: Routledge.

Rivera, M. 2014. "Hate it or Love it: Global Crossover of Reggaetón Music in the Digital Age." PhD diss., University of Illinois.

Robertson, Roland. 1995. "Glocalization: Time-Space and Homogeneity-Heterogeneity." In *Global Modernities*, edited by Mike Featherstone, Scott Lash and Roland Robertson, 25–44. Thousand Oaks, CA: Sage.

Robinson, Sue. 2009. "'Searching for My Own Unique Place in the Story': A Comparison of Journalistic and Citizen-Produced Coverage of Hurricane Katrina's Anniversary." In *Journalism and Citizenship: New Agendas in Communication*, edited by Zizi Papacharissi, 166–188. New York: Routledge.

Rockwell, Geoffrey. 2011. "Inclusion in the Digital Humanities." *geoffreyrockwell.com* (blog), September 7, 2011. http://www.philosophi.ca/pmwiki.php/Main/InclusionIn-TheDigitalHumanities.

Rodríguez, Yusimi. 2013. "Documentary on Internet Access in Cuba." *Havana Times*, January 10, 2013. http://www.havanatimes.org/?p=85719.

Rogers, E. M. 1994. *A History of Communication Study: A Biographical Approach*. New York: The Free Press.

Ronfeldt, David, and John Arquilla. 1998. *The Zapatista Social Netwar in Mexico*. Santa Monica: RAND, 1998.

Rosner, Daniela K., and Morgan G. Ames. 2014. "Designing for Repair? Infrastructures and Materialities of Breakdown." *Proc CSCW 2014*, 319–31. New York: ACM Publications. https://doi.org/10.1145/2531602.2531692.

Sabatini, Francisco. 2000. "Reforma de los mercados de suelo en Santiago, Chile: Efectos sobre los precios de la tierra y la segregación residencial." *EURE: Revista Latinoamericana de Estudios Urbano Regionales* 26, no. 77: 49–80.

Sakr, Laila Shereen. 2009. "The R-Shief Initiative: Proof of Concept." *Parsons Journal for*

Information Mapping, The New School, 2009. http://piim.newschool.edu/journal/issues/2009/02/pdfs/ParsonsJournalForInformationMapping_Sakr-Laila.pdf.

Salazar, C. 1997. "La escuela ayllú y las concepciones educativas de Elizardo Pérez." *Warisata mía*. La Paz: Editorial Juventud.

———. 2005. *Gesta y Fotografía: Historia de Warisata en imágenes*. La Paz, Bolivia: Lazarsa Ediciones.

Sample, Mark. 2011. "The Digital Humanities Is Not about Building, It's about Sharing." *@samplereality* (blog), May 25, 2011. https://www.samplereality.com/2011/05/25/the-digital-humanities-is-not-about-building-its-about-sharing/.

Sánchez, Yoani. 2011a. *Havana Real: One Woman Fights to Tell the Truth About Cuba Today*. Translated by M. J. Porter. Brooklyn, NY: Melville House.

———. 2011b. *WordPress: Un blog para hablar del mundo*. Madrid: Anaya Multimedia.

———. 2013. "Operación verdad (Entrevista de Yoani Sánchez a Eliécer Ávila)." *14ymedio* (blog), November 2, 2013. http://www.14ymedio.com/blogs/generacion_y/Operacion-Verdad_7_1285741414.html.

Sansone, Livio. 2013. "Challenges to Digital Patrimonialization." *Virtual Brazilian Anthropology* 10, no. 1: 343–386. http://www.vibrant.org.br/issues/v10n1/livio-sansone-challenges-to-digital-patrimonialization/.

Schiller, H. 1991. "Not Yet the Post-Imperialism Era." *Critical Studies in Mass Communication* no. 8: 13–28.

Schreibman, Susan, Ray Siemens, and John Unsworth. 2004. "The Digital Humanities and Humanities Computing: An Introduction." In *A Companion to Digital Humanities*, edited by Susan Schreibman, Ray Siemens, and John Unsworth, xxiii–xxvii. New York: Blackwell.

Scott, James. 1999. *Seeing like a State: How Certain Schemes to Improve the Human Condition Have Failed*. New Haven, CT: Yale University Press.

Sedano, Michael. 2011. E-mail message to author [Jennifer Lozano]. April 19, 2011.

———. 2012. Interview by Sonia Gutiérrez. "Face-to-face with *La Bloga*." *La Bloga* (blog), January 10, 2012. http://labloga.blogspot.com/2012/01/guest-columnist-sonia-gutierrez-getting.html.

Severin, Eugenio, and Christine Capota. 2011. *One-to-One Laptop Programs in Latin America and the Caribbean: Panorama and Perspectives*. Inter-American Development Bank Education Division (SCL/EDU), April 2011. Technical Notes No. IDB-TN-273. http://idbdocs.iadb.org/wsdocs/getdocument.aspx?docnum=35989594.

Shachtman, Noah. 2002. "Hacktivists Stage Virtual Sit-In at WEF Web Site." *AlterNet*, February 7, 2002. https://www.alternet.org/2002/02/hacktivists_stage_virtual_sit-in_at_wef_web_site/.

Sherman, Matthew. 2009. *A Short History of Financial Deregulation in the United States*. Washington, D.C.: Center for Economic and Policy Research. http://www.cepr.net/documents/publications/dereg-timeline-2009-07.pdf.

Silvernail, David L. 2005. *Does Maine's Middle School Laptop Program Improve Learning? A Review of Evidence to Date*. Center for Education Policy, Applied Research, and Evaluation, University of Southern Maine. https://files.eric.ed.gov/fulltext/ED509480.pdf.

Sims, Christo. 2017. *Disruptive Fixation: School Reform and the Pitfalls of Techno-Idealism*. Princeton, NJ: Princeton University Press.

Sinclair, J. 2004. "Geo-Linguistic Region as Global Space: The Case of Latin America." In *The Television Studies Reader*, edited by R. Allen and A. Hill, 130–138. London: Routledge.

Singer, N. 2015. "The Digital Disparities Facing Lower Income Teenagers." *New York Times*, November 3, 2015. http://bits.blogs.nytimes.com/2015/11/03/the-digital-disparities-facing-lower-income-teens/?smid=fb-share&_r=0.

Sleep Dealer. 2008. Directed by Alex Rivera. USA: Likely Story/This is That Productions.

Smith, Martha Nell. 2007. "The Human Touch." *Textual Cultures: Texts, Contexts, Interpretations* 2, no. 1: 1–15.

Somos más (blog). n.d. http://somosmascuba.com/.

Somos +. n.d. http://somosmascuba.com/quienes-somos/.

Spence, Louise, and Vinicius Navarro. 2010. *Crafting Truth: Documentary Form and Meaning*. New Brunswick, NJ: Rutgers University Press.

Squires, C. 2013. "Race/Ethnicity in Media History." In *The International Encyclopedia of Media Studies*, edited by A. N. Valdivia. Vol. 1: *Media History and the Foundations of Media Studies*, edited by J. Nerone, 122–149. New York: Wiley-Blackwell.

Stalbaum, Brett. 1998. *The Zapatista Tactical FloodNet*. http://www.thing.net/~rdom/ecd/ZapTact.html.

Stephanidis, Anthony, Andrew Crooks, and Jacek Radzikowski. 2013. "Harvesting Ambient Geospatial Information from Social Media Feeds." *GeoJournal* 78: 319–338.

Straubhaar, Joseph. 1991. "Beyond Media Imperialism: Asymmetrical Interdependence and Cultural Proximity." *Critical Studies in Mass Communication* 8: 39–59.

———. 2007. *World Television: From Global to Local*. Los Angeles: Sage.

Straubhaar, Joseph, Jeremiah Spence, Zeynep Tufecki, and Roberta G. Lenz. 2012. *Inequity in the Technopolis: Race, Class, Gender and the Digital Divide in Austin*. Austin: University of Texas Press.

Suchman, Lucy A. 1987. *Plans and Situated Actions: The Problem of Human-Machine Communication*. Cambridge: Cambridge University Press.

Sunder-Rajan, Kaushik. 2006. *Biocapital: The Constitution of Postgenomic Life*. Durham, NC: Duke University Press.

Taal, Maya. 2013. "CPJ Risk List: Where Press Freedom Suffered." *Committee to Protect Journalists (CPJ)*. https://cpj.org/2014/02/attacks-on-the-press-cpj-risk-list-1.php.

Takhteyev, Yuri. 2012. "Coding Places: Software Practice in a South American City." *Nature* 452 (7185): 272. https://doi.org/10.1177/0094306114539455vv.

Taussig, Michael. 1992. *Mimesis and Alterity: A Particular History of the Senses*. New York: Routledge.

Taylor, Claire. 2014. *Place and Politics in Latin American Digital Culture*. New York: Routledge.

Taylor, Claire, and Thea Pitman. 2007. *Latin American Cyberculture and Cyberliterature*. Liverpool: Liverpool University Press.

———. 2013. *Latin American Identity in Online Cultural Production*. New York: Routledge. http://hemisphericinstitute.org/hemi/en/e-misferica-91/taylor.

Taylor, Diana. 2010. "Save As. Memory and the Archive in the Age of Digital Technologies. September 30, 2010." YouTube video. 1:09:52. UC Berkeley Events. October 11, 2010. https://www.youtube.com/watch?v=xGurF1Rfj0U.

———. 2012. "Save As." *On the Subject of Archives, E-Misférica* 9, no. 1–2.

Telemundo and The Weather Channel. 2014. *Muriendo por cruzar.* August 2014. https://www.youtube.com/watch?v=aYyBbmYuLnw.

Terras, Melissa. 2011. *Quantifying the Digital Humanities.* UCL Centre for the Digital Humanities infographic, December 2011. http://www.ucl.ac.uk/infostudies/melissa-terras/DigitalHumanitiesInfographic.pdf.

The Afrolatin@ Project. Accessed May 12, 2015. http://afrolatinoproject.org/.

The Da Vinci Code. 2006. Directed by Ron Howard. USA: Columbia Pictures.

The World Bank Group. 2016. "World Development Report 2016: Digital Dividends." http://www.worldbank.org/en/publication/wdr2016.

———. 2018. "International Tourism, Number of Arrivals." https://data.worldbank.org/indicator/ST.INT.ARVL.

Thompson Klein, Julie. 2015. *Interdisciplining Digital Humanities: Boundary Work in an Emergent Field.* Ann Arbor: University of Michigan Press.

Tironi, Manuel, and Javiera Barandiarán. 2014. "Neoliberalism as Political Technology: Expertise, Energy, and Democracy in Chile." In *Beyond Imported Magic: Essays on Science, Technology, and Society in Latin America,* edited by Eden Medina, Ivan da Costa Marques, and Christina Holmes, 305–329. Cambridge, MA: The MIT Press.

Tomlinson, J. 1991. *Cultural Imperialism.* Baltimore: John Hopkins Press.

Torres, Edén E. 2003. "Donde hay amor, hay dolor." *Chicana without Apology: The New Chicana Cultural Studies.* New York: Routledge.

Torres, Jason. 2013. "Marca país genera críticas y dudas en varios sectores." *CRHoy,* September 4, 2013. http://www.crhoy.com/marca-pais-desata-criticas-en-el-congreso/.

Toyama, Kentaro. 2010. "Can Technology End Poverty?" *Boston Review.* https://boston-review.net/archives/BR35.6/toyama.php.

Treviño, Marisa. 2014. "NBC Latino Shuts Down—Failed Experiment or Successful Test?" *New America Media,* January 23, 2014. http://www.thehartfordguardian.com/tag/nbc-latino/.

Trucano, M. 2012. "Evaluating One Laptop Per Child (OLPC) in Peru." *World Bank Blogs,* March 23, 2012. http://blogs.worldbank.org/edutech/olpc-peru2.

Tsing, Anna Lowenhaupt. 2004. *Friction: An Ethnography of Global Connection.* Princeton: Princeton University Press.

Twain, Mark. 1889. *A Connecticut Yankee in King Arthur's Court.* New York: Charles L. Webster & Company. http://www.gutenberg.org/files/86/86-h/86-h.htm.

Unión Patriótica de Cuba (blog). n.d. http://www.unpacu.org/.

Unruh, Vicky. 1994. *Latin American Vanguards: The Art of Contentious Encounters.* Berkeley, CA: Univ. of California Press.

Unsworth, John. 2002. "What is Humanities Computing, and What is Not?" *Jahrbuch für Computerphilologie,* 4, edited by G. Braungart, K. Eilb, and F. Jannidis, 71–84. Paderborn: Mentis Verlag.

Valdivia, A. N., ed. 1995. *Feminism, Multiculturalism and the Media: Global Diversities.* Newbury Park, CA: Sage.

———. 1996. "Is Modern to Male as Traditional is to Female? Re-Visioning Lerner and Schramm's Gender Construction in International Communications." *Journal of International Communications* 3, no. 1: 5–25.

———. 2013. *Latina/os and the Media.* Cambridge, MA: Polity Press.

———. 2014. "Latina/os and the Media: A National Category with Transnational Implications"/ "Latina/os e a mídia: Uma categoria nacional com implicações transnacionais." *MeEL: Mestrado em estudos de limguagen.*

———. 2016. "Implicit Utopias and Ambiguous Ethnics: Latinidad and the Representational Promised Land." In *The Routledge Companion to Latina/o Media Studies*, edited by I. Casillas and M. E. Cepeda, n.p. London and New York: Routledge.

Varas, Eduardo. 2014. "Enchufe TV, fenómeno ecuatoriano en Internet." *Revista Soho,* September 16. http://www.revistasoho.com.ec/revistasohoecuador/?p=2162. Link no longer active.

Vargas, L. 2009. *Latina Teens, Migration, and Popular Culture.* New York: Peter Lang.

Venegas, Cristina. 2010a. *Digital Dilemmas: The State, the Individual and Digital Media in Cuba.* New Brunswick, NJ: Rutgers University Press.

———. 2010b. "Liberating the Self: The Biopolitics of Cuban Blogging." *Journal of International Communication* 16, no. 2: 43–54.

Vich, Cynthia. 2000. *Indigenismo de vanguardia en el Perú.* Lima, Peru: Pontificia Universidad Católica del Peru, 2000.

Villazana, L. 2014. "Transnational Virtual Mobility as a Reification of Deployment of Power: Exploring Transnational Processes in the Film *Sleep Dealer.*" *Transnational Cinemas* 4, no. 2: 217–230. DOI: 10.1386/trac.4.2.217_1.

Voces Cubanas. n.d. http://www.100yaldabo.com/voces.htm.

Vota, Wayan. 2007a. "Is OLPC the Only Hope to Eliminate Poverty and Create Peace?" *OLPC News,* November 30, 2007. http://www.olpcnews.com/people/negroponte/olpc_poverty_world_peace.html.

———. 2007b. "One Pornographic Image Per Nigerian Child." *OLPC News,* July 19, 2007. http://www.olpcnews.com/countries/nigeria/pornographic_image_child.html.

Wabgou, Maguemati, Jaime Arocha Rodriguez, Aiden Salgado Cassiani, and Juan Alberto Carabalí Ospina. 2012. *Movimiento social afrocolombiano, negro, raizal y palenquero.* Bogotá: Universidad Nacional de Colombia.

Wade, Peter. 2005. "Rethinking Mestizaje: Ideology and Live Experience." *Journal of Latin American Studies* 37, no. 2: 239–257.

@walfridolopez' blog (blog). n.d. http://www.walfridolopez.com/.

Warschauer, Mark. 2008. "Laptops and Literacy: A Multi-Site Case Study." *Pedagogies: An International Journal* 3: 52–67.

Warschauer, Mark, and Morgan G. Ames. 2010. "Can One Laptop per Child Save the World's Poor?" *Journal of International Affairs* 64, no. 1: 33–51.

Warschauer, Mark, and T. Matuchniak. 2010. "New Technology and Digital Worlds: Analyzing Evidence of Equity in Access, Use, and Outcomes." *Review of Research in Education* 34: 179–225. https://doi.org/10.3102/0091732x09349791.

Wolf, Eric R. 1982. *Europe and the People without History*. Berkeley, CA: University of California Press.

Wolf, Jim. 2001. "'Hacktivism' credited to Zapatistas." *Reuters*, November 2, 2001. http://archives.openflows.org/hacktivism/hacktivism00722.html.

Yoanislandia. n.d. www.yoanislandia.com.

Yuan, Elaine J. 2012. "A Culturalist Critique of 'Online Community' in New Media Studies." *New Media and Society* 15, no. 5: 1–15. http://nms.sagepub.com/content/early/2012/11/22/1461444812462847.

Zevallos, Juan. 2002. *Boletín Titikaka: Indigenismo y Nación*. Lima, Peru: Instituto Francés.

Contributors

Paul Alonso is assistant professor in the School of Modern Languages at the Georgia Institute of Technology in Atlanta.

Morgan Ames is lecturer and postdoctoral scholar with the School of Information and the interim associate director of research for the Center for Science, Technology, Medicine and Society at the University of California, Berkeley.

Eduard Arriaga is assistant professor in the Department of Global Languages and Cross-Cultural Studies at the University of Indianapolis.

Anita Say Chan is associate research professor of communications in the Department of Media and Cinema Studies at the University of Illinois, Urbana-Champaign.

Ricardo Domínguez, the founder of Electronic Disturbance Theater, is an American artist and associate professor in the Department of Visual Arts at the University of California, San Diego.

Orlando Luis Pardo Lazo, a Cuban writer and artist, is a graduate student in the comparative literature program at Washington University in St. Louis.

Héctor Fernández L'Hoeste is professor of world languages and Latin American cultures at Georgia State University's World Languages and Cultures Department. He is the author of *Lalo Alcaraz: Political Cartooning in the Latino Community.*

Jennifer Lozano is assistant professor in the Department of English at the University of North Carolina, Wilmington.

Ana Lígia Silva Medeiros is a research librarian and archivist at the Fundação Casa de Rui Barbosa in Rio de Janeiro, Brazil.

Gimena del Río Riande is a researcher at the Seminario de Edición y Crítica Textual of the National Scientific and Technical Research Council in Buenos Aires, Argentina.

Juan Carlos Rodríguez is associate professor in the School of Modern Languages at the Georgia Institute of Technology in Atlanta.

Isabel Galina Russell is a research librarian at the Institute for Bibliographic Studies at the Universidad Nacional Autónoma de México in Mexico City.

Angharad N. Valdivia is research professor of communications in the Department of Media and Cinema Studies at the University of Illinois, Urbana-Champaign.

Anastasia Valecce is assistant professor in the Department of World Languages and Literature at Spelman College in Atlanta.

Cristina Venegas is associate professor in the Department of Film and Media Studies at the University of California, Santa Barbara.

Index

REFRAMING MEDIA, TECHNOLOGY, AND CULTURE IN LATIN/O AMERICA

Edited by Héctor Fernández L'Hoeste and Juan Carlos Rodríguez

Reframing Media, Technology, and Culture in Latin/o America explores how Latin American and Latino audiovisual (film, television, digital), musical (radio, recordings, live performances, dancing), and graphic (comics, photography, advertising) cultural practices reframe and reconfigure social, economic, and political discourses at a local, national, and global level. In addition, it looks at how information networks reshape public and private policies, and the enactment of new identities in civil society. The series also covers how different technologies have allowed and continue to allow for the construction of new ethnic spaces. It not only contemplates the interaction between new and old technologies but also how the development of brand-new technologies redefines cultural production.

Telling Migrant Stories: Latin American Diaspora in Documentary Film, edited by Esteban E. Loustaunau and Lauren E. Shaw (2018; paperback edition, 2021)

Mestizo Modernity: Race, Technology, and the Body in Postrevolutionary Mexico, by David S. Dalton (2018; first paperback edition, 2021)

The Insubordination of Photography: Documentary Practices under Chile's Dictatorship, by Ángeles Donoso Macaya (2020; first paperback edition, 2023)

Digital Humanities in Latin America, edited by Héctor Fernández L'Hoeste and Juan Carlos Rodríguez (2020; first paperback edition, 2023)

Pablo Escobar and Colombian Narcoculture, by Aldona Bialowas Pobutsky (2020)

The New Brazilian Mediascape: Television Production in the Digital Streaming Age, by Eli Lee Carter (2020)

Univision, Telemundo, and the Rise of Spanish-Language Television in the United States, by Craig Allen (2020; first paperback edition, 2023)

Cuba's Digital Revolution: Citizen Innovation and State Policy, edited by Ted A. Henken and Sara Garcia Santamaria (2021; first paperback edition, 2022)

Afro-Latinx Digital Connections, edited by Eduard Arriaga and Andrés Villar (2021)

The Lost Cinema of Mexico: From Lucha Libre to Cine Familiar and Other Churros, edited by Olivia Cosentino and Brian Price (2022)

Neo-Authoritarian Masculinity in Brazilian Crime Film, by Jeremy Lehnen (2022)

The Rise of Central American Film in the Twenty-First Century, edited by Mauricio Espinoza and Jared List (2023)

www.ingramcontent.com/pod-product-compliance
Lightning Source LLC
Chambersburg PA
CBHW020826270326
41928CB00006B/453